THE RULE OF THE MASTER

The Rule of the Master

Regula magistri
Translated from the Latin by
Luke Eberle
Monk of Mount Angel Abbey

Introduction by
Adalbert de Vogüé
Monk of La Pierre-qui-Vire
and translated by
Charles Philippi
Monk of New Camaldoli

Cistercian Publications
1977

This translation has been made from the critical Latin edition of Adalbert de Vogüé, published as *La Règle du Maître* in the series, *Sources chrétiennes, Série des Textes Monastiques d'Occident, n°XIV & XV (Sources chrétiennes, n° 105 & 106)*, Paris: Les Editions du Cerf, 1964.

Cistercian Publications are available in Europe and the Commonwealth through A. R. Mowbray & Co. Ltd., St. Thomas House, Becket Street, Oxford OX1 1SG

Library of Congress Cataloguing in Publication Data

Regula Magistri. English
  The rule of the Master = Regula magistri.

  (Cistercian studies series ; 6)
    1. Monasticism and religious orders—Rules.
I. Eberle, Luke. II. Title. III. Series.
BX2436.5.M3E5   1977   255   77-3986
ISBN 0-87907-806-5

Printed in the United States of America

CONTENTS

PREFACE

WHEN ONE PERUSES the collection of ancient monastic rules compiled in the ninth century by Benedict of Aniane, there is one rule which immediately attracts attention because of its monumental proportions. Far lengthier than most of these short writings and three times longer than the Rule of St. Benedict, it surpasses by half again the second longest work of the collection, the Rule of St. Basil.

Size alone does not distinguish this *Regula Magistri*, as Benedict of Aniane called it. An examination of the content reveals an impressive and rich multiplicity of parts, a thoroughness of treatment, and a methodical organization.

The *Regula Magistri* is not a pure regulation like the Rule of Pachomius nor a simple anthology of advice and counsel like that of Basil, but it is a veritable rule of life encompassing the entire existence, material and spiritual, of the monastic community and the individuals within it. By turns are treated the monks' virtues and the monastery's organization, grand perspectives of the Christian life and minor details of observance—and these not at all cursorily or by allusion, as is so often the case in the short monastic rules, but at length and in depth, with no fear of systematic expositions and large developments or even digressions and repetitions.

No less characteristic is the care the 'Master' took to order and inter-relate the various parts of his work. Ordinarily nothing is less organized than a monastic rule. Material is usually arranged according to simple associations of ideas. Here on the contrary we can trace an overall plan and recognize a logical order which is explicitly and repeatedly announced. This methodical order conveys a well thought-out concept of cenobitism. Not only do the principles and internal structure of cenobitism stand out clearly, but an endeavor is made to relate them to the goals of the individual, to the whole of monasticism and to the Church itself.

In many respects then the Rule of the Master is unusual. And yet it curiously resembles another, similar work, the Rule of St Benedict. From the prologue to the treatise on humility, these two texts often correspond verbatim. After that each rule follows its own course, though some correspondence may still be observed in the sequence of material and, at times, in the substance of the regulations.

Until recent times these similarities aroused little interest among critics, who thought they could explain them easily as the dependence of the Master on St Benedict. Just before the last war, however, Dom Augustin Genestout rethought the problem and reversed direction; he asserted that St Benedict had depended on the Master. Since 1938, the year this new theory became widely known, a controversy has raged between defenders of the two theses. Soon a third was added: those who maintained the middle solution by hypothesizing a common source for both the Master and St Benedict. The debate has not let up in more than a quarter century, and has occasioned a mass of studies, no doubt the largest which a question of this sort has stirred up in our times. The traditional thesis has been championed successively by J. Perez de Urbel, J. McCann, C. Lambot, A. Lambert, R. Weber, H. Frank, M. Cappuyns, P. Blanchard, and E. Franceschini.[1] The new thesis has been upheld by M. Alamo, F. Cavallera, J. Froger, C. Gindele, H. Vanderhoven, F. Masai, P. B. Corbett, G. Penco, A. Mundó, and E. Manning. Hypotheses supposing a common source for the two rules or some sort of interdependence are to be found in various forms in the work of B. Capelle, F. Renner, F. Vanderbroucke, O. J. Zimmermann, Th. Payr, and R. Hanslik.[2]

The discussion has caused so much commotion that many of our readers, in opening this volume, may be expecting us to summarize it all. We shall not. In the present work reference is not made to St Benedict save in a few instances where comparison of the two texts serves to illumine some detail of the Master's work which would otherwise escape notice.

We shall devote our attention here only to the Rule of the

Master. It offers abundant material by itself, as the size of this volume witnesses. Little studied in its own right until now, it will lay open its secrets and with them elements which will increase our understanding of St Benedict only if we commit ourselves to the patient labor of exegesis on the Rule of St Benedict. It is not our intention to evade the important problem of the relationship between the two rules, but to prepare ourselves to deal with it more seriously.

It remains for us to thank those who have helped render this work less imperfect. Our grateful recognition goes to professors M. Diaz y Diaz, J. Fontaine, C. Mohrmann, to the reverend Fathers C. Batlle, B. Fischer, J. Froger, B. de Gaiffier, A. Genestout, J. Gribomont, J.-C. Guy, C. Lambot, A. Mundó, H. Vanderhoven, and R. Weber, who have so amiably responded to our questions and furnished information, documents, and numerous suggestions.

Though lacking immediate contact with them, we cannot neglect the number of learned men who have preceded or accompanied us in the study of the Rule of the Master. We owe them much, and if their very number does not permit us to cite them as we would like, they may be assured of the place they hold in our grateful recognition and esteem. With his study on the Latin of the *Regula Magistri,* meant as a guide in the establishment of the text, Mr. P. B. Corbett in particular has been for us a constant companion whom we never consulted without profit, even though we finally went separate ways. Thanks to him and to all who have accumulated treasures of wisdom and erudition in regard to this text, this edition seems to us less a personal work than the result of joint effort. May this edition in its turn assist the understanding the Rule of the Master, which is not merely a great literary enigma, but an important source for the history and knowledge of the life consecrated to God.

Adalbert de Vogüé osb

Abbaye de la Pierre-qui-Vire
Saint-Léger-Vauban

NOTES TO THE PREFACE

1. On the history of this controversy, see G. Penco, 'Origine e sviluppi della questione della *RM*' in *Studia Anselmiana* 38 (1956) 283–306; also by the same author, *S. Benedicti Regula* (Florence: 'La nuova Italia' Editrice, 1958) pp. xix–xxxi. Here we would only recall that the signal for this controversy was sounded by M. Alamo, 'La règle de S. Benoît éclairée par sa source, la Règle du Maître' in *RHE* 34 (1938) 739–755, who was the first to make a case for the new thesis conceived by Dom Genestout.

2. R. Hanslik, *Benedicti Regula* in *CSEL* (Vienna: Hoelder-Pichler-Tempsky, 1960). We reviewed this work in *RHE* 56 (1961) 909–915.

3. On this subject see our work *La communauté et l'abbé dans la Règle de saint Benoît* (Paris: Desclée de Brouwer, 1961) 27–37 and 505–511.

TRANSLATOR'S NOTE

This English translation of the Rule of the Master has been made from the Latin text issued by Adalbert de Vogüé, OSB (*La Règle du Maître*, Sources Chrétiennes No. 105, Paris: Les Éditions du Cerf 1964). I must state at once, and gratefully, that Fr Adalbert's French translation proved to be an invaluable, indeed indispensable, norm and guide in rendering the very difficult Latin into English.

The objective assigned and pursued was an English text that would be clear and readable, faithfully reproducing the original. I have tried to retain the 'flavor' of the Latin in its turns of thought and mode of expression, without adhering slavishly to the involved grammatical and syntactic constructions. No liberties were taken with regard to the substance of RM, but for the sake of clarity its many inconsistencies and vagaries of style were occasionally remedied to spare the reader the labor any translator has to accept in wrestling with a text. Some of the interminably long sentences were broken up, with no damage to the meaning, and it was of course frequently necessary to use equivalent English constructions for active and passive voice, indicative and subjunctive mood, infinitives and participles, etc., where the linguistic styles differ. So too regarding verb tense; the present indicative is used, for example, in ceremonial directives whereas the Latin may use subjunctive, future or future perfect.

The footnotes, except for those pertaining directly to the English translation, were excerpted from the many given in Fr Adalbert's scholarly work. The aim in selection was to help the reader understand the text, rather than to provide the scholar with sources, parallel texts, analysis of the Latin grammar and syntax, variations in mss readings, and the like. It may be added that Fr Adalbert's three volumes offer a bibliography, a lengthy introduction analyzing RM, text and French translation of RM, critical notes, many more cross-references than accompany the English translation, indexes, and a verbal concordance (the last a complete volume by collaborators).

Luke Eberle OSB

Mount Angel Abbey
St Benedict, Oregon

DIVISIONS AND SIGLA OF THE TEXT

The close connection which exists between the Rule of the Master and the Rule of St Benedict necessitates the use of the same system of references within the two texts. For some twenty years, principal editors of St Benedict have concurred on a standard division into 'verses.' A similar system of divisions in the text of the Master has been followed in the Latin edition and in this translation. All references in the Introduction and in the notes cite chapter and verse of the text as follows:

$$12{:}4 = \text{chapter 12, verse 4}$$

References to the Prologue (Pr) and to the Theme are listed in similar fashion. The length of the latter calls for subdivision, and we have reckoned its three parts separately, entitling them: Theme (Th), Theme *Pater* (Thp), and Theme sequence (Ths). These tags have only a utilitarian importance. Though not conforming to the real meaning of the word Theme or to the genuine character of this introduction, they (the first two at least) have the advantage of being in current use among scholars working with the Rule of the Master over the last twenty-five years.

INTRODUCTION

CHAPTER ONE

INSTITUTIONS

THE COMMUNITY

THE COMMUNITY PORTRAYED in the Rule of the Master is not very numerous. The author has in mind only two 'decades' or groups of ten monks, each directed by two deans: twenty-four religious; and, if the abbot and cellarer are also counted, twenty-six persons in all. The number is not limitative. In several places the Master allows for the possibility of further increase.[1] Such development would be a sign of 'God's favor.'

The decanal system in force in the monastery was not an invention of our author. The institution is as ancient as cenobitism itself and may even claim Jewish precedent.[2] Whether it is Jewish or Christian, the monks were continually mindful of the example set in the desert by Israel, whom Moses divided into groups of hundreds and of tens.

In assigning two deans to each group of ten monks, the Master may equally have been inspired by Pachomian precedent. For the Master, however, these two officers are simple colleagues on an equal footing, not a head and his assistant as they were with Pachomius. A double preoccupation motivated this collegial system: to enforce surveillance over the brethren and to share the honor between two subjects in such a way that neither might rank himself the abbot's assistant and designated successor.[3]

Besides their duty of surveillance, the deans had real authority over their men. By weekly turns, they organized (*ordinare*) community services and manual labor, as well as the instruction given the illiterate and the brothers who did not know the psalter.

The cellarer belonged to neither decanal group. He came under the immediate surveillance of the abbot. His department was the 'cellar' or storeroom—food provisions, kitchen utensils, plateware. He was not the general financier he is today in benedictine monasteries. Equally, if not more, important was the *custos ferramentorum* (17) who was simultaneously warehouseman, wardrobeman, sacristan, treasurer, librarian, and trustee.

Only two porters (95) and some craftsmen of undetermined number (50 and 85) held permanent charges. Other community services were filled on weekly rotation. Each week two brothers were appointed to serve in the kitchen, veritable domestics of the community who not only prepared and served the food, but did the washing and cleaning as well. A weekly reader was assigned for the refectory, as were two *uigigalli* or 'watchmen' who announced the day and night offices, and two guestmasters. All belonged to the same 'decade', and took turns according to the deans' arrangements.

At the office, the 'antiphons' (antiphonated psalms) were said in turn by the brothers who knew the psalter, beginning with the abbot and the deans, and then in descending order. For readings, on the other hand, the order was ascending: first the provosts (reading from the Apostle), then the abbot (the gospel). No order of precedence seems to have existed among the other brothers within the groups of ten.

In the absence of an order of seniority or of merit, the *minores* or ungraded religious were divided into several categories on the basis of age, level of education, technical competence, and virtue. On the basis of age, men were distinguished from boys. The boys seem to have been mixed in with the older brothers within the groups of ten, though special regulations governed their nourishment, *lectio*, and punishments. With regard to food regulations, boyhood was considered as lasting until the twelfth year (*perinfantuli*); for punishments, it lasted until the fifteenth year.

By education, the brothers are classed as illiterate, *litterati* (they can read), and *psalterati* (they know the psalter by heart). These last enjoyed the privilege of being eligible to be invited to the abbot's table, at least if they were professed. And only they had the right to the *lectio* at the hours prescribed by the rule, while the others learned how to read, or applied themselves to the psalms.

By professional skill, there were the *artifices* or skilled craftsmen (they knew a trade), and those who lacked this qualification. The latter were employed in the garden or to run errands outside. To receive a commission or be sent on a journey was a mission of confidence requiring a good deal of virtue (11), but at the same time it was a laborious task and little appreciated, and sometimes provoked refusals (57).

Finally, the Master was fond of distinguishing degrees of virtue in his subjects (2). We shall see the importance he attached to the 'spiritual man.' This is the ideal to which he tried to lead all the brothers. The community was also separated into the *abstinentes* and the *comedentes*, sometimes openly segregated in the refectory; into those who kept vigil and those who slept in; into the diligent and negligent, and so on. In the matter of obedience and silence, there were special rules for the perfect and the imperfect.

In this portrayal of community, the absence of certain officers is noticeable. Nothing is said about a boys' master. Their moral formation is entrusted to the deans, their instruction to the *litterati* who succeeded one another by turns; nothing about a *secundus* or assistant-abbot for the whole community unless some accident should intervene in the abbatial succession. Not a word about a specially appointed wardrobeman: the brother custodian kept articles of clothing in his storage closet, and the deans, it seems, looked after the clothing needs of their men (11:107, 81:9–20). This suggests a not very numerous community in which functions were scarcely differentiated or specialized.

THE MONASTERY

The diminutive architectural layout corresponds with the small number of brothers. The storeroom is so close to the oratory that the cellarer can hear the brothers at prayer without leaving his place of work.[4] Most of the brothers worked at very little distance from the oratory. They assembled so swiftly for the office that any brother more than fifty strides away (about seventy-five yards) was dispensed from coming:

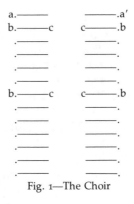

Fig. 1—The Choir

a. The abbot.
a'. The abbot's assistant (93:64).
bb. Deans and brethren (22:9).
c. Prayer mats (19:25; 69:10).

otherwise he would have been obliged to run and would have arrived late (54–55).

What does the layout involve? First the oratory, in which the altar—the real center of the monastery—stood. Here the brothers split into two choirs, each apparently formed by a group of ten. The abbot's place was not in the center but to one side,[5] in such a way that one of the provosts was normally next to him. This much envied place 'at the abbot's side' was given each day to a different provost or even to a simple brother.[6] The two choirs probably faced one another, with sufficient space between for the brothers to have prostrated themselves full length after each psalm.

The refectory with its attendant facilities (kitchen and storeroom) seems to have been adjacent to the oratory.[7] This room did not in fact bear a proper name, but was designated by the paraphrase *ad mensas*.[8] There the abbot had his *cathedra*. He invited to his table, in addition to guests, the brothers who knew the psalter, being careful, as in the oratory, to change his neighbor every day. Each group of ten was seated at a table presided over by the provosts. The reader had no permanently constructed podium from which to read, but took his place at a portable bench centrally located between the tables.

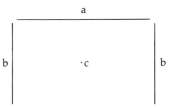

Fig.2—The Refectory

a. Table of the abbot, porters, and guests (84:1).
bb. Tables of the deans and brothers.
 c. Reader's bench (24:13).

The dormitory is called the *atrium lectorum* or simply *atrium*. The U-shaped arrangement of its beds is reminiscent of ancient dining halls. The abbot was in the center, watching over all those entrusted to him. A lamp or night-light illumined the place. Reading after nocturns in the last hours of the long winter nights was done here, and did not seem to disturb the repose of those sleeping. The fact that this is the only dormitory confirms what we already know about the small numbers of brothers. This place too seems to have been adjacent to the oratory (32:7–8).

A single storage closet likewise sufficed to accommodate all the monastery's possessions (17). It bears no special name, but is occasionally called the *uestarium* (81:10). Also listed is a lodging by the door for the porters, another *cella* or separate

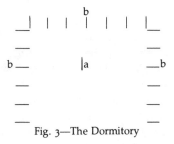

Fig. 3—The Dormitory

a. The abbot's bed (29:3).
bbb. Beds of the deans and brothers.

building for guests and the brothers who look after them, workrooms (*officinae*), a bakery, and latrines (*refrigerium*) located, it seems, apart from the other buildings. All these places were to be found within an enclosure into which only one door (*regia*) provided entrance. The enclosure contained a garden cultivated by the monks. No leased-out farmhouse adjoined the monastery (86:1–2), but there were some dogs and horses stabled not far from the door (95:10–11).

The absence from this list of certain traditional places, such as library, *scriptorium*, and chapter room, may occasion surprise. Books were kept in the one and only storage closet, previously mentioned, with all the monastery's other possessions (17:13). The work of the *scriptores* (54:1) was no doubt performed in one of the *officinae*. Readings made in common were designated for at least two different places, one for each group of ten monks (50:10), but common rooms such as the dormitory and refectory were also perhaps employed for this purpose. In them the council meetings were certainly held (2:41–50). All these places seem located at ground level; there is no mention of a stairway.

THE OBSERVANCES

In the spatial area we have traced out, the Master's community led an existence known down to its least detail. We do not intend to create a lifelike picture of it here, however, but only to sketch the main lines of observance and their place in the history of monastic institutions.

Three-quarters of the day was occupied with manual work. Work had to conform to the demands of prayerful quiet and fasting—hence the exclusion of field labor (86). Only skilled crafts and gardening were practised. Business trips or errands must be mentioned too. The Master's desire to impose a monastic behavior on expeditions outside the enclosure led to minute regulations on the absent brothers' quantity of food, hour for meals, manner of praying the divine office, ceremonials for visits and for brief encounters, time reserved for *lectio*. Nothing was left to chance.

Lectio, which occupied the first or the last quarter of the day,[9] was a community exercise. Brothers gathered together in their respective groups of ten and listened to the reading. Each took his turn as reader, for there was only one *codex*. At the same time, the *litterati* were teaching the boys and the illiterate how to read, while those who had not yet learned the psalter by heart applied themselves to it. All of this constituted the *opus spirituale*. The Master attached such importance to it that he dispensed no one from it, not even those on journeys. Reading might take the place of manual work in the case of physical indisposition or supererogatory fasting.

Intellectual activity was not confined to these three hours a day. Throughout the day's manual work, the brothers were urged to 'ruminate' the psalms and Scripture.[10] This 'meditation' was an oral exercise done in a low voice. Subjects of spiritual interest might also be discussed, except in the abbot's presence. Most important of all, the manual work was accompanied by reading if the workers formed a sufficiently large group. Thus the entire day was immersed in prayerful quiet and attention to the word of God.

In addition to the prescribed hours, the brothers had at their disposal free time which they might devote to study. The last hours of the night after nocturns in winter, and all day Sunday were such times.

In the matter of fasting, the Master shows himself faithful to the ancient principle of a single meal at the hour of none.[11] Like the first generations of monks, he knew no variation but the stricter Lenten fast and the Paschaltide relaxation. At Christmas, however, he established a time of penance and remission analogous to that of Eastertide. And he excepted Thursdays from the fast, except in Lent. Apart from these innovations, RM preserves the primitive system of the year-round fast, as distinguished from more modern systems in which food arrangements vary with the seasons.[12]

Maintenance of a fast on weekdays in summer could not but be an onerous practice. An echo of certain complaints can be perceived in the considerations which open chapter twenty-eight. Arrangements made for the boys and for travelers, moreover, are like stepping stones to a more general mitigation. By Caesarius and Aurelian of Arles as well as by St Benedict, the summer fast was in fact reduced to two or three days a week—a mitigation not yet granted in RM except to special categories.

Abstinence, on the other hand, was not as rigorous as one might expect.[13] Meat was served on Holy Thursday, and everyone might select meat courses at meals during the Easter and Christmas seasons. Apart from Lenten penances, the alimentary rules of the community were, on the whole, quite liberal.[14] Wine was taken at meals in all seasons, and the brethren gathered in the refectory in the evening for a beverage whenever the time remaining after the meal was a bit long.

Regulations about punishments are notably more complex than in Cassian. Cassian made provision only for excommunication or for whippings, according to the gravity of the fault.[15] The Master prescribed in addition a series of private warnings.[16] Furthermore, he distinguished two kinds of excommunication where Cassian knew only one. As for whippings, they were not dealt out to grown men except rather rarely and reluctantly.[17] For ordinary faults the Master preferred prolongations of fasts and curtailments on bread and wine.

In the matter of vigils, the Master preserved a primitive observance: the great vigil on the night of Saturday–Sunday (49). If this custom is more commonly associated with earlier times,[18] it was still a common practice in the first half of the sixth century, when the legislators of Arles prescribed two great vigils a week. Regulations about vigils in RM are very moderate for the other six nights of the week, especially when the Master's nocturns are compared with those of the *Ordo lirinensis*. It was always permissible to sleep during the last hours of the night, a custom which would still prevail in certain roman monasteries at the height of the eighth century.[19] In summer the whole community availed itself of this second period of sleep, and a nap at the hour of Sext compensated for the shortness of the night. This nap seems to have been an innovation since the first generations of monks. Neither Jerome nor Cassian nor any of their contemporaries mention it.

The cycle of the hours of the office included Prime. This hour is wholly ranked with Terce, Sext, and None, with noth-

ing to suggest its recent origin. Yet it is known that Prime
made no explicit appearance in the West before Caesarius of
Arles, and even at Arles became a daily office only with Aurelian. Even Cassiodorus does not mention it.[20] These facts
would seem to prevent us from dating the Master's *ordo* before the first decades of the sixth century. The *ordo* on which
St Benedict depended seems also to have known Prime, both
the name of the hour and its conformity with the other little
hours.

One distinctive characteristic of the office *horarium* is its
simplicity. Solar hours were strictly observed, without those
retardations and anticipations that give so complicated a
physiognomy to St Benedict's horarium. The only concession
of this sort which the Master permitted was to advance Vespers a bit, especially in summer.[21] This fidelity to the primitive *horarium* is a sign of the Rule's antiquity.

Viewed as a whole, this observance does not seem particularly hard when compared with other Rules of antiquity. A
genuine concern for discretion inspires it. But two salient
traits distinguish its legislator. The first is his inclination to
regard all types of dispensation with suspicion. With pitiless
severity he tried to uncover all false pretexts of indisposition. Office, work, abstinence, and fast, all the points of observance were to be jealously maintained by the abbot. The
abbot was to be suspicious of anyone seeking exemption from
any of these points.[22]

Secondly, the Master displays extreme sollicitude for
minutiae. Not a detail goes untreated, no eventuality is left
unforeseen, no situation escapes being made the object of
precise regulations. The most amusing result of this tendency
is the extraordinary chapter sixty-one, where the hour for
meals taken outside the enclosure is determined upon consideration of three variables: the status of the person who
extends the invitation, the persistence of the invitation, and
the day of the week, all of which then provide material for ten
different solutions! Our author often betrays this tendency
towards juridicism and casuistry. Even his vocabulary indicates a juridical formation and a tendency to see everything
from this angle.[23] Surely nothing has so detracted from his
influence as the minute precision of his rules. Such rigid and

detailed legislation could hardly spread beyond the narrow enclosure for which it had been conceived. But we do ill to complain, because this abundance of precise details is in fact what makes the RM an incomparable document for the historian.

NOTES

1. See 19:18, 22:3, 8; cf. 23:5, 86:19, 92:44. According to 11:20, the decanal system is to be instituted only 'of the community is numerous'. Can we conclude that the author was unsure of finding in his monastery the actual minimum of two groups of ten monks?

2. See *La communauté et l'abbé . . .*, p. 302.

3. The deans' complete equality appears not only in the lack of an order of precedence between the different groups of ten (22:1–2), but also in the provision for turn-taking decreed for the two deans of the same group of ten (23:28, 27:1).

4. RM 16:48–9 (the rubric is conditional), 20:10–11 (pertains not only to the cellarer but to any absent brother (cf. 20:1–2). Note that the absent brother seemed able to follow the office from his place of work.

5. See 93:64. The abbot led one of the choirs and his assistant, if there was one, the other.

6. 22:1,9; cf. 92:35–6.

7. See note four above, and compare with 22:2–7. This coming and going between oratory and kitchen was supposed to be very swift, lest it disrupt ceremonies.

8. See 24:title, 1. *Ad mensam* is also found (24:38), *mensis* (23:title) and other passages use the word *mensa,* which never loses its primary sense of 'table'. It can also mean, besides the refectory, the meal itself (23:40–2, 77:5).

9. The normal time for *lectio* was at the beginning of the day. See Caesarius of Arles, *Regula monachorum* 14, and *Regula virginum* 19–20 (cf. *Reg. virg.* 69). The reason is well stated by Pelagius, *Ep ad Demetriadem* 23 (PL 30:37B): the best part of the day, that is, the first three hours, were to be devoted to *lectio.* In *Ep 2 ad virginem*, the same reason is attributed to Caesarius (PL 30:1132C). Gallican rules of the fifth and sixth centuries all placed reading at the beginning of the day. See the texts analyzed by G. Holzherr, 'Die Regula Ferioli', *Studia Anselmiana* 42 (Rome, 1957) 227–8. The augustinian *Ordo monasterii,* however, prescribes reading from Sext to None (chapter 3; see *Revue Benedictine* 42 [1930] 319). It may be that the Master borrowed both observances—the morning and the afternoon lectio—from these two varying traditions, allocating them by season and giving this allocation a practical meaning of his own.

10. Except at leaving the oratory after office (68). 'Meditation' has been a constant and universal practice of monasticism.

11. Jerome, *Ep* 22.35. The Egyptians whom Cassian described likewise observed a uniform fast all year round without seasonal variations (*Conf.* 21,

29–30). Yet they dispensed themselves from fasting not only on Sundays but also on Saturdays (*Inst.* 3, 10–12). So the Master introduced no innovation by conceding two days' dispensation from the fast each week. He substituted Thursday for Saturday, which was a fast day at Rome.

12. See the rules of Caesarius and Aurelian.

13. 53:26–33, cf. 45:3. Compare with Caesarius, *Reg. mon.* 24: *pullos et carnes nunquam sani accipiant*—this sets the tone for all of ancient monasticism.

14. RB prescribes an almost identical menu, but takes a restrictive attitude toward second portions and wine. No trace of these reservations appears in the Master.

15. Inst. 14, 16.

16. These prescriptions of gospel origin are missing in Cassian but are present in Pachomius, Basil, Augustine, and in all later legislators.

17. A very grave fault (14:87); refusal to make satisfaction (13:69–72). Caesarius says flatly that anyone coming to office late is to be punished with the rod (*Reg. mon.* 11). For Columban, beatings were the ordinary thing. In this, there is radical opposition between the RM and Columban's monasticism.

18. The great vigil was to disappear in the RB and the roman office. Mention of it had already been omitted in the augustinian *Ordo monasterii*.

19. See the *Ordo romanus* XVIII, 19 (Andrieu, 3:207, 19). Cassian strongly opposed this custom (*Inst.* 3, 5).

20. *Comm. Ps* 118, 164; PL 70:895C.

21. 34:12–13.

22. See RM 69, 28:17, 53:5. The same attitude is found towards guests (78–79) and postulants (87–91).

23. It is met with when studying, for example, the uses of *debitus, iuste, iniuste, digne, dignus, indigne.*

CHAPTER TWO

LITURGY[1]

THE LITURGICAL SECTION of the RM is composed of two parts, followed by appendices (45–49). The first part deals with the number of psalms (33–38), the second with how they are said (39–44).

The first part is dominated by the constantly recurring structural law of the 'twenty-four impositions'. Since each psalm was followed by silent prayer and a *Gloria*, which involved kneeling,[2] the brothers knelt twenty-four times in the course of the day offices and an equal number of times during the night hours. The generic name *impositio* is given to every recited text (antiphon, response, or canticle) which concluded with the brothers kneeling, and thus is included in the calculation of the twenty-four occasions when the brothers kneel. The following table shows the division of the twenty-four impositions. Both here and below, conjectural figures are placed within brackets.

	Night		Day	
	Winter	Summer		
Nocturns:	[13][3] antiphons	9 antiphons	Little Hours:	3 antiphons
	3 responses	3 responses		1 response
	16 impositions	12 impositions		16 impositions
Matins:	6 antiphons		Evensong:	6 antiphons
	1 response			1 response
	1 Gospel canticle			1 Gosp. cant.
	8 impositions			8 impositions

As we see, the nocturnal system fails to meet the twenty-four impositions in summertime. The shortness of the nights then required that the antiphons be reduced to nine. And the hour of Compline, which goes to make up part of the seven-fold day office (34; 42), falls outside the calculation of impositions. Aside from these exceptions, the entire cycle merits admiration for its harmony. The little hours (Prime, Terce, Sext, and None) which punctuate the day correspond to the unique night office of nocturns. Evensong, the office at the end of day, corresponds to Matins, the office of the end of night.

The second part of the liturgical section treats of the times when alleluia is said. Antiphons, which occasion the greatest number of impositions, are divided at each hour into two groups, those without alleluia, and those with alleluia. There are two antiphons without alleluia for each antiphon with alleluia. We call this the two-to-one structural law which dominates this second part.

Uniform structural division into threes appears throughout, winter nocturns alone excepted. Antiphons are arranged in threes or multiples of three, and these are divided according to the two-to-one ratio. The Master was not the only one to build such a structural design. Similar structure is found in the majority of ancient monastic *ordines*.

At each hour there was ordinarily one response, without alleluia except in Paschaltide and Christmastide, on Sundays and feasts.[4] But at nocturns, besides the introductory response which conforms to the rubric just-mentioned, two responses were said, the first without, the second with, alleluia, each following a group of corresponding antiphons. The Gospel canticles (*euangelia*) which concluded Matins and Evensong were to be said by the abbot without alleluia, except on Sundays.[5] During Easter and Christmas seasons, day and night, as well as on Sundays and the patronal feast of the oratory, all antiphons and responses received the alleluia, beginning with the *benedictiones* of Matins.[6]

Epiphany brought a change regarding the alleluia. This feast marked the end of Christmastide, wholly comparable to the preceding Paschaltide. On the day after Epiphany, the alleluia which had been joined to all antiphons and responses ceased.[7] Whether partial or total, cessation of the alleluia at Epiphany was related to Easter preparation: on the day after Epiphany, the *centesima Paschae* commenced.[8] So Epiphany not only closed Christmastide, it also inaugurated a time of special austerity which would intensify until Easter.

Throughout these two parts the treatise on the divine office progressively develops the structure of each of the canonical hours. The outlines which follow will give an idea of it.

I. NOCTURNS:
    { Opening versicle (three times)
     Exhortatory response (Ps 95)
     Antiphons without alleluia: [9] in winter
                                6 in summer
    { Response without alleluia
    { Antiphons with alleluia: [4 in winter]
                            3 in summer
    { Response with alleluia
    { Reading from the Apostle
    { Reading from the Gospel
    { Verse
    { *Rogus Dei*[9]

II. MATINS AND EVENSONG:
    { Four antiphons without alleluia
    { Two antiphons with alleluia
    Response
    Verse
    { Reading from the Apostle
    { Gospel (canticle)
    Rogus Dei

III. PRIME, TERCE, SEXT, NONE:
    { Two antiphons without alleluia
    { One antiphon with alleluia
    Response
    { Reading from the Apostle
    { Reading from the Gospel
    Verse
    Rogus Dei

IV. COMPLINE:
  {Two antiphons without alleluia
  {One antiphon with alleluia
  Response
  {Reading from the Apostle
  {Reading from the Gospel
  Rogus Dei
  Closing verse

One can see at a glance that the hours of the office are all constructed on the same pattern. Identical elements succeed one another in the same order. Two exceptions may be observed, however: nocturns were introduced by a versicle and response, and the place of the versicle varied with the hours. The versicle at Compline 'closed' the brothers' mouths just as that of nocturns 'opened' them. It ought then to have concluded Compline. The position of the versicle at Matins and Evensong may be related to the special role of the gospel canticle at these hours, though this relation cannot be further elucidated. [10]

Is it possible to determine *which psalms* were said at each hour? An often-repeated rubric answers this question summarily: *currente semper psalterio,* the order of the psalter ought to be followed. The Master did not therefore include a preferred distribution of psalms—which psalm at which hour on which day—nor the saying of the psalter in a given period, a week for example, as is the case in the RB and the roman office. He was content to prescribe a continuous recitation of psalms, psalms were probably resumed at whatever point in the psalter they had been relinquished at the preceding hour. This principle, however, affects only antiphons, never responses, and at Matins and Compline it did not apply even to antiphons. The custom of assigning at Compline special psalms which relate to nighttime and sleep is found almost universally in ancient monastic *ordines,* [11] but we are ignorant of the psalms the Master wanted to have recited. For Matins, the Master indicates the psalms: Ps 51 (50) and the *Laudes,* [12] probably at the two extremes of the antiphonated psalmody and some canticles, as is the case in the benedictine rite (39:4).

One of the canticles is specified: on Sundays and feasts the *Benedictiones*[13] are recited (39).

What critical assessment can be made of all this liturgical legislation? From the point of view of form, its clarity and order arouse admiration. Furthermore, it is short. The two readings at each hour were probably brief, unlike those of vigils.[14] As for psalms, their number is very moderate: three antiphons at the little hours, six at Matins and Vespers, nine or thirteen at nocturns; one response at the day hours, three at the night office.[15] On the whole, these numbers correspond with the egyptian and oriental measure recommended by Cassian. They compare with the augustinian *Ordo monasterii* and, above all, with the roman office. But they contrast sharply with the much larger quantities of the entire liturgical tradition of Gaul from the time of Cassian's contemporaries (whom he did not hesitate to criticize) up to the Council of Tours in 567, and of the irish office, which includes the Lérins *ordo* of the two bishops of Arles, Caesarius and Aurelian.

Noteworthy also is the fact that antiphony predominated over other types of psalmody. Antiphons accompanied most psalms at each hour. Whereas three successive antiphons were always considered a minimum, responses were mere isolated units. In the entire office, responsorial psalmody amounted to only a fourth or a fifth of the antiphonal psalmody. The preponderance of antiphony is a new trait which distinguishes the Master's office from that of Arles-Lérins. The complete absence of hymns in RM is another factor; hymns figure in all the hours of Caesarius and Aurelian.[16] Lastly, the Master ignores the distinction between Vespers and *duodecima*; for him they are one and the same office, not two separate hours as at Arles. But this is not the place to treat at length the ancient monastic offices and the position the Master's office holds among them. In pursuing this research, let us content ourselves with pointing out a trail of capital importance: the roman office, as it was already attested to at the beginning of the sixth century by the benedictine office (which seems to be derived in large measure from it). Often the Master's *ordo* displays the clearest relationship with the roman *ordo* and that of St Benedict.[17]

THE EUCHARIST

The Master's community received the Eucharist daily under both species. Communion took place at the conclusion of the hour of the office which preceded the meal, that is, as a general rule, at the end of None. Thus the sacrament was received just before the monks went into the refectory. Communion terminated the fast, and this divine food led to physical nourishment.

Communion was a community rite. To abstain from it was considered arrogance and provoked punishment (22). Only a brother who had a nocturnal pollution on his conscience could abstain for two days, after having confessed his fault to the abbot (80).

We do not possess detailed knowledge of the ceremonial of this important rite. We can only catch a glimpse of certain customs regarding the hebdomadaries' communion (21): how they washed their hands in preparation—the consecrated bread was received in the hand—the kiss of peace and the community 'standing before the abbot' as it did at other times in the refectory. [18] We note too the order observed for communion: first the abbot, then hebdomadaries, finally each group of ten with its deans leading. It seems to have been the abbot who, though a layman, distributed the sacred species. That would hardly be surprising at a time when the faithful still gave themselves communion at home during the week with the bread they received at the Sunday Eucharist.

Reception of the eucharist was normally associated with the meal. It did not ordinarily imply celebration of Mass: there was no Mass except on Sundays, [19] the patronal feast of the oratory, [20] and the blessing of the abbot. [21] The communitarian rite of communion *extra missam* is well attested by sixth-century documents. [22] It was prescribed for Sundays and feasts by Aurelian of Arles, [23] while it seems to have been daily in the *Regula Pauli et Stephani*. [24] With the Master it was certainly daily. As for receiving the Blood of Christ as well as his Body even outside of Mass, it too is found in several contemporary or even subsequent documents. [25] In many cases it is not possible to say how the Precious Blood was made available. Reservation of consecrated wine, still men-

tioned for Holy Saturday by Chrysostom,[26] seems hardly to
have existed at all later on. The custom of reserving hosts
previously immersed in wine existed here and there, but the
Master's manner of speaking supposes a chalice from which
the wine is drunk.[27] This chalice had perhaps been sanctified
immediately before by the immersion of consecrated hosts,
according to the ancient procedure of 'sanctification by contact' which was to continue in use at Rome and elsewhere for
several centuries.[28]

Mass itself was celebrated in the monastery only on the
occasions of the patronal feast and the blessing of the abbot.[29]
This is suggested first by the expression *missas ecclesiae* used
to designate it.[30] *Ecclesia*, habitually contrasted with
monasterium, meant to the Master the secular church in the
twofold sense of society[31] and edifice.[32] Consequently, the
missas ecclesiae[33] were no doubt celebrated outside the
monastery, at the seculars' church.[34] Had Mass been celebrated in the monastery oratory, the Master would have
avoided this expression, as in fact he does in speaking of
Masses to celebrate the patronal feast of the oratory and the
blessing of the abbot.[35]

This is confirmed by a number of facts which seem to have
passed unobserved until now. The Master has the verse *Exultabunt sancti in gloria, laetabuntur in cubilibus suis* (Ps 149:5)
recited on Sundays. The significance of this verse, according
to him, is that 'wherever are these couches of saints, in other
words, churches, the exultation of Mass is celebrated.'[36] The
ecclesiae in which Mass is celebrated therefore are provided
with saints' relics. This is re-affirmed, with the aid of the
same verse, when the Master treats of visits to churches by
brothers on journeys.[37] Now, the oratories of monasteries
seem not to have possessed relics. The profession rite, which
took place in the oratory, carries no allusion to them, though
the altar itself is cited as a witness.[38] The Master observes
equal silence about them when he deals with visits to monastic oratories by brothers on journeys.[39] It therefore seems that
the verse *Exultabunt* recited on Sundays alludes solely to the
celebration of Sunday Mass in secular churches.[40] Nothing
indicates that monastic oratories were the site of similar celebrations.

This necessity for going out apparently explains why the Master prescribed 'nicer' feastday raiment to be worn only *in processionibus*.[41] Certainly the word *processio* may designate any sort of liturgical assemblage, even in the oratory of the monastery.[42] But it really seems here as if the Master were thinking of an actual trip out. It is in fact with regard to such trips that Benedict, in the corresponding chapter of his rule,[43] speaks of giving the brothers clothing 'somewhat better than usual'. Still more precisely, the Master's prescription reminds one of the nun in the *Lausiac History* who refused all new clothing or footwear so as to have, in her shabby clothes, a pretext for not going out to receive communion on Sundays.[44] For monks and nuns as for seculars, going to church demanded suitable attire.

There was really no permanently resident priest in the Master's monastery. Neither the brothers nor the abbot himself took holy orders. As for guest priests, their presence was not a permanent and assured fact. Celebration of Mass, moreover, does not figure among the prerogatives granted them.[45] Eucharistic liturgy was therefore celebrated in the oratory only by priests from outside on the two exceptional occasions previously mentioned. Ordinarily, the Master's community went to the parish church to assist at offices celebrated by diocesan clergy. This state of affairs seems fairly archaic in all respects. In daily communion, absence of priests in the community, and the necessity for going out for Mass, the RM appears to look towards the past rather than the future. In Gaul at almost the same period, communion was less frequent,[46] monks were ordained priests for the service of the community,[47] and Mass was celebrated in the monastery itself.[48]

These latter two traits likewise characterize the benedictine rule. Unlike the Master, Benedict received priests into the community[49] and forsaw the ordination of priests and deacons from among the monks.[50] These new arrangements correspond to a change of attitude toward the eucharistic celebration. It is consequently understandable why the benedictine rule makes no further mention of special clothing to be worn in 'processions'. Significantly, it replaces this particular prescription with a different arrangement: somewhat better clothing was to be given those about to set off on journeys.[51] And when the monastery oratory became, like the 'churches', the scene of regular eucharistic celebrations, its altar received relics just as did the altars of churches.[52] Clergy, Masses, relics—nothing was lacking in the oratory of Benedict's monastery. From the RM to the RB we witness an evolution which equates the monastery to secular churches, and confers on it, under the bishop's supervision, a sort of sacramental autonomy.

RITUAL

The Master's ritual is found dispersed in segments throughout the length of his rule.[53] It has a richness and a precision unsurpassed, to our knowledge, by any liturgical document of antiquity prior to the first *Ordines Romani*.[54] Structurally, these rites may be divided into two great categories: *prayers* and *blessings*.

PRAYERS. Let us take as an example the prayer offered on the completion of one's weekly kitchen assignment. It occurred in the refectory on Saturday evenings (25):

> When the abbot has been seated, as well as the whole community, the hebdomadaries together say: 'Please, brothers, pray for us, for we have completed our week of humble service.' All then rise with the abbot and kneel, and pray for them in common with them. And when they have risen, the hebdomadaries say this verse: 'Let those who hate us behold, and be confounded, because you, Lord, have helped and consoled us.' Then, after the abbot has pronounced a conclusion, they give the kiss of peace to him as well as to the provosts and the whole community.

This rite involves essentially prayer in common. Other elements all turn around this one. The following outline may be sketched:
1. Request for prayer.
2. Prayer, terminated by a verse and conclusion.
3. Kiss of peace.

This pattern is found every time the Master describes what may be styled a rite of *entrance* or of *exit*, one marking the beginning or the end of an assignment. These rites are numerous. Beginning with those which are connected closely with the exit of the kitchen servers, we may single out for attention the entrance of these same brothers (19:1-8) and the weekly reader's entrance (24:6-12).[55] Embarkation on and return from journeys are similarly commemorated (66 and 67), as are arrival and departure when a visit is made to a monastery (57:19-24) or to a church (57:25-7), as are the encounters with and bidding good-bye to other religious in the course of a journey (71 and 63), the arrival of guests at the monastery (65),[56] and the reception of gifts blessed by a bishop or priest (76). To the rites relating to journeys and the world outside must be adjoined those which sanctify work: prayer before and after manual work (50:47-50), and before and after spiritual work or 'meditation' (50:65-9). This sort of prayer also precedes and follows meals (23 and 38; cf. 73), accompanies the washing of feet at bedtime (30; 4-7, cf. 30:26), and the awakening by the abbot (32:4-5). There is also the communion rite for the weekly kitchen servers (21), which resembles that of visits to churches, and the prayer for a tempted brother (15:19-27, 5).

We would mention finally several rites distinguished by their complicated appearance, though their elements and the act they solemnize classify them fundamentally in the category of *prayers*. First is the entrance into monastic life which is profession (89:3-28), then the entrance into office or 'ordination' of the abbot[57] (93:6-42), finally re-entrance into the community or the reconciliation of the excommunicate (14:1-73). Of these three entrance rites, the last two have counterparts, exit rites, which correspond with them. Ordination of the new abbot is matched by the absolution of his predecessor (93:39-42), and reconciliation pairs up with a ceremony in which excommunication is imposed (13:1-41). Profession, on the contrary, has no corresponding rite mark the end of monastic life, other than death. The complete absence of a funeral rite is a curious characteristic of this ritual, otherwise so complete.

BLESSINGS. These form a type of rite characterized by brevity. Silent prayer, which constitutes the nucleus of the prayers, is suppressed. With it disappear the verse and kiss of peace. Only a request remains, ordinarily reduced to a single word, *Benedicite*[58] or *Benedic,*[59] and a response consisting of a formulaic blessing, sometimes accompanied by a sign of the cross.[60] A simple inclination of the head accompanies the request, and the superior normally stands to impart the blessing.[61] This is the position prescribed for the conclusion of the prayer rites.

Blessings, then, are like prayers in miniature, prayers reduced to a request and a conclusion. The brevity of the rite is in keeping with its frequency. Blessings are in fact numerous. To cite the more principle ones: the superior's blessing is sought every time a brother wishes to speak (RM 9); before one is seated at the reader's bench (24:13); before one occupies the abbatial chair (93:37); before the various chores of kitchen duty (19:8). But it is above all in the course of meals that blessings abound. They are repeated before each item eaten and before each drink; the beverage is blessed not only before its distribution, but also at table when each brother seeks his provost's blessing before drinking. The servers cannot even sample the beverage without a special blessing (23).

What critical assessment can be passed on the Master's ritual? At first glance it appears excessive and a little suffocating. Closer examination reveals, however, that this impression comes more from the meticulousness of the description than by the real quantity and breadth of the rites. It is because he takes such pains to note each detail, as though he were compiling a ceremonial or a book of customs, that the Master produces this impression of an overdone ritual. On an equal literary par, any ceremonial, including those of the twentieth century, creates the same impression. It is necessary, then, to get beneath appearances and to try to evaluate the real dimension and importance of this collection of rites.

There are about twenty prayer rites, some daily, several weekly, the greatest number without periodic determination. Some are mutually exclusive, being without periodic determination. Some are mutually exclusive, being performed in different circumstances. Thus, when a brother is sent on a journey, he fulfils the rites for embarking upon it and for completing it on their respective days, but he does not fulfil the prayers before and after work prescribed for those remaining in the monastery.

Of rather limited number, the prayers are chiefly short and simple rites. Few words are spoken. As a general rule, the only formulas are those of the request and conclusion. In the heart of the rite comes the silent prayer, whose length is determined by the gravity of the circumstances. This intimate, wordless prayer confers on the rite a character of interiority which in later times came, unfortunately, to be effaced, when the 'horror of the void' led liturgists to fill up this silence with an Our Father and some verses.

Prayer rites are distinguished in addition by their homogeneity. The same structure recurs throughout, easily adapted to various circumstances. Even the three 'great ceremonies' (reconciliation, profession, and the blessing of the abbot) are ultimately based on this unique plan, the elements of which they repeat or combine in an original manner. Even the longest of them all, the blessing of the abbot, remains an astonishingly quick ceremony, lasting not more than a quarter of an hour. Its style is that of ancient ordinations, whose simplicity contrasts sharply with the proliferation of rites and formulas of the roman-germanic ritual and of the roman pontifical rite still in use until recently.

Homogeneous in itself, the Master's ritual manifests the same quality in the divine office. The elements which compose it—request, prayer, verse, conclusion—are likewise found in the office. Silent prayer, with its spoken conclusion, follows each psalm of the office just as it constitutes each function of the ritual. The request for prayer is likewise made at the beginning of each prayer of the divine office, in behalf of the sick, the absent, or guests about to depart.[62] The versicle plays an integral part in all the hours of the office. Certain versicles—*Domine labia* and *Exultabunt sancti*—are even used in both office and ritual. Moreover, the fact that all the versicles of the ritual are taken from psalms alone is enough to establish profound continuity between them and the divine office. Although psalmody properly so-called does not enter into the ritual except before and after meals, the versicle may be considered a fragment of psalmody. This drawing upon the psalter fuses the ritual to the hours of the office. Like the office, the ritual is made up of psalmody and prayer. Thus the two great forms of monastic prayer, prayer which sanctifies the hours and prayer which sanctifies actions, are fundamentally alike.

Blessings themselves pertain not only to the ritual. They are found as well in the office, where the superior's blessing was to be sought before each psalm.[63]

The monastic ritual as it appears in the *Regula Magistri* seems to us one of the most remarkable attempts ever made to put into practice the apostolic precept *omne quodcumque facitis in uerbo aut in opere, omnia in nomine Iesu Christi.*[64] One or another aspect of the ritual which might seem to us too onerous must be judged in the light of concrete living conditions in the Master's monastery. The kiss of peace, repeated after each prayer, could not have taken very long in a relatively small community. Other aspects can be explained by reference to the customs of ancient times. The numerous blessings in the course of meals only match the profane order and ceremonial in use at meals in the roman world.

NOTES TO CHAPTER TWO

1. This chapter has been considerably abridged. See *Translator's Note.*

2. See 33.

3. This figure is missing in 33:29. We restore it in accordance with the sum-total of impositions. See our study 'Lacunes et erreurs dans la section liturgique de la *RM,*' in *Rev. Bénéd.* 70 (1960) 410–413. We therefore reject the sum, twelve, indicated by *A* in 44:2, as well as the eleven furnished by *P* in the same passage. As surprising as the figure thirteen may be, it is confirmed by the absence of symbolic notation in 33:29. The figure twelve could not have failed to provoke comparison with the twelve apostles. Cf. 33:30,40.

4. RM 45. The rubric seems to come into play only on the patronal feast of the oratory (45:18), not on that of any saint (38:5–7, 45:16).

5. RM 39:2, 41:3.

6. It is probable that the *euangelia* of Matins-Vespers is included in this general law for feastdays, though only Sundays are immediately envisaged in 39:2, 41:3.

7. RM 45:2–3, 8–11.

8. RM 45:11.

9. This, probably meaning a silent prayer, has been translated as 'Prayer to God'.

10. The benedictine and roman offices both have the verse of Matins-Vespers before the gospel canticle, though after the *capitulum.*

11. Perhaps already in Cassian, *Inst.* 4, 19, 2: *psalmos quos quieturi ex more decantant.*

12. No doubt Ps. 148-150. Cf. Cassian, *Inst.* 3, 6 and Caesarius-Aurelian.

13. Dan 3:52-56, 57-90. This is the second of the three canticles of Easter Matins for Caesarius-Aurelian. In the roman and benedictine offices it is found on Sundays. The Master makes it his point of departure for a dispensation from kneeling and for the general use of the alleluia. Should we conclude from this that it comes at the beginning of the office rather than at the end?

14. RM 44:9. Two readings were already to be found in the egyptian office described by Cassian, *Inst.* 2, 4-6. But the Master generalized this prescription which in the egyptian offices prevailed only at Vespers-nocturns. Moreover, these readings had only an optional character in Egypt: for the Master they were obligatory. Finally, Egypt had one reading from the Old Testament and one from the New, except in Paschaltime and on Sundays when both were taken from the New Testament. The Master adopted this last system and extended it to the whole year.

15. We admit that, in the Master's terminology, *antifana = psalmus cum antifana*, that is, each antiphon corresponds to a single psalm. Another interpretation has been sustained by C. Gindele in a series of articles, in particular 'Die Struktur der Nokturnen in der lateinischen Mönschregeln vor und um St Benedikt' in *Rev. Bénéd.* 64 (1954) 9-27, and 'Die römische und monastische Ueberlieferung im Ordo Officii der *RB*,' *Studia Anselmiana* 42 (Rome, 1957) 171-222. According to this author, each antiphon corresponds to three psalms, a thing which would enormously expand the size of the office. We have criticized this interpretation in the article 'Le sense d'antifana et la longeur de l'office dans la *RM*,' *Rev. Bénéd.* 71 (1961) 119-124. The same conclusion of non-acceptance has been proposed against C. Gindele by V. Janeras, 'Notulae liturgicae in *RM*,' *Studia monastica* 2 (1960) 359-364, and by O. Heiming, 'Zum monastischen Offizium von Kassianus bis Kolumbanus,' *ALW* 7 (1961-1962) 89-156.

16. However, the care with which the two bishops note the *incipit* of each hymn could indicate innovation. It is not sure that the *ordo* of Lérins included these hymns.

17. Further evidence supporting this relationship may be found in my article 'Scholies sur la Règle du Maître,' *RAM* 44 (1968) 122.

18. RM 23:4, 27:13.

19. 45:14-15, 75:5 (*missas ecclesiae*).

20. 45:17 (*processionem missae . . . agendae . . . a sacerdote*).

21. 93:8 (*missae altaris*). The new abbot presented the bread and wine to the priest.

22. On this point see my article 'Problems of the Monastic Conventual Mass,' *Downside Review* 87 (1969) 327-338. In earlier generations, the rite of daily communion at home is attested by Basil (Ep 93), Jerome (Ep 49, 15 [cf. Jerome, Ep 71, 6]), Augustine (Ep 54, 3-4). This usage seems to have held on tenaciously in Egypt, according to Basil's testimony, and at Rome, according to Jerome's testimony. The remainder of this section on the Eucharist is a moderately abridged translation of some further insights of the author which

were published in 'Scholies sur la Règle du Maître,' *RAM* 44 (1968) 122–127.

23. Aurelian, *Reg. mon.*, PL 68:396B; *Reg. virg.*, PL 68:406G. The question of Sunday communion occurs also in the *Reg. Cuiusdam* 32; PL 66:994, but we cannot affirm that it treats here of communion *extra missam* as in Aurelian, though this is possible.

24. *Reg. Pauli et Stephani* 13, ed. by J. Vilanova (Montserrat, 1959) 113.

25. Gregory, *Dial.* 2, 37; 3, 26; 4, 11; 4, 36 (communions *in articulo mortis*); *Vita S. Mariae Aegypt.* 35 (22). Cf. Gregory, *Dial.* 4, 16, in which mention is not made of the Blood. Basel, Ep 93, likewise means communion under both species.

26. Chrysostom, *Ep* 1 *ad Innocentium* 3; *PG* 52:533 (reservation of the species in church, not at home). According to the *Gelasian Sacramentary* 418 (cf. 390), it seems the consecrated wine was still reserved on Holy Thursday for the Good Friday communion, unlike what the *Ordo Romanus* and later *Ordines* would prescribe.

27. 21:7 (*confirmment*).

28. Cf. Ambrose, *De officiis.* 1, 41 (ministry by a deacon). See M. Andrieu, *Immixtio et Consecratio* (Paris: A. Picard, 1924), and especially J. P. De Jong, 'Le rite de la commixtion dans la messe romaine,' *ALW* IV/2 (1956) 245–278, and V/1 (1957) 33–79; 'La commixtion des espèces,' *QLP* 45 (1964) 316–319.

29. 45:17, 93:8–11. The monastery oratory was no doubt considered a private sanctuary in which Mass could be celebrated only rarely and with the express authorization of the bishop, who designated the celebrant in each case. This statute for private oratories is well formulated in two rescripts of Pelagius I, Ep 86 and 89 (Gassó-Battle p. 210–216), as well as by the formulas of the *Liber Diurnus* and of Gregory, which repeat its terms.

30. 45:14, 75:5.

31. 1:83, 11:8,9,11, 83:2, 18, 93:6.

32. 45:15, 53:64, 57:25.

33. See C. Mohrmann, *Études sur le Latin des chrétiens*, III (Rome: Edizioni di Storia e Letteratura, 1965) 363–364. *Ecclesiae* is a genitive of departure for Etheria, *Pereg.* 25, 2 and 28, 2, for whom *missas ecclesiae* signifies 'dismissal from church' (cf. *missa de ecclesia* in *Pereg.* 27, 3 and 46, 6). In the Master, however, it seems that *missas* designates not so much the final 'dismissal' as the whole of the liturgical action, as RM 45:14 shows (*usque ad missas ecclesiae adimpletas*), and also 93:11 (*celebrantes oratorio missas*). Cf. 46:6 (*ordine quo missae a clericis celebrantur*). The meaning of *missas ecclesiae* is therefore 'Mass at church.'

34. It is true the expression designates Mass celebrated in the *monastic* church in Scete, in *Vitae Patrum* 5, 4, 27: *Post missas ecclesiae fugite fratres*. But this sense, which corresponds to Scete's particular situation, is highly improbable in the case of RM, in view of the Master's terminology in its totality (see notes 10, 11, 14).

35. 45:17 *processionem missae ibi agendae ipso die a sacerdote*; 93:8: *missae altaris in oratorio*; 93:11: *celebrantes oratorio missas*.

36. 45:14–15: *hoc est quod per omnium sanctorum cubilia, id est ecclesias, missarum exultatio celebratur.*

37. 57:25–26.

38. 89:6–11. Compare RB 58:18–19: *coram Deo et sanctis eius . . . ad nomen sanctorum quorum reliquiae ibi sunt.*

39. 57:19–24.

40. In addition, it seems Mass was celebrated in churches only on Sundays. This tends to confirm that the daily rite described in RM 21 is really a communion *extra missam.*

41. 81:7.

42. 45:17: *usque ad processionem missae ibi agendae ipso die a sacerdote.* However, the procession *ibi agendae ipso die* shows the event was not customary. Ordinarily Mass was said elsewhere.

43. RB 55:14.

44. Palladius, *Lausiac History,* 59, 2.

45. 83:5: *nihil aliud eis in monasteriis liceat, nisi orationes colligere, conplere et signare.*

46. See above, note 23.

47. Aurelian, *Reg. mon.* 46.

48. *Vita S. Johannis Raeomensis* 15 (*AA SS,* Jan. 28). According to this *Life,* the Mass celebrated in the monastery was reserved strictly for the monks, in their interests. No secular might assist. The same rule is laid down in the *Liber Diurnus* V, 13; PL 105:92B. Leaving the enclosure to go to church had been customary during the first monastic generations. See *Les Vies Coptes de S. Pachôme,* ed. L. Th. Lefort (Louvain: Bureaux du Muséon, 1943) 96; Jerome Ep 108, 20; Augustine, *Reg.* 10, 67. Though Pachomius attests this usage at Antinoean (*Lausiac History,* 59, 2), he reveals a different custom in use at Tabenna, where a priest and a deacon went to celebrate on Sundays with the nuns (33, 2). Previously Pachomius had had a priest come to his monastery, at least on Sundays (*Vies Coptes,* p. 96).

49. RB 60.

50. RB 62.

51. RB 55:14.

52. RB 58:18–19 (above, note 38).

53. This reproduces, in much abridged form, a study published in *Rev. Bénéd.* 71 (1961) 235–252.

54. In this respect the RM can be compared to the *Apostolic Tradition* of Hippolytus or to the *Itinerarium Egeriae.*

55. No ceremony is foreseen for the reader's exit, this, no doubt, because of the slight importance attached to this service. Other weekly servers such as the *uigigalli* (31) and guestmasters (79) have no ceremony either at entrance or exit, apparently for the same reason. The same applies to permanent officers of a rank inferior to the provosts: cellarer (16), the brother custodian (17), and porters (95).

56. Departure of guests is not treated, but see 20, 88 (departure of a postulant).

57. The term 'ordination' is not reserved only to the abbot. It recurs in reference to deans (11:15), the cellarer (16:62), and hebdomadaries (18:10, 13). A ceremony was foreseen for the *ordinatio* of deans 11:15–19), but the description of it is sketchy. Only the handing over of the *uirga,* the insignia of this function, is indicated.

58. 1:51; 19:8; 23:29; 65:3; 95:20.

59. 27:8 (a unique case). The request for a blessing in either of these forms is itself sometimes called *benedictio*.

60. 23:18.

61. 27:16 *antequam sedeat.* Yet in 23:2-3 (blessing of bread), it seems the abbot remained seated.

62. 20 and 57. If travelers returned while the office was in progress, they introduced the prayer request upon their return at the beginning of the prayer following the psalm. In this case, the prayer prescribed by the ritual became identified with that of the office (67).

63. 56:2. Cf. 22:13, 14; 46:1, 2.

64. Col 3:17.

CHAPTER THREE

DOCTRINE

T HE MASTER'S ASCETICAL doctrine rests on an anthropology and a soteriology. Set within its historical context, this accumulation of ideas on human nature, on redemption by Christ, and on the ascent to perfection contains nothing original. The Master only appropriated to himself thought common to antiquity. But a brief résumé of this doctrine will be useful here, both because some themes, too little known today, require elucidation, and because one aspect of the author and his work shall then become manifest. The RM presupposes a rather broad culture and some personal reflection on it.

Following the concept current since St Paul's time (1 Th 5:23), the Master considered man composed of three elements: *body, soul,* and *spirit.* [1] The inferior element is very often called 'flesh' with the pejorative evaluation attached to this term in the pauline vocabulary of flesh as the unruly corporal appetite which stands in opposition to the law of God and in which sin reigns. The spirit, on the contrary, is the noble and sound inclination by which man loves God and adheres to his will. Between these two rival yearnings, the soul is the basis of liberty which alternatively obeys one or the other. The soul's oscillation between flesh and spirit is the whole drama of human life, or christian life, and of monastic life.

Salvation depends on this choice. The body is but earth and dust, the soul alone gives it human form and consistency. [2] Man's whole life originates in the soul. It is the soul that senses, that moves, that acts. Nothing the body does escapes its control and its responsibility. [3] In consequence, human life in its manifold spheres falls within the compass of free will,

43

and is answerable to the judgment of God. Each human action, from the greatest to the least, requires that the soul choose for or against the spirit, that is, for or against God. When death comes, the cast-off body reverts to dust, but the soul bears the full weight of earthly works which, good or bad, set their seal on it for all eternity.

Material goods, which cannot follow the soul after death, are therefore unimportant.[4] The only thing which lasts is the soul and the account it shall have to render for all its actions. The prospect of a judgment which determines eternal happiness or damnation is what drives a man to conversion, drives him, in other words, to enter a monastery.[5] This also determines the whole structure of the monastic community and the *ascesis* imposed on each of its members. The monastery is nothing but a school where one learns to serve God, a workshop where God's commandments are practised, an army battling against the flesh.[6] Everything is calculated with the view of accomplishing the divine will and of eliminating entirely the sin in each individual. It is an offering of souls beyond reproach, of blameless lines to the God who beholds us even now and shall one day summon us to judgment.

Nothing original, we repeat, comes out in these perspectives. Then as now, notions of eternal salvation, divine law, sin, and judgment formed the mental framework of all Christian existence. What is unique is the intensity with which these thoughts are here 'realized', in the newmanian sense of the word. In the Master's monastery, the individual and the collective conscience are, as a matter of fact, haunted by such thoughts. The rule incessantly proposes the theme of struggle against sin. Does the monk happen to be on his way to the oratory to celebrate one of the little hours? The avowed motive for the celebration is to render thanks to God for the last three hours passed free of sin.[7] Is he organizing the use of time? The primary end assigned to work is so to occupy the spirit as to dispel evil thoughts.[8] Do the monks pray before beginning any work? They do so to implore divine assistance not to commit sin or displease the Lord at any moment.[9]

What lends sharpness to this obsession is the consciousness of fighting not only against flesh and blood, but against the terrible power of the devil, who is bent on men's destruction. In the world, Satan reigns undisturbed over a mankind entirely his. But in the monastery he unleashes furious attacks on men intent on resisting him.[10] To enter the service of God is therefore to enter into open warfare with the devil. One meets him at every turn of monastic life: during psalmody, when the devil manages to provoke repeated coughing and spitting;[11] during the prayers after psalmody, when besides these physical embarrassments he causes the imagination to wander;[12] during kitchen service, when he tempts to gluttony;[13] outside the enclosure, where he capitalizes on a brother's isolation in the course of a journey to entice him to evil actions.[14] Above all the devil works for the apostasy of postulants and professed, to make them return to the world.[15] These multiform and incessant schemings not only menace each individual, they increase the weight of the cares borne by the abbot and provosts, who are obliged to continual surveillance.[16] The community life is wholly and completely dominated by this preoccupation with the struggle against the flesh, against sin, and against the devil.

In the face of these powerful enemies, the brothers are not left to their own resources, happily for them. God not only arbitrates the combat, he intervenes powerfully, for he is good and the savior.[17] His grace is really the principal, universal agent of all good things done in the monastery despite the devil.[18] The sign of the cross puts evil thoughts to flight,[19] and dispels temptations[20] and material misfortunes as well.[21] God's blessing reduces the accursed devil to impotence.[22] In serious cases, recourse to prayer is imperative, and, whether individual or communitarian prayer, it proves sovereign.[23] Christ's promises about the efficacy of prayer are the object of unshakable faith.[24] The dogma of his redemptive passion gives assurance of victory.[25] Christ is truly the Rock upon which all the forces of evil are dashed.[26]

Yet confidence in God does not exclude recourse to social pressure to sustain the tottering virtue of individual brothers. The monastery is literally a school where men of all ages are trained in a way that one would hardly dare to train children today. The abbot not only teaches by word and example: either personally or through the provosts, he sees to it that the brothers put his teaching into practice. The continual presence of the provosts with their men is one of our author's fixed ideas. He reverts to it constantly.[27] Provosts have the mission of not letting pass any failing, and they are armed with short ready-made discourses appropriate to each mistake. Should a brother manifest resistance, the offender was brought before the abbot, punished with excommunication, and obliged to humiliating penance after harsh privations. Refusal to make satisfaction brought expulsion after thee days. Little faults—a negligence, simply being late—could set this penal procedure in motion.[28]

Fear of punishment was not the only means devised. Shame was also employed.[29] Throughout his rule the Master seemed to set high hopes on a spirit of rivalry for succeeding to the abbacy. He organized a contest of virtue among the brothers, refereed by the abbot; the winner of it was awarded first place.[30] This pedagogical stratagem, of which our author seems very proud, seems to us today an aberration. In spite of certain extenuating circumstances, it is unlikely his contemporaries judged differently.[31]

Whatever we may think of this odd invention, we must recognize that the educative theme permeating RM falls well into line with all ancient cenobitism. The *coenobium* was, in our fathers' eyes, an institution that educated men in simple and vigorous methods. This must be borne in mind, however disagreeable it may be to our modern sensibilities. If the RM, more than any other rule, disconcerts us in this respect, this is not because it accentuates abnormally the pedagogical aspect of training, but simply because, being much more detailed and methodical than any other document, it lifts these realities in much sharper relief by treating them more exhaustively. The disciplinary element is not hypertrophic; it is only described with unmatched precision. To cry out against the seemingly childish or tyrannical character of certain proceedings as if they were only odious novelties resulting from the author's pedagogical mania would be a mistake. Were the benedictine Rule three times longer, it would also reveal many details of which we are happily ignorant.

Collective discipline cannot completely eliminate sin. The individual must supply personal effort. The element of individual *ascesis* appears chiefly in the first part of the rule (3–10). Following the lists of good works, of virtues, and of vices in chapters three–five, three great treatises describe the three governing virtues: obedience, silence, and humility. Obedience is not only the fundamental attitude of the disciple who places his will in the hands of a 'teacher' so that the latter might make the will of God reign in his life; it is also an imitation of Christ, a participation in his passion, the equivalent of martyrdom.[32] One of RM's rare summits is encountered here where something like a breath of mysticism may be sensed. Moreover, obedience is not pleasing to God unless it proceeds from the depths of the heart, and fulfills the order given with a good will and without interior murmuring.[33] It is therefore very much more than mere external discipline.

The opposite of obedience is 'self-will'. By this is meant all manner of resistance to the divine will and to the will of the superior, it being taken for granted that the disciple would not know the will of God except through his 'teacher'. Self-will, therefore, properly means sinful will. A synonymous expression, often linked with self-will, is the 'desire of the flesh.' It refocuses our attention on the flesh-soul-spirit trichotomy.[34]

Although obedience provides the remedy for self-will, that is, for the root of all sin, it is not on that account less necessary to keep a special eye on certain dangerous areas where sin readily asserts itself. The Master follows a picturesque scheme in describing human activities: the soul is lodged in the heart, which is the seat of thinking; with the eyes the soul looks out and takes in the objects it covets; with the tongue it manifests to the world what it has conceived in the heart. But although heart, eyes, and tongue serve as organs of sinful activity, the soul has the power to control these organs, which ought to be used for good. The Master indicates in turn how the evil thought, the impure glance, and the sinful word are to be mastered—treating this last fault at great length because of its social repercussions. The considerable development given to 'taciturnity' (this virtue alone is mentioned in the titles of chapters eight and nine) should not blind us to the whole ascetical program of which it is but one element. Taciturnity is one aspect of the vast plan of resistance against sin, a plan which equally involves exercising recollection of God and custody of the eyes.

This plan of *ascesis* receives further enlargement in chapter ten. Within a framework of 'marks of humility' which he took from Cassian and, according to his custom, transformed into a picturesque 'heavenward ladder'', the author blends all the material from the two previous treatises on obedience and taciturnity. This amalgam is to be found from the first degree to the list of faculties needing surveillance (thoughts, tongue, hands, feet) which comes from the treatise on taciturnity. Self-will and the desires of the flesh are added to take up again thereby the doctrine on obedience. This doctrine is further developed in degrees two–four, just as the doctrine on taciturnity constitutes degrees nine–eleven. The twelfth degree, entirely original when compared with Cassian, repeats the prescriptions on custody of the eyes. Humility, the title of the chapter, occupies only a very limited placed in this synthesis (degrees five–seven). These twelve degrees are presented as an ascent from fear of God to the perfect love which casts out all fear. By the time it reaches the summit, the soul has acquired a sort of facility for doing good. Virtue has become second nature, 'the love of good habits' reigns in it and renders inferior motivations impotent. To these notions derived from Cassian, the Master adjoins a precious remark: it is the Lord who brings about this marvelous state in his servant, the Holy Spirit who thus purifies the humble brother of his vices and sins.[35] Here, for the second time, an almost mystical touch may be felt.

Manifestly, the great exposition of spiritual doctrine which fills chapters seven–ten does not consist of three independant treatises simply juxtaposed. Although obedience, taciturnity, and humility are brought up in their turn, these virtues are nevertheless all studied from the same viewpoint of the *fight against sin*. The last phrase of chapter ten sounds the tone which dominates throughout: *mundum a peccatis et uitiis*. From beginning to end, purification of the whole man is the subject. Obedience puts an end to self-will and carnal desire; custody of the heart, custody of the eyes, and taciturnity all put a stop to sin in the most vulnerable faculties of the human constitution; humility accomplishes its task both by embracing the other virtues and by furnishing a specific remedy for the chief vice, pride. If the Master judge it to his purpose to refuse special attention to other faculties, such as sins of the hands and feet (theft and homicide),[36] or to gluttony, or sexual appetite, this is because the monastic observance set forth in the second part of the rule by itself serves as an adequate check against offenses of this nature. Only the main features of personal *ascesis* are laid down in the first chapters. We must not delude ourselves, however, into thinking that the Master is merely recommending three important virtues with no precise mutual relations. His purpose is to present a complete and methodical defense against sin.

Flee sin to avoid hell; accomplish God's will to obtain eternal glory. Under a twofold aspect, negative and positive, this fundamental concept confers unity on the whole spiritual treatise. The accent may seem to fall more often on the negative. Is avoiding sin not always at issue? Without denying the predominance of *declina a malo* over *fac bonum,* which can partly be explained by the elementary nature of this *ascesis* designed for new converts, we must at any rate note that, in the presentation of the Last Things, the heavenward perspective shines forth much more clearly than the prospect of hell. A great reader of the *Visio Pauli,* the Master could have drawn, had he wished, from that apocalypse its frightful images as well as its paradisiacal visions. But in fact, while portrayals of paradise are developed at length on three occasions in RM,[37] hell is not once described.[38]

Along with this positive eschatological expectation, the disciple has before him a life-long program which he ought normally to follow here below. The RM not only organizes the suppression of sin, it guides the brother in an ascent towards the spiritual ideal. The passage from fear to love in chapter ten has already been mentioned. Between these two extremes, one is unfortunately hardly able to recognize successive stages in the 'degrees' of the Master, any more than in the 'marks' of Cassian, despite some semblances of progression.[39] We must instead gather from the entire rule indications of the brothers' spiritual progress.

The first step of monastic *ascesis* is renunciation of the

world. The plan our author selected does not permit him to speak of it in its natural place at the Rule's beginning. Only at the end of the work, when he deals with the admission of postulants, does the Master speak of it *ex professo*. Absolute despoilment is required. The postulant's every possession, present or future, must be abandoned. Several ways of achieving this are suggested: distributions to the poor, an offering to the monastery, legacies to relatives. By no subterfuge may the newly-arrived keep anything for his personal use, whether in the monastery or in the world.[40] The purpose is clear: the postulant's first concern is to burn his bridges behind him, to cast off every thought of returning to the world, and in this way to assure his perseverance.[41] The brother is not to have the least thing over which he could exercise his own will: poverty conditions obedience.[42] Ultimately, renunciation of personal property signifies a turning away from all material anxieties. In other words, the brother has entrusted his material existence as well as his spiritual management to the abbot; he takes no further thought for his own body. Leaving to the monastery the trouble of providing for him, he henceforth gives no thought to anything except the salvation of his soul.[43]

To renounce all possessions is to carry out the words of Christ, 'Go, sell what you have and give the money to the poor, and come, follow me.'[44] But once everything has been sold, the second part of the program, the following of Christ, remains to be accomplished. So the second step of monastic *ascesis* is renunciation of one's own will, obedience. In fact, our author understands Christ's words, 'Let him who wishes to be my disciple renounce himself and follow me!' as obedience.[45]

Like renunciation of material things, obedience ought to be absolute. No pains are spared in making the newly-arrived brother understand its demands. That this is really a kind of martyrdom is not concealed from him. It is not easy to glimpse the concrete tests the author has in mind when he speaks of 'various and hard things commanded by the abbot' and of 'various mortifications of our wills'.[46] Certainly the mortifications imposed by the rule, of which the abbot is guardian, are the first to suggest themselves. Among these, renunciation[47] and enclosure[48] are apparently considered especially costly, for enclosure prohibits visits by parents and relatives. In addition to these points of common observance, the subject ought to obey the particular orders given him by the abbot. In this domain, the only points of friction the rule singles out for attention are errands outside the monastery—a tiring occupation which the skilled craftsmen might consider below their dignity[49]—and supererogatory ascetical practices performed without permission.[50] But many others no doubt existed.

Obedience admits of no qualifications on the subject's part. No liberty of judgment is left him, the eventuality of a conflict between the order given and divine law is never even envisaged. Nor is it allowed that the material execution of an order be accompanied by interior reservations and holding back. One must obey with all one's heart. If there are any limits to obedience, they exist only in virtue of certain concessions permitted by the Rule itself. Accordingly, brothers may choose their occupations on Sundays[51] and during the intervals separating nocturns from Matins in wintertime.[52] To some extent they may also determine their food consumption during Lent and the rest of the year.[53] This leaves a margin to spontaneity. Moreover, the rule grants a certain latitude even in the exercise of obedience. Whereas the 'perfect' obey at the first word, the 'imperfect' are granted the right of not complying until the second command. Similar concessions are made in the matter of silence.[54]

Classifying brethren as 'perfect' and 'imperfect' may seem simplistic to us, and the casuistry too naive. Yet such distinctions do at least manifest the author's genuine concern to adapt his pedagogy to the diversity of graces and characters, in keeping with directives he gives to the abbot.[55] At the outset, the Master does not place all the members of his little world on an equal footing. He knows conversion is a progressive thing, and makes prudent allowance for gradation on the way to perfection. Theoretically he demands 'perfect' and 'irreproachable' observance from the novice during his year of probation.[56] But in fact perfection is to be met with only only in a small number of religious; these, by their example, ought not to dishearten the weak, but to incite them to progress.[57]

Obedience to rule and abbot embraces within itself all the renunciations of monastic life. But once consent has been given to this radical sacrifice, which alone is mentioned in the act of profession,[58] it is necessary to prepare to fight each of the evil tendencies residing within sinful man. This combat against 'vices and sins'[59] is the very substance of monastic life, as has already become apparent. The brother ought to wage war particularly on pride, loquacity, laughing and horse-play, on carelessness of external deportment, on gluttony or appetite, on nocturnal pollutions and the unruly activity of the imagination which occasions them, on the shame which hinders confessions, on sleep itself. May this incoherent enumeration be pardoned: the Master himself is hardly more orderly. If he tried to arrange certain aspects of ascesis logi-cally in chapters seven–ten, it was with the help of pictur-esque schemes (the soul lodged in the body; the heavenward ladder) rather than with a truly profound and coherent sys-tem of concepts. Moreover, these chapters of the synthesis leave out plenty of tendencies (desire for food and sleep, sexuality, etc.) about which only occasional instruction is proffered in the course of the Rule. Nor need a closer exam-ination be made of the order or extent of the lists of good works, of vices, and of virtues in chapters three–five and ninety-two. The author is satisfied with a chain of scriptural passages, St Paul in particular, finished off with some recol-lections of his reading. The absence of the theory of eight principal faults is striking: it had served as Cassian's framework in the *Institutes*. When we consider the great debt the Master owes to Cassian, nothing shows us better than this omission how little our author is interested in systems.[60]

Whatever the reason for the absence of speculation, the important fact for us here is the intense ascetical effort the Rule required of each brother. It corrected him of all his faults. This effort tends towards a goal: to make the brothers *spiritual men*. The ideal of the 'spiritual brother' is what con-fers a certain unity on this ascetical program otherwise so little systematized.

To understand fully what the author means by the word *spiritalis*, a term very dearly esteemed by him, the trichotomic conception of man explained at the beginning of this study must be recalled. Man is flesh, soul, spirit. His whole religious adventure, as we explained, consists in the oscillation of the soul between flesh and spirit, and in his choice for one or the other of these mutually opposed tendencies. The spiritual man is one who has made the spirit triumphant in himself.[61]

This concept appears in the Rule for the first time in a quotation from St Paul: 'You who are spiritual' writes the Apostle to the Galatians in exhorting them to gentleness.[62] Later on, the Master adverts to the same text when he sets down the law of daily fasting: 'Let us who are spiritual be ashamed to evade fasting.'[63] Here the term applies to the entire monastic community. By their profession, all monks are spiritual, at least in principle. They may therefore be designated generically by this word, in distinction to seculars who are in principle 'carnal'. This generic sense is found several times in the RM: the 'spiritual brothers' are simply the religious, as distinguished from seculars, whether they are brothers of the monastery (56, 15), monks from elsewhere (57, 61), or both (63).[64] This is not merely a social label. Awareness of the profound significance of the term and its demands is maintained. This has already been noted with regard to fasting. It appears again when the Master exhorts his 'spiritual men' to detachment from money.[65] and abstention from worldly affairs,[66] or when he offers the following definition, in regard to abnegation as concerns clothing: *ideo spiritalis homo Dei est, non carnalis* (81:20).

But besides this general sense, *spiritalis* has a more restricted meaning. Instead of general application to every monk insofar as he belongs by profession to a determined social category, it is reserved to those monks who show themselves really worthy of the name. This limited use already appears in regard to guests, whether monks or priests: 'if they are spiritual' (again alluding to Gal 6:1) they set to work to earn their keep, as St Paul would have them do.[67] Similarly, *spiritalis* is employed several times in its restricted sense for members of the community who distinguish themselves for their delicate sensibilities and their fervor. Thus, after a nocturnal pollution, the brothers, 'if he is truly spiritual' (the recurrence of this expression is noteworthy) will not be ashamed to confess his fault (80:4). Again, a brother who voluntarily renounces sleep after nocturns is *quasi spiritalis*, acting like a spiritual man: such a brother 'loves the spirit more than the flesh'.[68]

The quality of the 'spiritual man' is recognizable not only by reductions of sleep and food. It appears also in certain movements of spontaneous sorrow brought on by events which seem to separate the brother from God. For example, when a brother is condemned to eat without a blessing for having been late, then, 'if he is spiritual, he will suffer for having to take his meal apart from God' (23:48). The 'spiritual brother' will weep for himself even to 'despair' when he finds the office finished after he has hurried to get there (55:13).

Clearly, for the Master monastic *ascesis* has the goal of forming 'spiritual men' of this type. Spiritual not only by reason of profession, in virtue of the common observance, but spiritual in heart, because of the inmost reality of their virtue. Indispensible to the attainment of this goal is the education of freedom, beyond sheer drilling. The Master's comments on 'purity of heart' come to mind here—the goal of the ascetical effort, or rather the gift of the Holy Spirit to those who have labored in *ascesis*. At the summit of the ladder of humility, when the cenobite has attained to perfect charity, the Holy Spirit purifies him of his vices and sins.[69] This state is comparable to that of the authentic hermit: one who, by dint of inurring himself within the community, has become capable of solitary combat 'with God and the spirit' against the vices of the flesh and of the thoughts.[70] The Master sees such 'purity of heart' not only as the condition for entrance into heaven (10:122), but also as the state of a small number of religious whom he has presently under his eye. These are the 'perfect', the 'pure of heart', those who are 'purified of sin'.[71] For the others, he never ceases recalling how they have to 'purify the depths of the heart' if they would have their being and activity undefiled.[72] Upon his entrance into the monastery, the postulant is urged to 'make pure the depths of his heart' before he is invested with the monastic habit.[73]

The Master cherished this ideal so much that he made it a constant rule of life for his monks. This is the law of the primacy accorded spiritual things. As strongly as the obligation to manual work is maintained, it must nevertheless not hinder the deans in their surveillance of the brothers. Even here the 'cause of God' or the 'cause of the spirit', in other words, the repression of vices, is uppermost. To this the 'profits of the flesh' ought never to be preferred, that is, results of manual labor. The Master cites a Gospel text: *quaerite regnum Dei*.[74] The same idea recurs with regard to manual labor during Lent. A brother who imposes a voluntary fast on himself was to be exempted from community work.[75] This is because fasting is a 'spiritual work'[76] and as such it takes preference over manual work. Those who fast must not be left idle, however, but should read for those working. This act of reading is itself a 'work in the spirit'[77] superior to manual work.

The primacy of things spiritual demands that field work be sacrificed, incompatible as it is with prayerful quiet, indifference to earthly things, and the monastic fast (86). Many times the Master repeats his warning against 'secular affairs',[78] 'anxiety for the morrow',[79] 'distresses of the world'.[80] From all of these preoccupations the inhabitants of the monastery should be totally freed, in order to think only of their soul and the things above. This was pushed to the length of selling products at cheaper prices to merchants, in order to affirm emphatically the detachment proper to 'spiritual men'.[81]

THEOLOGY OF MONASTIC LIFE

One of the RM's most perceptible qualities is the clarity with which monastic life is understood and situated within the Church. By 'monastic life' we mean cenobitism, since eremitism was not mentioned by the Master except briefly in an opening paragraph—the importance of which should not, however, be minimized.[82]

Earnest reflection pervades the very organization of the Rule. By studying the Rule's plan, we shall see it. Everything is methodically arranged according to an over-all concept of the monastery and its government. What we need to highlight here is how monastic life thus constituted is situated within the history of salvation and the Church.

The prologue, first of all, introduces the Rule. The authority of the document and its author is forcefully affirmed. The author frankly introduces himself as God's spokesman.[83] His intention is to set forth a doctrine which is nothing else than the 'narrow way', that is, pure Gospel. Evocation of the Last Things finally determines the nature of the work and the author's purpose: nothing less than eternal salvation or damnation is at stake!

The same breadth characterizes the second introduction, the *Theme*. Here is introduced the *schola dominici servitii*, that is, the monastery. But this comes only after original sin, sinful life in the world, and baptismal regeneration have been evoked. The sacrament has enabled us to throw off the burden of sin: how could we once again take it upon our shoulders? The voice of Christ calling to 'take up his yoke' and 'find rest' had drawn the weary sinner to the baptismal font; now the same voice invites him to leave the 'ways of the world'.

The commentary on the *Our Father* and that on the psalms only reiterate this summons with every echo of Scripture. It matters little that these passages are perhaps excerpts derived from a baptismal catechism. Whatever their origin, their presence in the Rule attests to a very remarkable intention to relate monastic life to the basic tenets of christian life, after having recognized it as baptism's prolongation. These two commentaries abound with lengthy, profound formulas which describe christian salvation history in all its dimensions.[84] At the same time, anyone familiar with the Rule perceives in these pages the declaration of several themes which the Master develops insistently in the most downright 'monastic' parts of his work.[85] The *Theme* is not therefore a vague, general exhortation, suitable for any Christian, which the author might have prefixed artificially to a body of legislation designed for monks. Even if a non-monastic source was used, it has undergone such transformation that it stands in solid continuity with the rest of the *regula*. The Master is offering us a genuine introduction to his Rule here. He grounds monastic *ascesis* in Scripture, puts the reader in the presence of great christian truths which, 'realized' with intensity, become the driving ideas of cloistered life: Christ is Father and Lord; Christ is calling us; Christ will judge us; his will ought to be accomplished and ours sacrificed; his providence foresees our needs; his grace makes us triumph over the devil; we must suffer with him to become partakers of his glory.

This invitation to monastic life brings us to the *schola dominici servitii* (Th 45). At the outset the Master gives a precise definition of the monastery and indicates its exact place in relation to the Church. He teaches us elsewhere that 'divine mansions' are of two kinds: churches and monasteries (11), churches of Christ and schools of Christ (1). These two kinds of institutions rigorously parallel one another. Both are defined by the hierarchy which govern them in the name of God: the one by bishops, priests, deacons, and clerics; the other by abbots and deans (11). The two hierarchies, though distinct, have in common their divine origin, the mandate of Christ who instituted them and who continues to assist them. In truth they may be said to form one sole hierarchical order, that of 'teachers' (1:82–83), solidly founded on the promises of Christ made to his apostles[86] and disciplines.[87]

To understand this theory of the abbot-teacher, which is the key to the definition of the monastery as a *schola Christi*, it is necessary to consider the interpretation of 1 Cor 12:28 and Eph 4:11, on which the theory rests. According to the received text, St Paul enumerates in nearly identical terms a series of offices exercised *simultaneously* in the Church, the Body of Christ: *primum apostolos, secundo prophetas, tertio doctores*. The order followed (*primum, secundo, tertio*) is one of descending dignity. But the Master had a different text before him. It inverts the first two terms of the list: *primum prophetarum, apostolorum secundum, doctorum tertium*.[88] In consequence, he understands the enumeration in a chronological sense in such a way that the offices of prophets, apostles, and teachers are exercised *successively* in the course of the history of the people of God. Prophets accomplished their ministry under the Old Testament. Apostles fulfilled theirs in the New Testament, at the time of Christ. Teachers have been at work since the departure of the apostles, to whom they have legitimately succeeded. They are the bishop and the abbot, each in his own domain (church or 'school'), assisted by his respective collaborators (priests, deacons, clerics, or provosts). 'Teacher' means, therefore, simply a successor to the apostles.[89] By giving the abbot this title, the Master equates him with the supreme pastor of the church, the bishop, just as he likens the monastery (or 'school of Christ') to a church.

This seems to pose a rather delicate theological problem: by what right is the abbot placed on an equal footing with the bishop? Can the promises made by Christ to the apostles and their successors be legitimately applied to him: To grasp the full import of these questions, it must be recalled that the abbot, according to the RM, is a layman (83). So it cannot be by reason of Holy Orders, priesthood or deaconate, that he claims to be a 'teacher'. This ought to belong to him in virtue of the abbatial function itself.

The study we made of this problem may be read elsewhere.[90] Today more than ever, the Master's thought seems to us rigorously orthodox and traditional. It may be seen without difficulty by noting the role the bishop plays in the abbatial 'ordination'.[91] It is clear that, for the Master, two acts in this long ceremony had decisive importance: inscription of the name of the abbot-elect on the diptych—which inscription was reserved to the hand of the bishop[92]—and prayers addressed to God by the bishop on behalf of the ordinand.[93] It is to these two essential rites that reference is made when the ceremony and its effects are recalled in the remainder of the chapter.[94] The first must be revoked by the contrary act: effacement of the name from the diptych by the hand of a priest,[95] if some day the new abbot's deposition were desired. As for the second, its importance is affirmed by a highly significant formula in the ordination rite itself: 'May the High Priest, by his prayers, *bind* in the acts of heaven what you have received on earth.'[96] This allusion to the power of 'binding' and 'loosing' (Mt 18:18) leaves no doubt about the meaning of the episcopal prayer: it is, it may be said, the constitutive rite of the ordination. Moreover, the presence of the bishop and his clergy is also required for the validity of the other rites involved. This is carefully indicated at each step of the ceremony.[97] It is really an ordination 'in the presence of the bishop',[98] or better, of an *ordinatio sacerdotalis,* an ordination of which the minister is the bishop.[99]

This ceremony of the blessing of the abbot is that to which the Master is making implicit reference, we believe, when he utters his solemn declarations at the beginning of the Rule about the abbot's powers. If the abbot is a 'teacher', an authentic representative of Christ, enjoying the same authority as a bishop, it is because he has been duly invested with the charge by the bishop himself. True, the three great texts on the abbot's authority[100] make no explicit allusion to the ordination ceremony, which is not described until right at the end of the Rule. As a result, the tie that connects the abbatial theory to its ritual foundation does not appear clearly. But this is only an illusion, the inevitable consequence of the plan followed.[101] As for the profound reality, there can be no doubt that the Master posits the same fundamental relation between the abbot's charge and abbatial ordination as he explicitly acknowledge between the 'ordination' of provosts, weekly kitchen servers, and reader, and their respective functions. The Master was wont to place at the beginning of a function as well as at the beginning of every action a prayer rite which commended the duty to God and grounded it spiritually. Description of this rite ordinarily comes *at the outset* of the treatise that deals with the particular function, as is natural. Some necessity forced a departure from this custom in the case of the abbot, but we are certainly justified in re-establishing the order mentally and in seeing in abbatial ordination the key to the theory of the abbot-teachers. Just as deans derived their power from the abbot who 'ordained' them,[102] so the abbot received his from the bishop in the course of the ordination.

If this is, for the Master, the foundation of abbatial authority, we need not seek its justification in some charism directly imparted by the Holy Spirit to the abbot.[103] It is much more on the pattern of episcopal consecration, that is, by ordination and in virtue of a quasi-sacramental rite, that our author receives the abbot's investiture. This rite was undoubtedly the sensible sign which allowed everyone to recognize the authentic 'teacher',[104] and permitted him to demand from everyone the obedience due a representative of Christ. From this, the prologue's tone may be understood without difficulty. The author, who would have been a duly ordained abbot, was conscious of speaking in the name of Christ.

The great passages on the abbacy consequently stand apart from all polemic regarding sacerdotal authority; indeed, apart from any claim to this.[105] A parallel with priesthood is made only to quicken the monk's faith in the divine mission of their abbot. This parallel does not then signify that the monastic hierarchy is independant of the ecclesiastical hierarchy. On the contrary, it derives all its power precisely from the latter. If the abbot is really, as a teacher, a legitimate successor of the apostles, it is because he shares in the unique apostolic succession by reason of the ordination the bishop conferred on him. There is no apostolic succession within the monastery, even if the former abbot designates his successor.[106] Thus the abbacy is grafted into the ecclesiastical hierarchy, as the monastery is likewise engrafted into the Church.[107] In all that concerns the authority of its heads or the supernatural existence of its members, the monastic community depends entirely upon the unique *mater ecclesia*.[108]

This means that likening the monastery to a church will always remain in the area of analogy. The monastery is 'like a church',[109] but it is *not* a church properly so-called. Its true name is rather *schola Christi*, school of Christ.[110] The Master was certainly not unaware that this expression or its equivalent can designate the church itself, as may be seen in numerous patristic writings.[111] He knew too that Cassian loved to define the *coenobium* as *schola*, by which he meant a school that prepares for the sublime and solitary exercises of the hermit.[112] Yet the Master's terminology deviates from these precedents. For him, the monastery was a school not insofar as it was a preparation for eremitical life, nor insofar as it was a church properly so-called, but precisely because it was a community *sui generis*, similar to the church but distinct from it.[113] The expression *schola*, *schola monasterii*, and even *schola Christi* already appear profusely in authors of earlier times as synonyms for *monasterium*.[114] None of those texts, however, makes *schola* the proper name of the monastery insofar as it is distinguished from the church, as we find done here by the Master.[115]

The monastery is, therefore, a quasi-church. That means it ought to resemble an *ecclesia*, both in its external aspect of a house of prayer,[116] in its liturgical usages,[117] and in its hierarchical structure, as has already been seen. But this also means it should differ from a secular church by reason of a 'particular service of God', expressed both in the liturgy and in the style of clothing.[118] Explicit in some cases, this comparison was no doubt in the back of the author's mind in many another, under its double aspect of resemblance and dissemblance.[119]

Since the monastery was considered in comparison with a church, it is only to be expected that the Master would make references to the model church, the primitive Jerusalem church described in chapters two and four of the *Acts of the Apostles*. But no mention of it occurs, all the more strangely since the reference to the church of the apostles was in fact current in cenobitical literature.[120] This omission makes us take note of two very marked characteristics of the Master's concept of cenobitism. First, our author shows almost no interest in the relationships of the brothers among themselves. The only important thing in his eyes is the 'vertical' relation uniting the brothers to their superiors, the deans and, above all, the abbot.[121] This is the sense in which the monastery was for him a school, a place where disciples received the instruction of qualified masters. 'Horizontal' relationships binding the disciples to one another are scarcely discernible. Apparently such relationships were accorded no appreciable role in the formation of souls.

A second characteristic, related to the first, is the Master's lack of interest in the community as such. Seldom do we come across a remark about the communitarian aspect of renunciation of property[122] or of prayer.[123] Renunciation and prayer are ordinarily viewed within a perspective of purely individual *ascesis*, like all other cenobitical values: obedience, taciturnity, humility, vigils, abstinence,[124] work, chastity. The monastery was seldom viewed as a society of charity in the sharing of goods and the union of hearts on the model of the primitive church and in the image of the Trinity. First and foremost the monastery was a school, an institution where individuals were assembled for a time for educational purposes (but see the note to Th 45), without any provision or even possibility for deepening relations very much. A school is mainly orientated towards each student's future; together, the students form only a temporary assembly, provisory and somewhat artificial. The same might be said of the monastery. It was geared towards each monk's future. Educating each member in view of eternal life was paramount, rather than assembling them all in a community which would want in itself to reflect that of heaven.

This vertical and individualistic presentation of the *coenobium* might disappoint us by its poverty. Yet it holds an interest: it disentangles in all its purity the relationship of the monk to the abbot which is historically the source of a certain type of cenobitism generated from the spiritual paternity of the desert. The RM falls well within the line of the evolution which, nearly two centuries earlier, had made of some Egyptian solitaries the first fathers of semi-anchoretic or of cenobitical communities. For the RM, as for the first communities of monks, the abbot is the *raison d'etre* of the gathering of the brothers. They have come to the monastery seeking the sure, infallible direction of the man of God. He it is who ought to teach them the will of God. Even more, he ought to bring it to realization in them, the obedience of the brothers making of him, as it were, the only will acting in the monastery. Thanks to this transfer of freedom and responsibility,[125] each brother might justly hope his conduct would be entirely approved by God and crowned with eternal life. To go to God through the medium of the abbot was then the primary, almost the exclusive, concern of all who entered the community.

But if the prominence given the abbatial function is a fundamental characteristic drawing the Master's monastery close to the foundations of an Apollonius[126] or a Pachomius, two particular traits nevertheless distinguish the RM. First, the abbacy is not presented here as a charism directly bestowed on some solitary renowned for his sanctity. Instead of such charismatic investiture as was the case with the first Egyptian or Western fathers of cenobitism,[127] our Rule has the abbot ordained by the bishop. No doubt the former abbot who presented a brother to the bishop for ordination had made his selection on the basis of the brother's acquired perfection. But merit and ability do not suffice. Recognition by ecclesiastical authority was required to constitute the new spiritual father in his office of Christ's representative and of teacher.[128]

A second distinctive trait of the RM is the role the Rule plays, alongside and even above the abbot, as an expression of the divine will. We are made conscious of it right from the prologue, and the famous definition of cenobites heralds in all clarity: *militans sub regula uel abbate* (1:2). The Rule's authority was sovereign in the Master's monastery. Its observation served as a criterion according to which the abbot was chosen.[129] It stood at the center of the ordination ceremony.[130] The abbot would be judged on it.[131] The novice likewise promised its observance in the profession formula,[132] and the deans never ceased admonishing him to put it into practice.[133] The rule was for everyone truly the 'law of God' (93:15). So great was its importance that it was read continually in the refectory.

And so in the RM we are far from that sovereign liberty with which the Fathers of the Desert, in the name of the Spirit, ruled the disciples who entrusted themselves to them. The abbot's authority was encompassed by a written document that laid down for him—and with what precision!— what he was to do. The margin of interpretation left to his judgment by this almost tyrannical rule seems very narrow.[134] Even in the area of teaching, the Rule intended to furnish the community with a complete program, apparently leaving nothing to the superior except the solicitation of administering particular exhortations to brothers undergoing temptation.[135] The abbot's role was not to formulate, then, but to repeat the Rule's doctrine and see to its application, with the assistance of the provosts.

From where does the Rule's authority come? Apart from Scripture, the Master rarely makes reference to normative documents.[136] He makes his work rather a 'dictate' of the Lord.[137] The legislator is a man inspired. Ultimately, this conviction no doubt proceeds from his consciousness of being a regularly ordained abbot, hence a true teacher.

Nothing indicates that the faculty for composing a Rule, or changing an already existent one, is transmitted to successive abbots. Our author was therefore aware of his legislative power in virtue of a unique title, for example, in the capacity of founder.[138]

CONCLUSION: REALITY OR FICTION?

Singularly remarkable as it is for its breadth, inspired nature, precision, and methodical organization, was the legislation we have been studying written for a really existent community? Certain indications could make us doubt it. The author seems unsure of the minimum two groups of ten monks, which is something presupposed by the whole rule (11:20), as well as by the architectural layout (16; cf. 79; 95). He never mentions the name of the 'territory' in which the monastery is located (87; 93; 94), or even the name of the patron saint of the oratory (45).[139]

Are we dealing with a product of the imagination devoid of practical importance? Nothing is less likely. From all the evidence, the author was an abbot completely informed about monastic affairs and solicitous for practical implementation. His work supposes long experience with institutions and men. So precise an observance, an *ordo,* and a ritual, are not to be simply invented in their entirety; a block of juridical arrangements like that of the postulant's renunciation of property (87) is not to be formulated without previous experience of the various difficulties here intended to be rectified. But certain other parts of the work perhaps concede a great deal to the imagination, indeed, seem utopian.[140] The rule in its totality cannot, however, be regarded as a pure flight of fancy.

This twofold aspect of the RM, the determined and the undetermined, is perhaps bound up with a situation and a purpose that could be expressed this way: the author was the abbot of a small monastery which functioned pretty much as the rule describes it, but he was writing for other communities, some of which were perhaps still to be founded. This scope allowed him to employ profitably a rich experience, but in a systematic manner, following the demands of a nature extremely careful about logic. Some specific points had to remain uncertain or undefined in a work of this kind.

NOTES TO CHAPTER THREE

1. Theme 28; 1:80; 81:18–19. On this anthropology, see in *Théologie de la vie monastique* (Paris: Aubier, 1961) the notations of H. Crouzel in regard to Origen (p. 26–27) and our own references to Cassian (p. 227).

2. 8:11–17.

3. Cf. 8:24; 14:82–83.

4. 86:9–10.

5. Pr 6 and 17–21; Ths 2–4 and 42.

6. Ths 45 (school); 2:52 (workshop); 1:5 (troop force).

7. 50:16–17, and *passim*.

8. 50:3–5, 37–38. This same finality is ascribed to silence (50:24), to reading during work (50:29), and to edifying conversations (50:45–46): always it is a matter of *avoiding sin*, in the present context more precisely sins of the tongue.

9. 50:47–49. The prayer after work has for its purpose recompense for the divine help given (50:50).

10. 90:69–70. The concept seems to come from Faustus of Riez, *Hom.* 8; *PL* 50:852D–853A.

11. 47:24.

12. 48:6, 11.

13. 21:8; cf. 19:8.

14. 15:48–54.

15. 87:8; 90:85; 91:36.

16. 11:2–14; 11:28–30; 93:21–24.

17. See in particular the entire Theme in which the *pia vox* of Christ reverberates (Th 11); the *pietas* of the Father is also commemorated (Thp 43); the Lord is truly the 'good' God (Ths 38; cf. 14:13; 14:61, 64; 15:42–43).

18. 2:51. The role of grace is strongly underlined: see Thp 76–80; Ths 25–28; 1:5, 79, 92; 3:46–47; 9:48; 14:49–56; 14:61–62, 65–66; 23:56; 53:10, 14, 28, 90, 56. There are perhaps in certain of these passages echoes of anti-Pelagian writings, even though the necessity of grace is a common ground of the whole ascetical literature, both in the East (Gregory of Nyssa and pseudo-Marcarius come to mind) and in the West (notably Cassian). There is no trace either of semi-Pelagianism or its opposing doctrine in the RM. It would be a mistake to reckon the Master in the Augustinian camp (M. Cappuyns, 'L'auteur de la *Regula Magistri:* Cassiodorus' in *RTAM* 15 [1948] 209–268, especially 230–234), or in that of semi-Pelagianism (F. Masai, in *Édition diplomatique* [Paris: Les Publications de Scriptorium, 1953], *Prolégomènes,* p. 62, n. 5). In reality, there is in the Master no theological stand either one way or the other. To the Master can be applied the very prudent conclusions which C. Vagaggini arrived at in studying St Benedict ('La posizione di San Benedetto nella questione

semipelegiana', *Studia Benedictina, Studia Anselmiana* 18–19 [Rome, 1947] 17–84). Both rules use an ancient, common terminology nearly on a level with Scripture, if one may dare say. At most it might be conceded that this terminology does not exclude a semi-Pelagian interpretation, since our author displays no concern over excluding this error. But Augustine himself is not always at pains to rule out such an interpretation, not even in his later sermons, and Caesarius of Arles (*Serm.* 212, 2; Morin, 797, 25) copies some semi-Pelagian formulas of Faustus without so much as batting an eyelash! The most 'disturbing' texts of the Master are Ths 35 and above all 1:76–80 and 14:57–59, in which Zech. 1:3 and Lk 11:9 are employed. Read in context, they betray no doctrinal intention.

19. 8:27; 15:53–54.
20. 15:25.
21. 47:24.
22. 19:8.
23. Individual prayer: 15:54; communitarian prayer: 15:19–27.
24. 1:79; 14:57–58; 15:41. Cf. 3:77.
25. Thp 7.
26. Ths 24; 3:56.
27. 11:22, 28, 35, 40, 108, 121–122; 18:5–8; 24:2; 50:36–38; 84:3–4. In virtue of the same principle, the abbot was obliged to watch over the whole dormitory (29:4; 44:19), guestmasters ceaselessly to watch over guests (79:5–21), and an ill brother to be watched after by his neighbor in the oratory (69:11).
28. See 19:13 (but is it a matter of true excommunication here? Cf. 17:8, where the word is not used); 73:3–4, 7.
29. 23:56; 53:9–10, 33.
30. See chapter 92 in its entirety.
31. See *La communauté et l'abbé*, p. 356–358.
32. See 7:59 (*uelut in martyrio*); 90:12–59. On these two aspects of obedience, see *La communauté et l'abbé*, p. 266–268.
33. 7:67–74.
34. Moreover, 'all self-will is carnal and proceeds from the body' (90:51; cf. 13:15).
35. 10:91. On this final point in the chapter on humility, see P. Deseille, 'A propos de l'épilogue du ch. VIII de la Règle' in *Collectanea OCR.* 21 (1959) 289–301, notably the comparative table, p. 290, n. 5. Note that this phrase in the Master is not from Cassian; it reminds one of Gregory of Nyssa, *De Instituto christiano*; Jaeger, p. 84, 16–86, 1, as A. Kemmer noted in *Orientalia christiana periodica* 21 (1955) 466, who asks whether our author might not have been acquainted with a Latin version of *De Instituto christiano*, the existence of which remains hypothetical. Suggestive as these comparisons may be, they do not necessarily imply, in our view, a literacy dependence, any more than do the similarities between the Master and Gregory of Nyssa to which we have drawn attention in *La communauté et l'abbé*, pp. 105–107, 113–114, 117–119.
36. 8:24–25; 10:12; 10:23–29.
37. 3:84–94; 10:94–117; 90:16–27.
38. Save for a rapid allusion to eternal fire in 90:14–15.

39. Such as 10:45–49: *postquam ... non solum ... set et* at the passage from the second to third degrees; 10:52: *in ipsa obedientia* (fourth degree); 10:68: *non solum sua lingua ... sed etiam intimo cordis ... affectu* (seventh degree); 10:82: *non solum corde sed etiam ipso corpore* (twelfth degree). So there sometimes is progress from one degree to another, but only within fixed groups of degrees: obedience (2–4), humility (5–7), silence and exterior deportment (8–12). But from one group to another no progression can be ascertained.

40. See chapters 87 and 91.

41. 87:8–12, 15; 87:45; 91:11, 34–41. Cf. 90:92–93.

42. 87:17–18. Cf. 81:15–17; 82:18–19, 29–31.

43. 89:21–22; 91:58; cf. 82:1–17, 23–25; 7:34–35, 53.

44. Lk 18:22, cited by RM 87:13–15; 91:18, 44.

45. 90:10, citing Mt 16:24 blended with Lk 14:26. See also RM 7:52, where application of the Gospel text to obedience is no less explicit, and 3:10. In these three passages, the Master omits the words *tollat crucem suam*, to which he nowhere alludes.

46. 90:31–32.

47. 90:63. Cf. 2:48–50; 16:58–61; chapters 81–82.

48. 90:65–66.

49. 57:14–16, which goes on to recall the great text of Lk 10:16. Cf. 50:72–74.

50. 74. Cf. 22:5–8.

51. 85.

52. 44:12–19.

53. 53:11–15, 26–33, 38–41. Cf. 27:47–51.

54. 7:1–21; 9:41–50.

55. 2:11–12, 23–25.

56. 90:78 (*perfecte*) and 79 (*inculpabiliter*).

57. 7:10.

58. 89:8 (*per disciplinam regulae*) and 11–16 (*mihi ... obaudire*).

59. 1:5 (*uitia carnis et cogitationum*); 9:41 (*peccato*); 10:12 (*peccatis et uitiis*); 10:70 (*uitiis et peccatis*).

60. Nothing is more natural, however, on the part of the author of a monastic rule, a wholly practical document. Compared with other documents of similar nature, the RM rather surprises us by the importance it allotted to theoretical considerations. Few rules have as much. It may be asked whether the Master knew Cassian through some summary version like the one Eucher of Lyons wrote (Gennadius, *De uiris inlustribus* 63; PL 58:1096). This abridged version could have omitted or summarized the theory of the eight principal faults. Cf. G. Holzherr, *Regula Ferioli* (Einsiedeln, 1961) p. 103, n. 7. Besides the absence of the eight principal faults, the absence of the four cardinal virtues is noteworthy: these are much treasured by Ambrose and Julianus Pomerius.

61. One is tempted here to spell 'spirit' with a capital 'S'. In the RM, as in Scripture, this term is not univocal. Sometimes it designates the Holy Spirit, the divine person dwelling within the soul of the just man (Th 17; Th 7; 2:3; 3:1; 10:26, 91; 33:21; 42:4). Elsewhere it is instead the principle of the human composite-being (Th 28; 1:5; 1:80; 11:98; 27:47; 28:18; 32:15; 44:18; 53:40; 80:12;

81:20), usually opposed to the 'flesh' or the 'body'. But this superior principle of man's being is precisely that by which man adheres to God and to his Spirit, so much so that it is distinguished only imperfectly from the divine person. Man's spirit is joined to God so that identification is often struck between the 'cause of the spirit' and the 'cause of God' (1:80; 11:98; 27:47–48). The curious passage in which the spirit of man testifies against the soul on judgment day (13:15) must be set apart. This sort of ambiguity is reminiscent of certain passages in the *Visio Pauli,* which lies at the origin of these images (see note *in loco*). Lastly, certain scriptural quotations give *spiritus* a particular sense: Gal 6:1 (*in spiritu mansuetudinis*) in RM 15:21; 1 Jn 4:1 (*omni spiritui*) in RM 90:71; 1 Cor 14:15 (*psallam spiritu, psallam et mente; orabo simul et mente et spiritui*) in RM 47:19; 48:14.

62. RM 15:21 citing Gal 6:1.

63. RM 28:3.

64. Cf. also 78:9, with regard to guests. In all these cases, *spiritalis* only gives added force to *frater,* each of these words being able by itself to designate the monk. No doubt *spiritalis frater* is implicitly opposed to *frater carnalis.* Cf. 13:71 (*necessarios corporales*); Th 2 (*pater terrenus et mater carnalis*); Th 3 (*carnales parentes*). This designation thus serves to emphasize the religious character of this 'fraternity' not based on blood lineage.

65. 85:3 (*spiritales a saecularibus actorum distantia separari*).

66. 86:8 (*spiritales conuersi . . . non implicant se negotiis saecularibus*). Cf. 79:4: *cum putantur hospites spiritales, subito . . . fures inueniantur.* Here again the value of the term seems perceptible.

67. 78:25; 83:13. For 79:4, see preceding note.

68. 44:17–18. Compare with voluntary curtailments on food (27:47–51), in connection with which the same formula occurs: *spiritum plus agnoscitur amare quam carnem.* See also 53:7–10, 11–18 (Lenten 'abstainers'); 53:27–33 (Paschal-time 'abstainers'). Inversely, he who shows himself sluggish when rising from sleep is like a bee which 'deprives itself of the first fruits of honey in the spirit and makes only the wax of the body' (32:15).

69. 10:91.

70. 1:5.

71. 9:41: *puris corde et mundis a peccato.* Cf. 9:47: *ex toto mundi uelut angeli.*

72. 14:84; 15:1 (*purgari*).

73. 90:75 (*mundare*).

74. 11:94–106.

75. 53:38–41.

76. 53:12 (*pro anima sua spiritualiter laborare*).

77. 53:40 (*in spiritu legendo laborent*). Reading is itself called *opus spiritale* in 50:16. In 24:4, it is called *esca diuina* and opposed to corporal nourishment.

78. 2 Tim 2:4, cited by RM 82:18; 86:8; 91:11.

79. Mt. 6:25–34, cited by RM 11:101–106; 16:12–25; 82:12–15.

80. *Visio Pauli* 10 and 40, cited by RM 86:7; 91:29.

81. 85:1–7.

82. 1:3–5. Cf. 1:11–12. See the commentary on these pages in *La communauté et l'abbé,* p. 61–67.

83. See my article '*Sub regula vel abbate:* A Study of the Theological Signifi-

cance of the Ancient Monastic Rules', *Rule and Life: A Symposium*, CS 12 (1971) 21–64.

84. Thp 1–11, Ths 2–4.

85. Compare Thp 34–40 with 7:51–52; 10:43–49; 90:10–12, 48–54 (submission to the imitation of Christ). The enormous importance which the commentary attaches to the third petition of the *Our Father* should be noted carefully: the Master is clearly starting on the condemnation of self-will, the central theme of the whole Rule. Compare also Thp 55–56 (Providence) with 3:49; 11:99–106; 16:1–26; 23:2; 82:16–18. The beautiful 'christian' formula of Th 11 has its echo in the overtly 'monastic' passage of Ths 46. The paternity of Christ theme is found in both Th 9–11, 21–22 (the whole and entire Lord's Prayer is addressed to Christ), and in 2:2–3. The body-soul-spirit trichotomy is repeated in identical fashion in Thp 28 and 1:80; 81:18–19. The theory of the 'earthen' body constructed like a *machina* is duplicated in Thp 52 and 77, and in 8:1–5 and 12–16. For the same analogy between the Theme and the entire Rule from the viewpoint of doctrine of grace, compare Thp 76–80; Ths 25–28 with 1:5, 79, 92, etc. This similarity is not limited to themes; it extends even to ordinary vocabulary. Thus the Theme has the characteristic words: *digne* (Thp 13); *iuste* (Thp 60); *uidete fratres* and *rationes nostras* (Thp 20); *discussa* (Thp 30); *per formam faciendi in se* and *demonstrat nobis dicens* (Thp 34); etc.

86. Jn 21:17, cited by RM 1:85. Mt 28:20, cited by RM 1:86–88.

87. Lk 10:16, cited by RM 1:89; 11:11.

88. RM 1:82; cf. 14:14 (*post prophetas et apostolos*) and Thp 46 (*per prophetas et apostolos*). There is the same inversion in citing 1 Cor 12:28 by Jerome, *In Zach.* 1; PL 25:1438 b, as Dom B. Fischer kindly pointed out to me.

89. It is the same for *pastor* (1:84), which is associated with *doctor* (cf. Eph. 4:11) in 11:12; 14:14. Bishops and abbots together realize the prophecy of 'Isaiah' (Jer. 3:15): 'I will give you pastors according to my own heart' (1:85; 11:12).

90. See *La communauté et l'abbé*, pp. 132–138 and 176–186.

91. We have already singled out for attention the bishop's role in *La communauté et l'abbé*, p. 137, n. 2; p. 182, n. 3; p. 360–361, but without drawing out its full theological significance, which seems to us, today more than ever, of capital importance.

92. RM 93:7.

93. 93:29, 32–33.

94. 93:56.

95. 93:78. *Quiuis sacerdos* seems to mean a simple priest.

96. 93:26.

97. 93:6, 11, 13–14.

98. 93:46.

99. 93:59; cf. 93:62 (*istum ... sacerdos ordinauit*).

100. 1:82–92; 11:5–14; 14:13–15.

101. A similar occurrence came to our attention above when studying *The Spiritual Ideal: nuditas* or renunciation of goods receives no developed treatment until the beginning of chapter 87, though it constitutes the first step of monastic *ascesis*.

102. RM 11:15.

103. As we did in *La communauté et l'abbé*, pp. 136–138. See also B. Hegglin, *Der benediktinische Abt* (St Ottilian 1961) 34. This view rests upon that of Basil Steidle.

104. Nothing is more significant in this respect than RM 7:37. The *maiores* or *doctores* who remonstrate with the sarabaites are evidently official personages, recognizable by a visible criterion, which would have to be their proper 'ordination'.

105. Not until chapter 83 do we perceive a defensive preoccupation against encroachment by clerical authority. This reaction was rampant in ancient cenobitism. See *La communauté et l'abbé*, p. 327–347.

106. See chapters 92–93. It was also the former abbot who divested the present one if the latter came into disrepute (93:78). In both these circumstances, episcopal control (examination of the candidate, ratification of the choice or of the degradation) is not formally indicated, but must be supposed. How would it be possible for the bishop to remain silent? Was his role to be reduced to that of a mere liturgical officiator? Could his consent be by-passed? See *La communauté et l'abbé*, p. 360. According to chapter 94, the bishop also intervened indirectly in the election itself, in the instance where the former abbot had died suddenly.

107. See our reflections with regard to Cassian, in *Théologie de la vie monastique*, 223–225.

108. Thp 2.

109. 53:64 (which is dealing only with exterior appearances).

110. 1:83. Also to be found are *schola eius* (= *Domini*) in 90:12, 46; *schola Dominici seruitii* (Ths 45); *schola Dei* (92:26); *schola diuina* (92:29); *schola sancta* (87:9); *schola monasterii* (90:29, 55; 92:64).

111. See Basil Steidle, 'Domini schola seruitii', *Benediktinische Monatschrift* 28 (1952) 396–406. The most striking parallel is surely that of Augustine, *Serm.* 177, 2, in which the Church is called the *schola Christi* in distinction to the schools of philosophers. See also Augustine's sermon *De disciplina christiana*; PL 40:669.

112. Cassian, *Conf.* 3, 1, 2; 18, 16, 15; 19, 2, 4; 19, 11, 1.

113. RM 1:83.

114. Faustus of Riez, *Hom. ad monachos* 4 (pseudo-Eusebius 38); *PL* 50:841D, where *hanc scholam* means Lérins; *Homilia de S. Maximo* in *Biblioteca Veterum Patrum* (Lyons, 1677) 6:655D (where *schola Christi* again designates Lérins); *Ep* 7 *ad Ruricium*; PL 58:858b (*schola monasterii*). *Schola Christi* is again found applied to a monastery in the *Passio S. Eugeniae* 15; Mombritius 2:395, 28—a work well known to the Master.

115. The *ecclesiae-monasteria* doublet was familiar enough to Caesarius of Arles. See *Serm.* 136, 1: (Morin, 536, 3): *psalmus ille, qui per omnem mundum dicitur et in ecclesiis et in monasteriis*, and cf. *Serm.* 1 (Morin, 18, 5): *de sacerdotibus uel abbatibus.*

116. 53:64.

117. 46:6–7. This passage establishes besides a new parallel between the ecclesiastical hierarchy (minor cleric and deacon) and the monastic hierarchy (deans and abbots).

118. 81:6.

119. See the connections suggested, in regard to the RB, by Fr Schmitz, 'Règle Bénédictine', *Dictionnaire de droit canonique* 2:229, and in *Histoire de l'Ordre de Saint Benoît* (Maredsous 1942) t. I, 1:18–19. A further reflection on the church-monastery relationship may be consulted in my article 'Scholies sur la Règle du Maître' in RAM 44 (1968) 158–159.

120. See for example *Théologie de la vie monastique*, 67–71 (Pachomius); 202–212 (Augustine); 215 (Cassian). Basil might be added too, *Long Rules* 5–7. The only allusions the Master made to the first chapters of Acts are Th 46 (*in huius doctrina . . . perseuerantes*); 20:5 (the prayer for Peter); 82:20 (Ananias and Sapphira). These passages do not concern the life of charity of the first Christians sharing goods and union of hearts (Acts 4:32).

121. See *La communauté et l'abbé*, 74–75, 492–496. Very significant in this respect is the use the Master makes of the great pauline metaphor of the *body* and its members. The only notion he retains is the relation of head (abbot) to members (brothers). See 2:29, 47. Of the relations joining the members into one body there is not a word in the RM.

122. 91:53–54. It is here that a reference to Acts 4:32 would be expected. See also 2:48–50; 16:58–61 (*res monasterii omnium est et nullius est*).

123. 15:20–25 ('united' prayer for the tempted brother); 16:51–52; chapter 20 in its entirety (prayer for the absent). These last two passages express remarkably, probably in dependance upon Julianus Pomerius, the solidarity of all the brothers, present and absent, in prayer as in work. But the importance of these passages is limited to the *silent prayer* which is but one part of the office, and it does not offer any teaching concerning the public and communitarian character of the divine praise in general.

124. Abstinence and work surely have altruistic value (27:47–51; 50:7), but for the benefit of the poor, that is, people outside the community. This is the direction in which the Master's thoughts ordinarily turn when he considers the duty of charity. See *La communauté et l'abbé*, pp. 492–496.

125. RM 2:6, 33–36; 7:54–56; see *La communauté et l'abbé*, 88–89; 99–100; 231–233; 250–251.

126. *Historia monachorum* 7; *PL* 21:411B. Semi-anchorites are involved here.

127. One thinks of the two founders of Jura (Romanus and Lupicius) or of St Benedict.

128. In the *Vita S. Eugendi* 8; (*Acta sanctorum* OSB 7:555, towards the beginning of the sixth century, bishops assembled *orationis causa* around the abbot-elect. Likewise, the emperor Justinian reserved to the bishop the approbation and installation of the abbot-elect (*Cod. Iust.* 1, 3, 47, *anno* 530). After he had gone so far as to entrust even the election itself to the bishop (*Novella* 5, 9, *anno* 535), the emperor re-entrusted it to the monks, though still reserving installation of the abbot-elect to the bishop (*Novella* 123, 34, *anno* 546).

129. 92:8; 94:7, 10.

130. 93:12–19, 24–30. Cf. 83:7: it is by virtue of the Rule that the abbot is sole master of his flock.

131. 93:18–19.

132. 89:8.

133. 11:42; 11:50. Allusions to the precepts of the Rule abound in nearby corrections.

134. The abbot was the judge in the matter of excommunication (13:50, 64), of pardon (14:22), and of appropriate punishment (13:70; 57:15). He could grant extra food or drink (26:11–13; 27:44–46, 52–54; 60:1–4; cf. 53:30). Only in the administrative domain (management of revenue, work assignments) did the Rule leave his hands free (2:41–50; 19:9; 50:18). See also 24:21 (readings).

135. 15:28–29, 35. Cf. 93:22. The abbot also instructed the novices (ch. 87–90). Note that the Rule does not foresee conferences given by the abbot to the community. The only thing indicated are some explanatory comments on the Rule read in the refectory (24:19, 34–37). The absence of regular conferences is a curious trait which contrasts with their frequency and importance in the pachomian congregation.

136. *Instituta Patrum* (34:2); *a Patribus* (90:92); *regulae nostrae a Patribus . . . statutum consilium* (91:48). See also the interdict laid by Pope Silvester (28:43).

137. Similar expressions may be found elsewhere. See Paulinus of Nola, Ep 3, 2: *dictata diuinitus uerba* (Augustine's books) and Barsanuphus, Ep 31 (PO 31:486, 25): 'Heed, my son, the words that I have spoken, or rather, that the Lord has spoken', and the *Vie de Schenoudi* (F. Nau, *Une Version syriaque inédite de la Vie de Schenoudi* [Paris: Leroux, 1900] p. 30): 'He did not give these rules of himself, but the Messiah determined them and dictated them through his mouth.' Compare with the pachomian legend that of the Rule was dictated by an angel. The Master's pretention is therefore less exorbitant than it sounds.

138. See *La communauté et l'abbé*, 511–515. The author's familiarity with ecclesiastical institutions could also indicate a clerical formation.

139. Compare with the explicit mention of Feriolus as patron in the *Regula Ferioli* 38. The Master moreover readily names his favorite saints, Eugenia, for example.

140. In particular the treatise on abbatial succession (ch. 92–94).

CHAPTER FOUR

TIME AND PLACE OF COMPOSITION

THE TIME PERIOD

From sources used, the *terminus a quo* for the composition of the Rule can be ascertained with some precision. If the *Passiones* obligingly cited by the Master cannot be dated with certainty, there is general agreement that the *Vita Siluestri* was composed in the last years of the fifth century. This *Vita* is in fact cited by a Symmachian apocrypha of the year 501, the *Gesta Liberii*, in terms which indicate a very recent appearance.[1] This explicit citation accompanies a number of unacknowledged passages drawn from texts composed certainly at the beginning of the sixth century, such as the Creed *Quicumque*, the *Regula monachorum* of Caesarius, and especially the *De uita contemplativa* of Julius Pomerius.[2]

The *terminus ad quem* is more difficult to determine. From the age of the most ancient manuscripts, we know the RM was composed certainly before the end of the sixth century.[3] If the text itself is examined, the sources will once again furnish certain elements of a response at least probable. The Master liked to cite certain apocryphas either forbidden or discouraged by the so-called *Gelasian Decree*.[4] It is evident that our author did not suspect his preferred reading might be the object of this kind of critical evaluation. Now, the *Decree*, without being an official document, did nevertheless express the views and practices of the 'roman church', that is, of persons governing the clergy of Rome. Whether or not the compiler belonged to this milieu,[5] there seems to be no doubt about what he tells of the principles professed there. Consequently, the *Decree* permits us to know the works which enjoyed popularity among the roman faithful, and at the same time the judgment the clergy leveled on these readings.

This picture is especially interesting to us because, as we shall see below, the RM was composed in all likelihood in the vicinity of Rome. In fact, the literary interests of roman Christians which we see mirrored in the *Decree* are very much the same as those manifested by the RM.[6] But then, how do we explain our author's apparent indifference to the reservations and even interdicts which bear upon a number of his preferred readings?[7] Such an attitude, above all in the head of a community, would be incomprehensible unless the roman clergy has *not yet* taken a public position on the suspect works. The date at which the RM was composed should then be reckoned prior to that of the *Decree*, or more precisely, before the 'roman church' had taken the positions expressed in this document.[8]

If that be so, one would very much like to be able to date the famous *Decree* accurately. Unfortunately, its date is no more certain than is the compiler's homeland. Some historians speak of the years 520–530.[9] Others are inclined to posit an earlier and broader period.[10] At any rate, as unsatisfactory as this document is by the standards of modern science, it does suppose a labor of research and criticism that would fit in quite well with what we know of the intellectual movement inaugurated at Rome under Pope Gelasius.[11] It is, so it seems, during the two or three decades following his pontificate that the roman clergy thought of conducting a severe sorting of what was currently being read by the faithful. This *terminus ad quem*, though not precise, brings us back to the first quarter of the sixth century, that is, the period to which examination of sources had led us.

This dating accounts for St Benedict's use of the RM. And it is compatible with the few tenuous chronological indications to be gleaned from the Master's work. The Master lived at a time when 'infidels' still existed (95:21). We know from the Life of St Benedict that the evangelization of Cassino had not been achieved by the time the holy patriarch went to live there.[12] The Master also speaks of the 'emperor' (82:2) and of the 'Caesar-designate' (93:63). These allusions to the imperial regime do not compel us to date the RM prior to the fall of the Western Empire (476)[13] or after the byzantine reconquest of Italy (535–540). Even today Frenchmen speak of the 'king' and the 'dauphin' a century and a half after royalty disappeared. The Master's way of speaking is readily understandable at a time when, under the domination of gothic kings, the spirits of the 'Romans' of Italy remain proud in remembering imperial Rome and open to the hope of liberation by byzantine armies.

The date we propose is confirmed in some measure by certain indications of the liturgical cycle as well: the existence of Prime and Sexagesima, a commentary on the psalms within a baptismal context, a system of two readings from the New Testament at Mass, and the custom of not singing alleluia outside Paschaltime. Here, as will be seen, we have characteristics that are best situated in the surroundings of Rome and Campania in the course of the first decades of the sixth century.[14]

THE REGION

Let us re-examine the sources to gain whatever indications they may have to offer on the subject of the Master's homeland. The main fact is the author's use of four Lives of typically roman saints: Anastasius, Eugenia, Sebastian, and Silvester. These saints not only had a sanctuary at Rome and were the object of a cult there, but their Acts themselves are among the most characteristic of what has been called 'roman lore'.[15] Some years ago, H. Delehaye ruthlessly unmasked these legends as works of pure fancy made up around some meager data in Rome's liturgical tradition: a name, a cult place, an anniversary—nothing more was needed for the composers of these Passions to concoct, in a fashion as arbitrary as it was unvaried, entire stories replete with heroic feats, magnificent triumphs, and prodigious miracles.

That such literature could beguile a monk like the Master is readily understandable if one adverts to the ascetical tendencies it incorporates: virginity, fasting, vigils, and prayer, as well as martyrdom, are all held in great honor. It is evident these legends were composed by monks and, in large measure, for monks or fervent Christians who shared the same ideal. St Eugenia, the Master's favorite heroine, for example, passes through monastic life and abbatial office before she finally suffers martyrdom. These legends, roman by their historical and topographical ties, carry above all the stamp of the monastic milieux of the Eternal City of which they are the product.[16]

More important for us here is that the Master, in using so facilely these hagiographical accounts, imposes an initial roman impress on his work. Admittedly, even at this period diffusion of 'roman lore' to regions quite distant from Rome is conceivable.[17] But the Master's citations suppose a familiarity with the texts that would be inexplicable unless both author and auditors together had not been imbued with this literature through readings made in common. This communitarian interest in its turn seems to indicate a collective devotion such as is given to local saints. It is difficult to imagine far from Rome a community devoting so much attention to roman saints at a time when every region and almost every city was jealously maintaining the cult of its own martyrs.

One of the Master's favorite readings provided him with justification for an observance which is also typically roman: dispensation from Thursday fast.[18] The *Vita Siluestri* defended this dispensation against criticisms by the Greeks. This *Vita* testifies to the contemporary roman custom concerning weekdays particularly given to fasting. They are the very same days the RM indicates,[19] especially Saturday, which is not a fast-day in the East or in many churches of the West.

To pursue further the parallels existing between Rome's liturgical customs and those of the Master's monastery, it is necessary to inquire beyond the circle of books which served as sources for the RM. Although the gospel books, sacramentaries, and *Ordines Romani* provide us with direct information about the state of the roman liturgy only some century and a half after the Master's time, the tradition they represent usually dates back much earlier. It is very significant to discover that these liturgical books also accord with the RM on many points: the Saturday fast, a vigil for Pentecost,[20] the absence of offices on Good Friday and Holy Saturday,[21] the abolition of artificial light during the night separating these two days.[22] Both the RM and these liturgical books name feastdays identically: *Sabbatus Pentecosten* for the vigil of Pentecost,[23] *Ascensa* for Ascension,[24] *Theophania,* along with *Epiphania,* for Epiphany,[25] *uicesima* for mid-lent, preceded by *tricesima.*[26] Moreover, given the date we have determined, correspondence can be established between certain indications provided by the RM and what is known about the roman liturgy at the beginning of the six century. This is the case with the limitation of alleluia to Paschaltime[27] and the system of two readings from the New Testament at Mass.[28]

On the other hand, if there is no evidence for Sexagesima at Rome until later, Campania is, with Provence, one of the two regions where this anticipation of the Lenten fast made its appearance in the first half of the sixth century.[29] The commentary on Psalms thirty-four and fifteen which follows that on the Lord's Prayer at the end of the *Theme,* point just as much towards Campania, for, granted the baptismal character of this whole introduction, it is difficult not to associate this commentary with the handing over of psalms to catechumens, a rite apparently proper to the neopolitan church at just this time.[30] These two converging indications move us to situate the Master's monastery southeast of Rome, in the direction of Capua and Naples, especially as nothing gives the impression that it might have been within the city of Rome.[31] Is it merely by coincidence that St Eugenia and St Sebastian, whose Acts our author loved to cite, have their tombs on the Latin Way and Appian Way respectively, exactly on the two roads that lead off towards the region southeast of Rome?[32]

Besides these liturgical indications, certain monastic observances found both in the RM and in two *Ordines Romani* of the eighth century ought to be added. These are the period for sleep after Matins,[33] saying Compline in the dormitory and ending it with the verse *Pone Domine,*[34] and the numerous blessing in the course of meals.[35] These last two customs also occur in the *Ordo Qualiter,* a witness to the Cassinese observance at this period. What is more, this *ordo* preserves several traits characteristic of the Master's work.[36]

In the area of vocabulary, the expression *pullorum cantus,* in which some have wanted to see spanish or gallican influence, is very evident in the language of the roman monastic milieux of the fifth and sixth centuries.[37] The Master used other special expressions which up to now have been found only in roman or italian authors.[38] If to these facts is added the italian origin of the two RM manuscripts and the massive use of the RM by the abbot of Cassino not too long after it was written, we will agree that all these indications converge well enough to permit us to form a conviction. This localization can then explain several traits which, without being absolutely characteristic, would well be ascribed to the roman region of this time period. We are thinking here of the derision to which the monks are subjected by seculars,[39] and of the precautions taken to avoid a manichaean interpretation of fasting.[40] The importance attributed to oil in the diet is also in character for this country.[41] And lastly, the fact that our author uses almost constantly the roman psalter cannot be overlooked. This version of the psalms no doubt received its name only much later and perhaps far from Rome,[42] but the immemorial tradition of its use in roman basilicas for divine services sufficiently justifies this name and confirms that we are closing in on the land of our Rule's origin.

It would be to little purpose, we believe, to refute one by one the various other proposals which have been tendered in regard to the RM's place of origin. The only one of these hypotheses that merits some attention is the one which insists upon the relationships between the Master and the monasticism of Provence and especially of Lérins.[43] True, Cassian's writings exerted a strong influence on the Master, but by this time the *Institute* and *Conferences* enjoyed renown far beyond southern Gaul.[44] And if the *Regula IV Patrum*, the Rule of Caesarius of Arles, and Julianus Pomerius' work might have given the RM some of its characteristics, there is no connection between the two milieux in such matters as structure of the divine office, the practices of fasting, or community organization.[45] That the Master moreover cites a passage from the *Visio Pauli* which seems to have been very much to the taste of gallican monks[46] is hardly significant, since other passages of the same work are drawn upon, sometimes explicitly, by the RM, which proves itself very independant in its citations.[47]

We may therefore formulate the following conclusion with maximum probability: the RM was written in the first quarter of the sixth century in a region near Rome, to the southeast, where it would be open to the dominating influence of the Eternal City, and, more tenuously, to that of certain churches of Campania.[48]

NOTES TO CHAPTER FOUR

1. See L. Duchesne, *Le Liber pontificalis*, 2nd ed., t. I (Paris: De Boccard, 1955), *Introduction*, p. cxiv, n. 54. The *Gesta* entitle this *Vita* the *Liber Siluestri*, which is the title the Master uses (*libris*). This title appears again in a guidebook of the seventh century (*ibid.*, p. cxv).

2. See 91:70. Pomerius, who taught grammar to Caesarius in the last years of the fifth century, would enter clerical ranks towards 503. The *De uita contemplativa* was written at this period. See Fr. Riché, *Éducation et culture dans l'Occident barbare* (Paris: Ed. du Seuil, 1962) 70–71.

3. See F. Masai, *Édition diplomatique*, 59–60.

4. PL 59:157–180. We cite the text and divisions of E. von Dobschütz, *Das Decretum Gelasianum* (Leipzig, 1912) (*Texte und Untersuchungen*, 38, 4), reproduced by H. Leclercq, 'Gélasien (Décret)' in *DACL* 6: 740–745. Only chapters IV and V interest us here. The so-called *Gelasian Decree* rejects as 'apocryphal' the *Acts of Andrew* (those of John are not mentioned), the *Liber Proverbiorum sancti Sixti*, the *Reuelatio Pauli apostoli* (this is exactly the title the Master gives to the *Visio*) and other works, a considerable number of which come from well known authors such as Faustus of Riez and Cassian. 'Apocryphal' therefore signifies for this document 'forbidden, condemned' in a very general sense and whatever be the cause for the ostracism. The *Gesta sanctorum martyrum* receives more qualified judgment. One of the reasons for their removal from public reading is their anonymous character. The same reason prompts the reserve shown towards the *Actus beati Siluestri*, though this work is tolerated. Origen's writings were to be added to this list too (*Decretum*, IV, 5, 2; RM 11:62); the compiler of the *Decree* declared he was following St Jerome's judgment on Origen's works, rejecting some and admitting others. We use the word 'apocryphal' to designate not only works prohibited as such by the *Decree*, but also works censured by it more or less clearly as being anonymous or of doubtful authenticity.

5. See B. Altaner, *Patrologie* 3rd ed. (Freiburg: Herder, 1951) p. 414. He localizes the compiler in southern Gaul. So also E. Dekkers, *Clavis Patrum Latinorum* (Steenbrugge, 1951) 1676.

6. This appears not only with regard to writings discouraged by the *Decree* (cf. n. 4), but also when the *Decree* warmly recommends the *Vita Patrum* of Jerome (IV, 4, 2).

7. As regards what the Master took over from Cassian and Origen no difficulty arises, for the former is never named or even openly cited by the Master, and the latter is not condemned *in toto* by the *Decree*. Citations from the *Passions* are strictly compatible with the *Decree* (IV, 4, 1), which probably

had in view only the public reading of these Acts during liturgical offices, though the criticisms which pseudo-Gelasius levels at them contrast sharply with the Master's avowed esteem for them. Opposition heightens when the Master explicitly cites the *Acts of Andrew*, the *Enchiridion* of Sextus (without naming the author) and the *Reuelatio Pauli*, all of which are rejected as 'apocryphal' by the *Decree*. Moreover, both compiler and those who were the inspiration behind the *Decree* would no doubt have frowned to hear these writings cited as 'Scripture'.

8. Or at least some of these positions. The custom of not reading the *Gesta martyrum* in church no doubt dates back much earlier and is to be explained, above all, by Rome's liturgical conservatism. In this connection, note that the RM never speaks of a public reading of these *Gesta* during the office. Chapter forty-nine does not specify of what the *lectiones* of vigils consist. It is, then, possible that the Master's monastery conformed to the discipline of the roman church on this point.

9. Thus, in an unedited conference, A. Mundó, who in turn refers to conclusions of E. von Dobschütz.

10. Cf. R. Massigli, cited by H. Leclercq, 'Gélasien' in *DACL*, 6: 735-738; G. Bardy, 'Gélase (Décret de)' in *DBS*, 3: 587-588, who proposes the years 484-519. And C. Vagaggini, 'La posizione di S. Benedetto nella questione semipelagiana', *Studia Benedictina* (*Studia Anselmiana* 18-19, [Rome, 1947]) p. 37, indicates the first two decades of the sixth century.

11. Gelasius I (492-496) is the initiator of what has been called the *Gelasian renaissance*. It is he who summoned Denis the Little to Rome and set him to work.

12. Gregory, *Dial.* 2, 8; Moricca, p. 95, 8: *infidelium insana multitudo*.

13. It is known, moreover, that the byzantine emperor remained nominally sovereign of Italy at the time of the Ostrogoth kings (476-540).

14. On Prime, see above, and also J. Froger, *Les origines de prime* (*Bibliotheca 'Ephemerides Liturgiche'* 19) (Rome: Edizioni Liturgiche, 1946) p. 74 and p. 102, n. 221. As for the other customs, see below. In *La communauté et l'abbé*, p. 505, n. 1, may be found two complementary indications elicited from the sense of *praepositus* and from the institutions of the council in the RM (cf. *ibid.*, pp. 193-198 and 388-402).

15. H. Delehaye, *Etude sur le légendier romain* (Brussels: Société des Bollandists, 1936). What was just said pertains more strictly to the first three passions. The *Vita Siluestri* is distinguishable from other roman legends by several particular traits, as L. Duchesne has well demonstrated (above). Moreover, ascetical tendencies are less pronounced in this work, interest descends to other things.

16. We moreover possess a semi-acknowledgment of authorship by Arnobius the Younger, *In Ps.* 101: *scripsimus passiones eorum in progenies alteras*. Cf. *In Ps.* 123, which makes reference to the Passions. These and other similar facts have been brought to light by G. Morin, *Études, textes, decouvertes*, (Paris: A. Picard, 1913) 1:347, n. 1. The striking similarity between the juridically-sounding account in the *Vita Siluestri* (Silvester's controversy with the Jews) and Arnobius' *Conflictus cum Serapione* might be added. Besides

these ascetical tendencies common to both RM and the Passions, the place of honor accorded the theme of martyr by the RM in its doctrine on obedience is to be noted (7:59 and parallels). Even a flavor of wit, perceptible enough in the Master, may be perceived in the Passions. See for example the humorous scenes in the *Passio Anastasiae* 12–14, 28.

17. The *Passio Eugeniae* was known in southern Gaul before 518, as a passage of Avitus Viennensis testifies, *Poem.* VI; *PL* 59:378BC.

18. See 28:41–43, citing the *Actus S. Siluestri*. Compare this with the justification for sleep after Matins by recourse to the *Passio Eugeniae*.

19. Wednesday, Friday, and Saturday.

20. See note on 28:45.

21. See note on 53:48.

22. See notes on 53:61–63.

23. See note on 28:44–45.

24. See note on 28:41–43.

25. The RM employs *Epiphania* six times (Ch. 39–45 and 53), and *Theophania* only once (28:47). At Rome, *Epiphania* appears in a sub-heading of the Gregorian Sacramentary (Lietzmann, p. 16, no. 17), while *Theophania* figures in Gelasius (see note on 28:47). Even if these latter are considered unauthentic, and due to gallican influence (C. Mohrmann, *Études sur le latin des chrétiens* [Rome: Edizioni di Storia e Letteratura, 1961] 1: 269), the constant presence of *Theophania* in the *comes* of Würzburg remains to be explained (cf. H. Leclercq, 'Lectionnaire' in *DACL* 8: 2286), as well as that of Murbach, of Alcuin, and that in the three most ancient copies of the *Capitulare Euangeliorum*. Only in the most recent of these three copies, dating after 750 and interpolated with frankish elements, does *Epiphania* appear, without however wholly eliminating its rival (Klauser, p. 141, no. 11–12). It seems, therefore, that *Theophania* belongs to ancient roman vocabulary at least as much as *Epiphania*. The latter is characteristic of the lectionary of Capua and of Neapolitan lectionaries. Cf. H. Leclercq, 'Naples' in *DACL* 12: 759–763.

26. See 53:3–4; *Ordo Romanus* XV, 81 (Andrieu, vol. 3, 115, 1); the *Comes* of Würzburg also testifies to *uicesima* and *tricesima* at Rome.

27. See 28:46, and John the Deacon, *Ep ad Senarium* 13; PL 59:406, in which is attested the restriction of the alleluia to Paschaltime at Rome in the early sixth century, though, according to the same author, other churches sang it all year round.

28. See notes on 46:6–7.

29. See 28:11, and J. Froger, 'Les anticipations du jeûne quadragésimal', *Mélanges de science religieuse* 3 (1946) 207–234. Instead of Sexagesima, Quinquagesima is mentioned equivalently by the *Liber pontificalis*, 1: 129, 2, which attributes to Pope Telesphorus the institution of a seven-week fast before Easter. The author composed this work at Rome under Hormisdas (514–523). As L. Duchesne has noted (*ibid.*, n. 2), 'the author ... differed from the actual and obligatory discipline. He had no doubt wanted to create propaganda in favor of a stricter observance.' The RM evinces the same tendency to make Lent last forty days, but obtains this result differently. It was a question of devotional practices not yet approved by ecclesiastical authority in the official

customs of the roman church. Compare this with the distinction made regarding the alleluia between the custom of the churches and that of the monasteries (28:46–47).

30. See notes on Th 1 and Th 10–14. Cf. B. Egli, *Der vierzehnte Psalm im Prolog der Regel des Hl. Benedikt*, (Sarnen: Buchdruckerei Louis Ehrli & Cie, 1962) p. 99.

31. Expeditions on foot or by carriage, which are often mentioned, make more sense if the monastery was situated in an isolated place and had to make its purchases some distance away. In any center of importance, it would have been merely a matter of going to market. Moreover, field labor is envisaged as possible, though excluded for ascetic reasons (ch. 86). Lastly, the satire on gyrovagues seems to suppose a territory through which monasteries and hermitages are scattered, rather than an urban center.

32. We owe this suggestion and many others to an unedited conference of D. Mundó, the text of which he kindly sent us.

33. Notes on 33:9, 18. Cf. above, n. 19. Moreover, the Master previously relied on the *Passio Eugeniae*, which itself attests to Roman custom, just as he justified the Thursday dispensation from fasting with the aid of the *Vita Siluestri* (above, n. 18).

34. Note on 30:12. On the beverage provided before Compline, see note on 27:10.

35. Compare RM 23 with *Ordo Romanus* XIX, 5–15. The same system of blessings is set forth by the *Ordo Qualiter* (B. Albers, *Consuetudines monasticae* [Monte Cassino 1970] 1: 44–6).

36. Notes on 11:68 (*crede*); 19:8 (*Benedicite*); 47:21 (no spitting).

37. See Arnobius the Younger, *In Ps.* 129, PL 53:53c: *tertia (custodia, uigilia) pullorum cantus transit.*

38. Thus *pallios linostimos* (n. on 81:5), *sagos tumentacios* (n. on 81:31), *lenis et racanis* (n. on 81:32), *erigi* in the sense of to be excluded (n. on 13:41).

39. See note on 24:21.

40. See note on 53:27.

41. Cf. 15:44; 53:7–8. Abstinence from oil is one of the most burdensome mortifications. Another detail which may help to localize the Master's monastery: sea-food is never mentioned. This coincides with the absence of any allusion to the ocean or to a river.

42. See R. Weber, *La Psautier Romain* (Rome: Vatican Poliglot Press, 1953) viii–ix.

43. Hypotheses proposed or suggested in various forms by I. Schuster, *Regula monasteriorum* (Turin: Società Editrice Internationale, 1945) p. 9, n. 1; B. Steidle, 'Das Inselkloster Lerin und die RB' in *Benediktinische Monatschrift* 27 (1951), p. 386; F. Masai, 'La RM à Moutiers-Saint-Jean' in *A Cluny* (Dijon 1950) 192–202; P. B. Corbett, 'The RM and some of its problems', *Studia Patristica* (Berlin: Akademie-Verlag, 1957) 1: 82–93. Th. Payr, 'Der Magistertext', *Studia Anselmiana* 44 (Rome, 1959) 83–84; R. Hanslik, *Benedicti Regula*, pp. xiv and lxxv.

44. Cf. Ferrandus, *Vita Fulgentii* 23–24 for Africa; Cassiodorus, *Inst.* 29 for southern Italy. At Rome itself, the *Gelasian Decree*, by its condemnation of Cassian, testifies to his success.

45. On the offices at Arles and in the RM, see above. Fasting: the nuns of Arles fast on Monday, not Saturday. The decanal system seems not to have existed in the communities of Arles, nor was there consequently any dependence of the Master in this matter. See K. Hallinger, 'Papst Gregor der Grosse und der Hl Benedikt', *Studia Anselmiana* 42 (Rome, 1957) 305–306. *Praepositus* has consequently a different meaning in the two milieux. Other officers of which Caesarius speaks are for the most part unknown to the Master.

46. See note on 86:7.

47. We add as a reminder that the expression *porro a finibus aduenire Italiae* (1:36) may be equally well understood in the environs of Rome as in southern Gaul.

48. Further evidence supporting this conclusion may be found in my article 'Scholies sur la Règle du Maître', *RAM* 44 (1968) 151–157. See also 'La Règle du Maître et les Dialogues de S. Grégoire', *RHE* 61 (1966) 44–76.

THE RULE OF THE MASTER

THE RULE OF THE MASTER

END OF THE LIST OF CHAPTERS

PROLOGUE

[1]You who are reading, first of all, and then you who are listening to me as I speak, dismiss now other thoughts [2]and realize that I am speaking to you and that through my words God is instructing you. [3]We must willingly go to him, the Lord our God, by our good deeds and right intentions, [4]lest by disregarding our sins we be summoned and snatched away by death against our will.

[5]You, therefore, who hear me speaking, listen through what is written here to what is being said to you not by my mouth but by God. [6]Now, while you are still living, he is instructing you about that of which after death you will have to give him an account. [7]For while we are yet alive we are being given time, because God's fatherly love daily awaits our amendment and wants us to grow better from day to day.

[8]You, therefore, who are listening to me, pay attention so that my words and your hearing of them may, by your soul's meditation, meet where three roads cross in your heart. [9]When, as a result of my words, you come to these cross-roads, leave one of them behind—that of sinful ignorance—[10]and enter upon the two lying before you—those of obedience to the precepts. [11]And while we are seeking to go to God, let us pause at that crossroads of our heart and consider

---

1. The literary structure of the Prologue is curious. There are two alternating series of texts, the one using the second person singular, the other using the first person plural. Only once is the second person plural used. The translation follows the original in giving the frequent interchange of persons.

2. An allusion to the reading of the Rule to the community (24:15) and to the postulant (87:3, 89:8, 90:5).

8. The heart was considered the seat of the soul, the organ of thought and will. Hearing and seeing were thought to come to that centre through the ears and eyes. In this sense the heart is a 'crossroads'. For the theme of the two ways, see Ch. 7. Here the narrow way is not simply the christian life, but the life of cenobites living under a rule.

92

the two roads of knowledge we see before us. ¹²Let us consider upon which of these two roads we can attain God. ¹³If we take the one to the left, we have reason to fear, because it is wide, that it is the one which leads to perdition. ¹⁴If we turn to the right, we are on the correct road because it is narrow and is the one which brings loving servants to him who is their Lord.

¹⁵So free your hearing to follow my discourse. ¹⁶You then whose attention we urge, understand that it is God who admonishes you through what is written here, so that now, while you are still alive and have time for your amendment, you may run with all your strength and, ¹⁷when you are summoned by death you will not, on the day of judgment and in eternal punishment, offer God the excuse that during your lifetime no one told you about amendment, ¹⁸and you [then] begin to repent forever, without hope of relief because you can no longer help yourself.

¹⁹From now on, therefore, before you leave the light of this world, observe what you are hearing, ²⁰because after you have departed you will not return until the resurrection; if you have lived a good life during your time here, at the resurrection you will be assigned to eternal glory with the saints. ²¹If, on the other hand, you do not put into practice what is here written and which I am going to read to you, you will be consigned to the eternal fire of hell with the devil whose will you preferred to follow.

²²So hear and do what is good and just, that by which God is pleased, and put into practice what this rule points out to you. ²³This rule for doing what is right gets this name 'rule' from what the apostle says in his epistle: 'According to the measure of the rule which God has measured to us a measure to reach even unto you'. ²⁴For the rule begins in truth and ends in justice, as the prophet says: 'You shall rule them with a rod', that is, with the force of fear, ²⁵as the apostle again says: 'What is your wish? Shall I come to you with a rod or in love?'. ²⁶So also the prophet says: 'A tempered rod is your

23. 2 Cor 10:13
24. Ps 2:9
25. 1 Cor 4:21
26. Ps 45:7–8

royal scepter. You love justice and hate wickedness'. [27]And
again the Lord says: 'I will punish their sins with the rod'.

END OF THE PROLOGUE OF THE RULE

THE THEME

[1]The prophet says: 'I am going to speak to you in parable'.
[2]And again he said: 'I became a byword for them'.

[3]Born from the womb of Eve, our earthly mother, and generated by our father Adam in an excess of concupiscence, we
have come down to this world's way of life; [4]taking upon
ourselves the temporal yoke of pilgrimage, we travel the road
of this life in ignorance of good works and in uncertainty
about the experience of death. [5]Our journey through this
world has burdened us with many sins of negligence. [6]The
running sweat of labor, with our shoulders weary from the
weight of this baggage, has made us aware of the proximity of
death [7]and we gasp with a burning thirst threatening destruction.

[8]Suddenly, to the right, toward the east, we see unexpectedly a spring of living water, [9]and while we are hastening to
it the divine voice issues from it and on its own initiative
meets us, calling to us and saying: 'All you who are thirsty,
come to the water!'. [10]And seeing us coming loaded with our
heavy baggage, it again says: 'Come to me, all you who labor
and are burdened, and I will give you rest'. [11]And hearing
this loving voice, we throw our burden to the ground and,
impelled by thirst, fall down greedily at the spring, drink
long, and rise refreshed. [12]After getting up, we stand there

---

27. Ps 89:32
1. 'Theme' seems originally to have applied only to the scriptural quotations
in the first two lines. It was subsequently extended to this entire section. Ps
78:2.
2. Ps 69:12
3. The christian law is our mother: an expression more familiar in antiquity
than now. RM equates Adam with our sinful free will.
9. Is 55:1
10. Mt 11:28

dazed by tremendous joy and wonder, looking at the yoke of the laborious journey just completed, namely, our baggage whose weight has exhausted us to the point of death because of our ignorance.

[13]While we are looking at these things and thinking about them for a long time, again we hear the voice from the spring of water which has refreshed us saying: [14]'Shoulder my yoke and learn from me, for I am gentle and humble in heart, and you will find rest for your souls. [15]Yes, my yoke is easy and my burden light'. [16]Hearing this, we now say to one another: [17]'After having been refreshed by such a spring and having heard the voice of the Lord inviting us, let us not take up again the burden of our sins which we have thrown off, [18]that is, which we renounced when we went to the font of baptism. [19]This baggage of our sins by its weight wearied us to death till now because of our ignorance of the holy law, and we despaired because we did not know the meaning of baptism. [20]Now, however, opening ourselves to the wisdom of God after having been burdened with the baggage of our sins, we have been invited by the voice of the Lord to rest. [21]Let us, therefore, reject the old baggage of sins. [22]Let the heedless ones on this world's road have the burden of their sins. [23]We regard as our mother no longer the Eve who came from the slime of the earth, but the Christian law calling us to heavenly repose. [24]So also we look no longer to Adam, in the will to sin, as our father, but to the voice of the Lord inviting us. [25]And not daring to rely on the merit of our desires, we nevertheless have now discovered where you are by our rebirth in your sacred font.'

[THEME PATER]

[1]'Our Father, who art in heaven.' [2]Therefore see, brothers, that if we have now found our mother the Church and have dared to call the Lord in heaven our father, it is right that we

---

15. Mt 11:28–9
1. Mt 6:9
2. Mt 19:29

should leave our earthly father and our mother according to the flesh, [3]lest being subject to both sets of parents we not only offend those who are citizens but, if we do not abandon the parents according to the flesh, we be considered adulterine offspring. [4]For because of the tree of scandal our race descended from paradise to the womb, from the womb to the world, and from the world to the portals of hell. [5]But we have been born anew through baptism and restored by the tree of the cross. The passion of the Lord effects the resurrection of our race [6]and its readmission by grace to paradise whence it had fallen by sin freely willed. [7]When Christ provided for us the refuge of his cross, the Lord destroyed the sting of death which was reigning over us. [8]After restoring us to the grace of adoption by him, he has moreover not ceased to invite us to the kingdom of heaven. [9]Hence the voice of the Lord says: 'If you keep my commandments, I will be your father and you shall be my sons'. [10]So it is that we, though unworthy but aware of our baptism, dare in his prayer to call him father. [11]Therefore it behooves us to share in his sufferings so that we may deserve to be made coheirs of his glory.

[12]So when saying, 'Our Father, who art in heaven,' brothers, let us now show that we are sons such as God wants to have, [13]and may the Divinity rightly grant us the title of sons, seeing our will conformable to his own. [14]For he who resembles his father not only in appearance but also in conduct is a true son.

[15]Since we have now deserved to say, 'Our Father, who art in heaven', we continue the prayer saying: 'Hallowed be thy name'. [16]Not that we want his name to be hallowed anew, since it is most holy from eternity to eternity, but rather that he may himself sanctify it in the good deeds of his sons, [17]so that as Father and Lord he may make his dwelling in our souls and send the Holy Spirit to live in us, [18]giving help to our hearts by his regard and ever keeping watch over them by his presence.

[19]Then we say, 'Thy kingdom come'. [20]See, brothers, how

9. Jn 15:10, 2 Cor 6:18
10. The 'Father' is Christ who suffered for us.
11. 1 Pet 4:13, Rom 8:17

we long for the coming of the Lord's kingdom and ourselves ask that his judgment be hastened, and yet we do not have our account in order. [21]We should therefore conduct ourselves at all times in such a way that, when the time comes, our Lord and Father will receive us and, [22]pleased with our daily good deeds in his presence, will separate us from the goats and place us at his right, admitting us into the eternal kingdom. [23]May we, in the judgment to come, find a propitious judge him whom in this world we have dared to call father.

[24]Then we say: 'Thy will be done on earth as it is in heaven'. [25]In this statement, brothers, our free will is expressed, [26]and whatever harm the persuasion of the ancient serpent has done us is removed, if we so will, for the will of the Lord heals us. [27]As the apostle says: 'You do not always carry out your good intentions'. [28]The spirit chooses to have the will of the Lord done in us, so that the soul no longer does what it had been persuaded to do by the concupiscence of corrupt flesh. [29]We therefore pray that the will of the Lord will be done in us. [30]If this his will is always done in us, on the day of judgment there will be no self-will to be condemned after being examined for faults. [31]For the will of the Lord is holy. [32]It knows how to remove fear of judgment. [33]This his will promises that those in whom it is accomplished will judge even angels.

[34]Our Lord and Saviour shows us this holy will by giving us the example of its being done in himself in order to suppress the free will of the flesh in us when he says: 'I have come not to do my own will, but to do the will of the one who sent me'. [35]And again he says in his holy passion: 'My Father, if it is possible, let this cup pass me by'. [36]This voice of fear in the Lord was that of the flesh he had assumed, and shows us

---

24. The length of the commentary on the third petition of the Lord's Prayer indicates the importance of this theme in the monastic theology of the Master. The very purpose of the cenobitical life, for him, was to substitute the will of God for the self-will of sinful man.

27. Gal 5:17

34. Jn 6:38

35. Mt 26:39

that the acts of life must always be well considered if death to come must be feared. ³⁷Too, it was a question the Lord addressed to the Father: whether what we ourselves wish can be done in us or whether what we do not wish may be justly imposed on us contrary to our desire. ³⁸Hence there follows the example of fidelity which the Lord gave by submitting to the will of the Father, saying: 'Nevertheless, let it be as you, not I, would have it'. ³⁹Then follows: 'If this cup cannot pass by without my drinking it, your will be done'. ⁴⁰See therefore that whatever we choose by our own will is patently unjust, and whatever is justly imposed on us against our will by the one who has command over us is accounted to our credit, ⁴¹because just as a man cannot see his face by turning his eyes upon himself, so he cannot be his own judge unless what is seen by another is judged with justice. ⁴²If no one can see his own face, then, how can he prove that his own will is right unless judgment is passed upon what is seen in us by another? ⁴³See, brothers, what loving care the Lord has devoted to our restoration and what way of salvation he has shown our waywardness; ⁴⁴so much so, that in his only-begotten Son he made manifest what he wished to accomplish in his servants.

⁴⁵'Thy will be done on earth as it is in heaven.' ⁴⁶From this, that he said 'in heaven', we can well understand, brothers, that just as the will of the Lord is fulfilled in all holiness by the angels in heaven, so should God's command given through the prophets and the apostles be obeyed by carnal men on earth too, ⁴⁷so that, as Holy Scripture says, in both spheres (that is, in heaven and on earth) the Lord may reign also in us according to his good pleasure, and there may be one shepherd and one flock.

⁴⁸So also we can understand in a spiritual sense what he says: 'Thy will be done as it is in heaven', ⁴⁹that is, that the will of the Father be done in the Lord, his Son, because he came down from heaven, the Lord himself saying, 'I have

38. Ibid.
39. Mt 26:42
47. Jn 10:16
49. Jn 6:38

come, not to do my own will, but to do the will of the one who sent me'. [50]Do you therefore see that if our Saviour, the Lord himself, shows that he came not to do his own will but to fulfill the commands of his Father, how can I, a wicked servant, the least of all, rightly do my own will? [51]Of him the apostle likewise says: 'When it says, "he ascended", what can it mean if not that he descended right down to the lower regions of the earth?'. [52]So by his saying, 'Also on earth' (that is, our bodily structure formed from the slime of the earth, to which God addressed the words, 'Dust you are and to dust you shall return', [53]the demand is justly made that the will of God be likewise done by us, so that by the daily accomplishment of the Lord's will in us, our own will is not found and therefore will not be condemned to punishment in the future judgment; rather, may the will of the Lord be in us, so that the crown of glory may be ours.

[54]Then continuing the prayer we say: 'Give us this day our daily bread', [55]Therefore, brothers, when the aforesaid will of the Lord has been daily fulfilled by us, excluding blame, and all the commandments have been observed in the fear of the Lord, [56]the petition that he give food to his workmen is worthily made, for he does not refuse the deserving laborer his wages.

[57]Then we say: 'Forgive us our trespasses as we forgive those who trespass against us'. [58]Brothers, praying thus, we should very much fear lest the Lord reply to these words of our prayer: 'The judgments you give are the judgments you will get, and the amount you measure out is the amount you will be given'. [59]And you who ask this, see whether you did to no one what you did not want done to you. [60]Therefore before we hear these words of the Lord, brethren, let us first examine our hearts as to whether we are with justice asking of the Lord what we have not denied to those asking us. [61]We ask that our trespasses be forgiven us. God hears and he wants to forgive us, but only if we first pardon those who ask

51. Eph 4:9
52. Gen 3:19
58. Mt 7:2
59. Tob 4:16

us to do likewise. [62]Or do I doubt, miserable man that I am, that divine recompense will be given me for my good deeds? [63]Look, give heed and consider, O miserable man, are you more loving than God? [64]Even though he charges you with duties of justice and charity, what you do is to your benefit over and above the reward and the gifts he gives you. [65]For there is nothing wanting to the power of the Lord nor does he need anything of yours in his strength or lack it in his glory. [66]The only thing he wants is our salvation, which he offers us by his grace, even though we cause him loss in us by our negligence.

[67]Then we say: 'And lead us not into temptation'. [68]These words, brothers, are warning enough that we should be on our guard. [69]We must therefore beg the Lord with many sighs, striking our hearts as well as our breasts, never to leave us his servants without his help, [70]lest we be open to the power and access of our enemy the devil, who is constantly prowling around us like a lion, looking for someone of us to eat, and who seeks to poison our hearts with his evil suggestions. [71]Therefore we must without ceasing pray to the Lord that he deign, by the protection of his assistance, to surround us with the wall of his grace and by his defence ward off the incursion of temptations in us, [72]so as not to permit the work of his hands to be taken captive and subjected to slavery by the enemy—[73]provided we do not on our part give our consent to the temptations of this same enemy and do not, [74]so to speak, make ourselves his captives, inclined to desire our enemy rather than flee him.

[75]Then we continue, completing the prayer: 'But deliver us from evil'. [76]Brothers, most holy, God desires to do this in us before we ask him, for he is powerful and nothing is difficult for him, but [he does it] only on condition that we deserve it. [77]He does not want this structure which we are and which he has made with his own hands to collapse. [78]He hastens to free us from the snare, if we do not on our part give consent

---

69. St Augustine, Sermon 351:6, places the striking of the breast during the recitation of the Lord's Prayer at the fifth petition and not, as here, at the sixth.

70. 1 Pet 5:8

to the enemy's suggestions, [79]but unceasingly ask the Lord to grant us the assistance of his grace so that we may rightly say: 'For with the Lord at our right hand nothing can shake me', [80]and confident in the Lord we say again: 'I will fear no evils, for you are with me'. [81]Thus may he, who at the beginning of the prayer shows us that we should dare, by his grace, to call the Lord our Father, deign now at the end of the prayer to deliver us from evil. Amen.

[THEME SEQUENCE]

[1]Having then completed the Lord's prayer, brothers, let us now, as the Lord commands, treat also the performance of our service [2]so that he who has deigned to include us among his sons may never be distressed by our evil deeds. [3]For by means of the good things he has given us we must always be so submissive to him that he will never, as an angry father, disinherit us, his sons, [4]and as a fearsome Lord exasperated by our sins commit us to eternal punishment as most wicked servants who refused to follow him to glory. [5]Let us, slothful as we are, finally arise, stirred by what Scripture says: 'It is now the hour for us to rise from sleep', [6]and with our eyes opened to the deifying light, let us listen with alert ears to what the divine voice ever crying out exhorts us, saying: [7]'If anyone has ears to hear, let him listen to what the Spirit is saying to the churches'. [8]What? 'Come, my sons, listen to me, I will teach you the fear of the Lord'. [9]'Run while you have the light of life, or the darkness of death will overtake you'.

[10]And the Lord, seeking from among the many people a workman to hear him, again calls out, saying: [11]'Which of you desires life, and takes delight in prosperous days?'. [12]You, who are listening, reply: 'I do'. And the Lord will say to you:

79. Cf. Ps 16:8
80. Ps 23:4
5. Rm 13:11
7. Rev 2:7
8. Ps 34:11
9. Jn 12:35
11. Ps 34:12

[13]" 'If you desire true and everlasting life, malice must be banished from your tongue, deceitful conversation from your lips. Never yield to evil, practise good, seek peace, pursue it". [14]And when you have done this, my eyes will be turned to you, the virtuous, and my ears to your cry, and before you call to me I shall say to you: "Here I am".' [15]What can be more delightful to us than this voice of the Lord inviting us, brothers? [16]See how in his loving kindness the Lord shows us the way of life. [17]Girded with faith and the performance of good deeds, therefore, let us under the guidance of the gospel go his ways, so that we may deserve to see him who has called us into his kingdom.

[18]If we desire to dwell in his kingdom, we must run to it by our good deeds; otherwise we shall never arrive there. [19]But let us with the prophet inquire of the Lord, saying to him: 'O Lord, who shall sojourn in your tent or who shall dwell on your holy mountain?' [20]Having asked this, brothers, let us listen to the Lord again replying and showing us the way to his tent, [21]saying: 'The man whose life is blameless, who always does what is right, [22]who speaks the truth from his heart, whose tongue is not used for slander, [23]who does no wrong to his fellow, casts no discredit on his neighbor'. [24]When tempted, he closes his mind to the malignant devil, together with his suggestions, and thus foils him, taking the thoughts which come from him and, before they have grown, dashing them on the rock, Christ. [25]Such persons, fearing the Lord, do not pride themselves upon their good observance; rather, aware that what is good in themselves cannot be their own doing but the Lord's, [26]they magnify the Lord working in them, saying with the prophet: 'Not to us, O Lord, not to us, but to your name give glory'. [27]Nor did the apostle Paul attribute anything of his preaching to himself, but said: 'By

13. Ps 34:13–14
14. Cf. Ps 34:15
19. Ps 15:1
23. Ps 15:2–3
26. Ps 115:1
27. 1 Cor 15:10

the grace of God I am what I am'. [28]Again he says: 'If there is to be boasting, it is not for me to do it'. [29]Therefore the Lord continues teaching us the way of the blessed life, saying: 'Who stands by his pledge no matter what the cost, [30]does not ask interest on loans, and cannot be bribed to victimize the innocent'. [31]And in the gospel the Lord further says to us: 'Everyone who listens to these words of mine and acts on them will never be shaken'. [32]Then we ask him: 'In what way, Lord, will he never be shaken?' [33]The Lord again replies to us: 'How? Because I will compare him with a sensible man who built his house on rock. [34]Floods rose, gales blew and hurled themselves against that house, and it did not fall: it was founded on rock'.

[35]Having said these things, the Lord is silent, waiting for us to respond daily to these his holy admonitions, as we must. [36]Therefore day after day the time of this life is protracted so that we may amend our evil ways, [37]as the apostle says: 'Do you not realize that the patience of God is meant to lead you to repentance?' [38]For the loving Lord says: 'I take pleasure not in the death of a wicked man, but in the turning back of a wicked man who changes his ways to win life'.

[39]So, brothers, when we asked the Lord about the dweller in his tent, we heard the conditions for living there, and that we must do what is required of a dweller. [40]Therefore our hearts and our bodies must be prepared for the battle of holy obedience to the precepts. [41]And as to what nature in us finds impossible, let us ask the Lord to ordain that his grace come to our assistance. [42]And if we desire to escape the punishment of hell and attain eternal life, it is now, [43]while there is still time, while we are yet in the body and while we have the chance to put all these things into effect by the light of this life, [44]that we must hurry and do what will profit us forever.

28. Cf. 2 Cor 12:1
30. Ps 15:4–5
31. Mt 7:24. Cf. Ps 15:5
34. Mt 7:25
37. Rom 2:4
38. Ezech 33:11

[45]We must therefore establish a school of the Lord's service, [46]so that, never rejecting his guidance but persevering in his teaching in the monastery until death, we may by patience merit to share in the sufferings of Christ so that the Lord may make us coheirs of his kingdom. Amen.

END OF THE THEME OF THE RULE

45. RB Prol. 45
46. Cf. Ac 2:42, Ph 2:8, 1 Pet 4:13, Rom 8:12

I The kinds, drink, conduct, and life of monks in monasteries.

[1]Of monks, it is well known, there are four kinds. [2]The first are the cenobites, namely, those who live in monasteries and serve under a rule and an abbot.

[3]Then the second kind are the anchorites, that is, hermits, who are no longer in the first fervor of conversion but by long probation in the monastery [4]have learned, taught by association with many others, to fight against the devil; [5]well-equipped, they leave the ranks of the brethren for the single combat of the desert. Fearless now, deprived of the encouragement of others, they are able by themselves with God and the spirit to do battle against the vices of the flesh and of thought.

[6]The third kind of monks the sarabaites, is the worst. I would do better to call them still of the world, except that the tonsure of their religious intent prevents me from doing so. Untested, as gold in the furnace, by any rule or by experience as a master, soft as lead, [7]they still keep faith with the world and manifestly lie to God by their tonsure. [8]Two or three together, or even alone, without a shepherd, enclosed not in the Lord's but in their own sheepfold, they have as their law the wilfulness of their own desires; [9]whatever they think and decide, that they call holy, and what they do not want, that they consider forbidden. [10]And while they want to have cells, chests and various things according to their own judgment, they are unaware that they are losing their own petty souls.

[11]Likewise there are those who, recently converted, in unrestrained fervor think that the desert is a place of repose. [12]Giving no thought to the devil's lying in wait to harm them,

1. *Conf.* 18. RB 1
3. in supposedly historical sequence. Cf. *Conf.* 18.
6. Wis 3:6, *Conf.* 18:4,7

untrained but confident, they go forth to single combat with him, doubtlessly only to fall victim to the jaws of the experienced wolf.

[13]The fourth kind of monks, who should not even be called that and about whom I would do better to keep silence than to say anything, [14]are called gyrovagues. They spend their whole life as guests for three or four days at a time at various cells and monasteries of others in various provinces. [15]Taking advantage of hospitality, they want to be received every day anew at different places. [16]They oblige their successive hosts, who rejoice at the arrival of a guest, to prepare choice dishes for them and to put the axe to poultry because of their coming—this, every day by different hosts. [17]They think that in this way they are not imposing on their successive hosts, since by changing hosts every day they aim at having one meal here, another there, prepared for them when, abusing charity, they arrive at a new place. [18]They force upon their various hosts, in spite of themselves as it were, the precept of the apostle wherein he says, 'You should make hospitality your special care'. [19]Making use of this precept, they demand care for their restless feet after their journey, but using traveling as a pretext, are thinking of their guts, defiled by endless drinking, rather than their feet, when they want a big supper or dinner. [20]And when, after the journey, the greedy guest has cleaned the table down to the last crumb, he shamelessly declares his thirst to his host, and if there is nothing there to drink, the host is asked to prepare it on the spot. [21]And when after the double excess of food and drink they are stuffed to the point of vomiting, they attribute to their laborious journey all that their gluttony has got them.

[22]And before a new bed receives his guest, exhausted from drinking and eating more than from traveling, they give their host an exaggerated account of the hardship of their journey, [23]and while they compel their host to offer them an abundance of food and endless drink as a reward for their visit, they pretend that the reason for their wandering is a pilgrimage and captivity. [24]Moreover they are soon inquiring whether there is a monk or a monastery nearby, so that after

18. Rom 12:13

leaving this place they can stop and stay there, [25]feigning fatigue, as if the whole world were shutting them out and as if in all of it there were neither place nor forest nor the wide expanse of the Egyptian desert itself to take them in, [26]not even any monastery to receive them for the service of God—as if, as we have said, the whole world were rejecting them. [27]Hence they say that it is with good reason they are wandering about and that nowhere at all can they find a place to stay, nor refreshment for their soul, nor full observance of discipline—[28]which amounts to their saying that they are so very wise that they alone are displeased by what is pleasing to God and to all others. [29]Therefore they choose instead to keep on the move, so that by changing hosts every day they may get a change and variety of meals and much to drink on the plea that traveling has caused their thirst. [30]It is therefore evident that they do this in order by their wandering to cater to their gullet rather than to their soul.

[31]And when after spending a couple of days with one host they are served less food, [32]and on the morrow see that their host is busy with work in his cell instead of cooking their meal, [33]they quickly decide to seek another host. Hardly arrived, they are off again. [34]They take hurried leave of their now stingy host, and while getting ready to leave this hospitality behind, they ask their host to say a leave-taking prayer. [35]Thus they hurry as if someone were pushing them, as if meals prepared for them by other hosts were already awaiting them.

[36]And if, not far from this monastery, they find a monk's cell, they stop there, saying they have come from far-off Italy. [37]With head bowed as if in humility, they lie again about pilgrimage and captivity to this new host, [38]forcing the good man out of sympathy for their long journey to use up his whole scanty means in cooking and serving them food, [39]most certainly only to be left destitute and plundered by these gluttons after a couple of days. [40]When the next day he himself, his cell, his customs and rule of life do not please them, [41]and when after two days he, like the others, reduces the fare, [42]he too is soon driven to give them back their pouches which have already been filled with bread baked and given them by various hosts. [43]Although the bread is fresh

when they take it from the table in the various hostels, they cause it by their avarice to become moldy by hoarding it.

⁴⁴After their pouches have been returned to them then, their poor donkey is called from the pasture. The poor thing was enjoying the pasture after the labor of the recent trip, and now after a couple of days its masters are dissatisfied with the hospitality they have received. ⁴⁵When it has again been harnessed and loaded with various tunics and cowls which their insolence has extorted from others or of which, taking advantage of the occasion, they have defrauded their various hosts—⁴⁶they make a show of wearing ragged clothing so that they can ask for a replacement—⁴⁷they say farewell to this host too. Hardly have they arrived when they leave again, for mentally they see themselves already invited to other guest quarters. ⁴⁸The poor donkey is whipped, prodded, singed, but it hunches its back and does not budge. ⁴⁹They beat its ears when its haunches are down. ⁵⁰And so the poor thing is almost killed and, [already] worn out, is beaten, because they are in a hurry and cannot wait to get to another monastery for a meal.

⁵¹As soon as they have arrived at another monastery or monk's cell, they cry out *Benedicite* gaily and loudly, from outside, ⁵²as if they already had in their hands the cup which they are going to request to assuage their thirst once they have entered the monastery. ⁵³Once inside and not yet announced and received, they unload. ⁵⁴As if they had come to discharge some obligation or as someone's delegate, their baggage is brought in before the guest himself has been received. ⁵⁵If they hurry to the oratory, it is only because they are driven to it by their desire for wine to satisfy the thirst caused by their traveling; knowing that you will, out of charity, offer wine to a guest, in the morning they ask for water.

⁵⁶When such as these, who ignore the fast because traveling, ⁵⁷arrive somewhere and find the monks fasting, they either force their hosts to break the fast for the sake of hospitality ⁵⁸or they brazenly tell them straight out that they are fasting out of avarice because they do not want to give their guests any refreshments after their journey. ⁵⁹Because of the

---

51. 'Bless [the Lord]³—a monastic salutation.

habitual gluttony which goes with their vagrancy, they force the settled monks to break their fast, ascribing this presumption to travel fatigue. [60]They ignore the fact that it is not necessity that compels them to travel so that they do not need to fast and abstain or remain anywhere for any length of time, [61]but that it is their deliberate gluttony that motivates them when they boldly come with the intention of eating bread earned by another's labor and love to wipe off their sweat on beds or couches provided at the various places for travelers.

[62]Once on these couches, they try to get the satisfaction of sleep while suffering from indigestion because of their surfeit of food and drink, [63]and even though they never bothered to pray the psalms because of their preoccupation with their gluttonous travels, [64]they bluntly say that their bones are so weary after the trip that getting up from bed [for prayers] is impossible—though they were manifestly hale and hearty at table the evening before. [65]As soon as the night office of the Work of God is finished they get up, groaning and feigning exhaustion. [66]After being warmed up by wine in the early morning and asking for a piece of bread or, pretending to be ill, requesting a potion, [67]they leave the monastery or cell, deceitfully bent over because of feigned weakness but secretly assured that the gait of a healthy man will be recovered as soon as they have left the place.

[68]Now, since they do not want to be under the regime of a monastery or to have an abbot to look after all their needs, [69]they should put up a cell somewhere and stay there, living as they please, and should provide the necessities of life for themselves. [70]If our way of life does not please them, they should let us see theirs. [71]As it is, never settling down, they are impelled always to go about begging, sweating, and groaning, instead of remaining in one place to work and live. [72]They are always coming anew to a succession of cells as humble guests with no more than their head bowed, only to leave again after a couple days as proud ingrates. [73]Since the manner of life at these various places and the discipline of all monasteries does not please them, they choose to travel rather than to settle down. [74]Always on the go from place to place, they do not know where they will next be a nuisance and, to top it all, they do not know where they will be buried.

[75]And now, in accordance with our high esteem for the first kind of monks, the cenobites, whose service and probation are the will of God, let us return to their rule.

[76]Brothers, the Lord cries out to us daily, saying: 'Return to me, and I will return to you'. [77]Therefore our return to God, brothers, is nothing else than a turning back from evil, as Scripture says: 'Turn away from evil, and do good'. [78]When we turn away from these evils we look toward the Lord, [79]and he, immediately causing the light of his countenance to shine upon us and coming to our assistance, gives his grace without delay to those who ask for it, shows himself to those who seek him, opens to those who knock. [80]These three gifts granted by the Lord are deserved by those who desire to do God's will, not their own, for what the Lord commands us in the spirit is one thing, what the flesh has in mind to force upon us is another—[81]and 'if anyone lets himself be dominated by a thing, then he is a slave to it'.

[82]Now, the Lord has given his Church, in conformity with the Trinity, three series of teaching: first, that of the prophets; secondly, that of the apostles; thirdly, that of the teachers. [83]According to their authority and teaching, the churches and schools of Christ are governed. [84]Like shepherds they enclose and teach the sheep of God in holy sheepfolds, as the Lord says through the prophet Isaiah: 'I will give you shepherds after my own heart, and these shall feed you on knowledge and discretion.' [85]And the Lord himself says to Peter: 'Simon, son of John, feed my sheep, [86]teaching them to observe all the commands I gave you. And know that I am with you always, even to the end of time'.

[87]Therefore all who still have folly as their mother ought to be subject to the authority of a superior so that, guided on their way by the judgment of a teacher, they may learn to

76. Zach 1:3
77. Ps 34:14
79. Ps 67:1. Cf. Mt 7:7, Lk 11:9
81. 2 Pet 2:19
82. 1 Cor 12:28
84. =Jeremiah 3:15
86. Jn 21:17, Mt 28:20
87. folly=*insipientia*:silliness

avoid the way of self-will. [88]The Lord gives us his commands through a teacher since, as he said above, he is always with these teachers, to the end of time, [89]certainly for no other purpose than to instruct us through them. As the Lord himself says to his disciples who are our teachers: 'Anyone who listens to you listens to me; anyone who rejects you rejects me'. [90]Thus if we put into practice what we hear from these teachers, we no longer do our own will, [91]so that on the day of judgment the devil will have in us no basis to claim us for himself in hell, [92]because the Lord has always accomplished in us what will be judged worthy of glory.

Question of the disciples:

II. WHAT CHARACTERISTICS THE ABBOT SHOULD HAVE.

The Lord has replied through the master:

[1]An abbot who is worthy to rule a monastery must always remember what he is called and be in fact what he is in name. [2]He is believed to be the representative of Christ in the monastery, for he is addressed by his name, [3]as the apostle says: 'You have received the spirit of sons, and it makes us cry out to the Lord, "Abba, Father!"' [4]Therefore the abbot must not teach or exact or command anything that is beyond the law of the Lord, [5]so that his bidding, admonition and teaching may enter the minds of his disciples like the leaven of divine justice. [6]Let the abbot ever be mindful that at the fearful judgment of the Lord there will be an inquiry into his teaching as well as into the obedience of his disciples, both the one and the other. [7]And let the abbot know that whatever the Father of the family finds lacking in the sheep will be laid to the blame of the shepherd. [8]On the other hand, if the shepherd has devoted his fullest attention to a troublesome and disobedient flock and has shown deep concern about its evil deeds, [9]this same shepherd will be acquitted at the judgment of the Lord and may say to the Lord with the prophet:

89. Lk 10:16
1. *abbas*:father. Cf RB 2.
3. Cf. Rm 8:15
9. Cf. Ps 40:10, Is 1:2

'Your truth I have not hidden in my heart and I have declared your salvation. But they have despised and rejected me'. [10]And then the fatal sickness will finally overpower the sheep who were unresponsive to his solicitude.

[11]Therefore when anyone receives the name of abbot, he must direct his disciples by a twofold teaching, [12]namely, make known all that is good and holy by his deeds even more than by his words. How? By declaring the Lord's commandments in words to disciples who can understand, but to the hard of heart and the simple-minded by demonstrating the divine precepts by what he does. [13]Let him make evident in himself, by his deeds, that everything he has taught his disciples at variance with these precepts must not be done, lest while preaching to others he himself should be rejected and [14]lest some day God should say to him while he is sinning: 'What business do you have reciting my statutes, standing there mouthing my covenant? You detest my discipline' [15]Or again: 'You observed the splinter in your brother's eye, but did not notice the plank in your own'.

[16]Let him make no distinction of persons in the monastery. [17]Let him not love one more than another, unless he finds that one excells in good works. [18]A freeman may not, by reason of his birth, be preferred to a slave who becomes a monk. [19]Why? Why? Because whether slave or freeman, we are all one in Christ and under the one Lord have the same obligation of service, for 'God has no favorites'. [20]God marks us out only if we are found better than others in our deeds. [21]Nevertheless, to show his loving kindness to all alike, God commands the elements to serve sinners as much as the just. [22]Therefore let the abbot's charity be the same to all, and let the one discipline be applied to everyone.

[23]In his teaching the abbot must always observe the proce-

---

13. Cf. 1 Cor 9:27
14. Ps 50:16–17
15. Mt 7:3
19. 'Why? Why?': this duplication may be a copyist's error, but the first 'Why?' may be that of the disciples and the second that of the Master introducing his reply.
19. Rm 2:11
23. 2 Tim 4:2

dure of the apostle as he states it: 'Reprove, entreat, rebuke';
[24]that is, alternating severity with gentleness, as the occasion
requires, he must show now the harshness of a master, now
the affection of a father. [25]Thus he must reprove the undisciplined and troublesome; he must entreat the obedient, meek
and very patient to advance in virtue; we admonish him to
rebuke the negligent and contemptuous.

[26]He should in himself exemplify for them that norm of
humility which the Lord presented to the apostles who were
quarreling about the first place, [27]namely, when he took a
child by the hand and brought him into their midst, saying:
[28]'If anyone wants to be great among you, let him be like
this'. [29]Therefore whatever the abbot enjoins his disciples to
do for God, he himself should first do, and thus when he
gives any orders the members will follow in line wherever the
head leads them. [30]He should have such love and kindness
toward all the brethren that he will not prefer one to another,
and will combine in himself the characteristics of both parents
for all his disciples and sons [31]by offering them equal love as
their mother and showing them well-considered kindness as
their father.

[32]The abbot must always remember what he is, remember
what he is called, and keep in mind that more is required
from him to whom more is entrusted. [33]And let him know
that he who has undertaken the ruling of souls must prepare
himself to render an account. [34]Furthermore, no matter how
great the number of brothers he knows he has under his care,
he may be sure that on the day of judgment he will have to
give the Lord a full account of all these souls, and most certainly of his own as well, [35]for, so as not to do their own will
in the monastery, the brothers always served in all obedience
to his commands. [36]When they are called to account for all
they have done they will say to the Lord at the judgment that
they did everything in obedience by command of the master.
[37]Therefore the master must always see to it [38]that everything
he commands, everything he teaches, every correction he
gives, is manifestly in accord with the precepts of God, as

28. Cf. Mt. 20:27
32. Lk 12:48

justice demands, so that he will not be condemned in the judgment to come. [39]Ever fearing the future examination of the shepherd regarding the sheep entrusted to him, he will, while concerning himself about his accountability for others, [40]be made careful about his own, and while correcting others by his admonitions, he will be freed from his own faults.

[41]Whatever the abbot wishes to do or have done for the good of the monastery is to be done with the counsel of the brothers. [42]When all the brothers have been called together, let there be a general discussion about the good of the monastery. [43]However, it is not on their own initiative or against the will of abbatial authority that the brothers happen to engage in deliberation, but by the command and direction of the abbot. [44]The counsel of all is to be sought because sometimes there are as many diverse opinions as there are people—[45]all at once the best advice may well be given by one from whom it was least expected, and this may redound most to the common good—[46]and from the many opinions the one to choose will be easy to find. [47]But if none of the brothers can give apt counsel, then let the abbot, after explaining his reasons, decide as he wills, and it is right that the members follow the head. [48]This is why we have said that all the brothers are to be called to the deliberation, according to the monastic maxim that the affairs of the monastery are the concern of all and not of any one person. [49]Of all, because the brothers expect to go on replacing one another in the monastery in the course of time. [50]Of no one person, because there is nothing in the monastery that any of the brothers can claim exclusively as his own, and no one determines or does anything by his own authority, but all live under the command of the abbot.

[51]The abbot is therefore the master of this holy art, not attributing the performance of it to himself but to the Lord, whose grace achieves in us whatever we do that is holy.

---

40. The subsequent paragraph does not belong to the previous instruction for the abbot but is an appendix. St Benedict detached it and made of it a separate chapter (RB 3).
41. Cf. RB 3
48. Cf. *Inst.* 4:14

[52]This art must be taught and learned in the workshop of the monastery, and it can be practised with the use of spiritual instruments.

Question of the disciples:

III. WHAT IS THE HOLY ART THAT THE ABBOT MUST TEACH HIS DISCIPLES IN THE MONASTERY?

The Lord has replied through the master:

[1]This is the holy art: first to believe in, to confess and to fear God the Father and the Son and the Holy Spirit, one God in Trinity, and three in one, three in the one divine nature and one in the threefold power of his majesty. Therefore, to love him with all one's heart and all one's soul. [2]Then in second place to love one's neighbor as oneself.

[3]Then not to kill, [4]not to commit adultery, [5]not to steal, [6]not to covet, [7]not to give false testimony, [8]to honor father and mother, [9]and not to do to another what one would not want done to oneself.

[10]To deny oneself in order to follow Christ. [11]To chastise the body for the sake of the soul, [12]to flee pleasures, [13]to love fasting. [14]To relieve the poor, [15]to clothe the naked, [16]to visit the sick, [17]to bury the dead, [18]to help the afflicted, [19]to console the sorrowing, [20]to make loans, [21]to give to the needy.

[22]To make oneself a stranger to worldly activities, [23]to pre-

52. Introduction to the following chapters. The abbot is the sole artisan of good works performed in the monastery since he is responsible for everything his monks do. The monks' personal responsibility is, however, indicated in the final line.

1. RB 4
2. Mk 12:31 par.
8. Dt 5:21. Cf. Mk 19:18–19, Lk 18:20. To honor father and mother is a rather remote precept for monks, so St Benedict substituted 'to honor all men' (RB 4:8).
9. Mt 7:12, Tob 4:16
10. Mt 26:24.
11. 1 Cor 9:27
16. Mt 15:36
17. Cf. Tob 1:20
20. St Benedict omitted 'to make loans, to give to the needy', no doubt because such activities were incompatible with monastic profession.

fer nothing to the love of Christ. [24]Not to give effect to anger, [25]not to await an opportunity for wrath. [26]Not to shelter deceit in one's heart, [27]not to make a consciously feigned peace, [28]to keep faith with a confrere, [29]not to love detraction, [30]to do what has been promised and not to deceive, [31]not to forsake charity. [32]Not to love taking oaths, for fear of perjury. [33]To speak the truth in heart and mouth.

[34]Not to return evil for evil, [35]to do no wrongs but to bear patiently those done to oneself, [36]to love enemies more than friends. [37]Not only to refrain from cursing those by whom one has been cursed but instead to bless them. [38]To bear persecution for the sake of justice.

[39]Not to be proud, [40]not given to wine, [41]not a great eater, [42]not a lover of sleep, [43]not lazy, [44]not a murmurer.

[45]To place one's hope in God. [46]When one sees anything good in oneself, to be aware that it is the work of God and not of oneself; [47]to regard evil as one's own doing and to ascribe it to oneself and to the devil. [48]To want one's desires be fulfilled by God. [49]To hope for one's sustenance not from the work of one's hands alone, but rather from God.

[50]To fear the day of judgment, [51]to dread hell, [52]to desire eternal life and the holy Jerusalem, [53]ever to keep death before one's eyes. [54]To be always watchful over the activities of one's life, [55]to be convinced that one is everywhere seen by God. [56]Immediately to shatter on Christ the evil thoughts which come into one's heart, [57]to keep one's mouth from evil and depraved speech, [58]not to love much talking, [59]entirely to avoid vain words or such as cause laughter, [60]not to love excessive or guffawing laughter.

[61]To listen willingly to holy reading, [62]to give oneself to frequent prayer, [63]in daily prayer with tears and sighs to confess to God one's sins of the past, [64]furthermore to correct these failings.

[65]Not to yield to the desires of the flesh, [66]to hate self-will, [67]to be obedient to the admonitions of the abbot.

26. Cf. Pr 20:13
32. Mt 5:34
34. 1 Pet 3:9
36. Mt 5:44
37. 1 Cor 4:21, 1 Pet 3:9
38. 1 Cor 4:12, Mt 5:10
65. Gal 5:16

[68]Not to wish to be called holy before one is so, but first to be holy so that one may and ought to be truly so called. [69]To fulfill God's precepts daily by one's deeds, [70]to love chastity, [71]to hate no one, [72]not to be jealous, [73]not to do anything out of envy, [74]not to love strife. [75]To be reconciled to an enemy before the setting of the sun, [76]to obey all good persons with all one's heart.

[77]And never to despair of God.

[78]Behold, this is the holy art which we must exercise with spiritual instruments. [79]When we have practised this holy art continuously day and night, [80] and when on the day of judgment each one has handed over to the Lord God what he has accomplished, [81]then this art, which issued from the will of God, when we have completed it and returned it without fault to the Lord on the day of judgment, [82]will be recompensed by the Lord with the reward which our faithful Lord promises to us. [83]This reward is prepared for the saints and those who fear God and fulfill these precepts by their deeds: [84]to dwell forever in a land seven times more brilliant than silver, [85]whose heavenly vault will be illumined not by the light of this sun or moon, nor of the stars, but by the eternal majesty of God himself. [86]In this land of splendor there are rivers of honey and milk, of wine and oil, flowing forever. [87]On their banks various trees bear a variety of fruits twelve times a year; they are cultivated not by man but by the divine bounty. [88]They do not give delight by satisfying the appetite for food, nor are they hungrily desired for eating, [89]but after the very sight of them has fed the eyes of the saints, each one receives into his mouth the taste which gratifies him. [90]There on the banks of these rivers are placed musical instruments constantly playing hymns which are sung to the praise of the king by the holy angels and archangels raising their voices in unison. [91]Hearing the sweetness of these voices so delights the saints that their heart, set to twittering with tremendous joy by the harmonious melody, wants to exult more and more, [92]while in the double splendor of heaven and earth divinely radiant, in this very brilliance of the terrestrial light,

85. *Visio* 21, cf. Rev 21:23
86. *Visio* 21, 23
87. *Visio* 22

the city of Jerusalem adorned with gold and precious stones glows with the brightness of its variety of pearls. [93]Its walls and gates, its streets and squares, resonant with the sweet harmony of the singing, forever cry out *alleluia,* the canticle of joy. [94]In this exultation the saints, resplendent in their heavenly transformation, rejoice that they have been set free from the perdition of the world and that God has found them worthy of these heavenly riches for all eternity.

[95]And now let us return to the text of the previous pages to learn the way which must be taken to arrive at all this.

Question of the disciples:

IV. WHAT ARE THE SPIRITUAL INSTRUMENTS WHICH WE CAN USE TO PRACTISE THE DIVINE ART?

The Lord has replied through the master:

[1]What are they? Faith, hope, charity; [2]peace, joy, mildness; [3]humility, obedience, silence; [4]above all, chastity of the body; a sincere conscience; [5]abstinence, purity, simplicity; [6]kindness, goodness, compassion; [7]above all piety; temperance, vigilance, sobriety; [8]justice, equity, truth; [9]love, measure, moderation, [10]and perseverance.

Question of the disciples:

V. WHAT IS THE SUBSTANCE AND CAUSE OF THE EVILS WHICH MUST BE EXPURGATED IN THE FURNACE OF THE FEAR OF GOD, AND WHAT IS THE RUST AND DIRT OF VICES FROM WHICH THE ABRASION OF JUSTICE MUST CLEANSE US?

The Lord has replied through the master:

[1]These are the vices which we must guard against: [2]first of all, pride, then disobedience, talkativeness; [3]falsehood, av-

---

92. Rev 21:10
93. Tob 13
94. Cf. 1 Cor 15:49
1. 1 Cor 13:13
2. Gal 5:22–3
6. Gal 5:22

arice, cupidity; [4]jealousy, envy, iniquity; [5]hatred, enmity, anger, quarreling, discord; [6]fornication, drunkenness, gluttony; murmuring, impiety, injustice, laziness, theft; [8]detraction, buffoonery, levity, impurity, idle speech; [9]excessive or guffawing laughter, humming; [10]covetousness, deceit, ambition, instability. [11]All these things are not from God but are the works of the devil which on the day of judgment will get from God what they deserve, the hell of everlasting fire.

Question of the disciples:

VI. WHAT IS THE WORKSHOP OF THE DIVINE ART AND HOW ARE THE SPIRITUAL INSTRUMENTS USED?

The Lord has replied through the master:

[1]The workshop is the monastery, [2]where the instruments of the heart are kept in the enclosure of the body, and the work of the divine art can be accomplished with assiduous care and perseverance.

Questions of the disciples:

VII. WHAT SHOULD BE THE NATURE OF THE DISCIPLES' OBEDIENCE?

The Lord has replied through the master:

[1]The first degree of humility is obedience without delay. [2]But this kind is proper to the perfect, few in number, those who consider nothing more dear to them than Christ; [3]because of the holy service they have vowed, for fear of hell, and for the sake of the treasures of eternal life, [4]as soon as they hear something commanded by the superior they can tolerate no delay in conforming. [5]It is of these that the Lord

5. Gal 5:20
11. 1 Jn 3:10,8
1. RB 5:1
5. Ps 18:44

says: 'No sooner do they hear than they obey me'. [6]And he likewise says to those who teach: 'Anyone who listens to you listens to me'. [7]Such as these, therefore, immediately relinquishing their own concerns and abandoning their own will, [8]disengaging their hands and leaving unfinished what they were doing, comply by their actions with the voice of the one who commands, falling into step with prompt obedience. [9]Thus in one and the same moment, so to speak, the command issued by the superior and what is done by the disciples, the two together, occur without any delay, in the swiftness of the fear of God.

[10]But this kind of obedience, proper to the few who are perfect, should not unduly alarm the souls of the weak and the indolent and make them despair, but, should inspire them to do likewise. [11]So keeping in mind that among us there are assorted embodiments of misery, since a sluggish nature is the source of a great deal of laziness in some persons—[12]for it is well known that the hearing of certain ones is dulled by insensibility of the ears, and we also note that the minds of some are immediately distracted and wander off into a jungle of thoughts—[13]we therefore indulgently moderate the strictures of obedience on the part of the teachers. Accordingly, the master should not be irked at having to repeat his command to the disciples, [14]as the Lord testified when, calling Abraham, he repeated his name a second time, saying: 'Abraham, Abraham'. [15]By this repetition the Lord clearly showed us that one call is possibly not enough to ensure [his] being heard.

[16]As regards questions, when the master's voice is twice directed to the disciples, it is only right to indulge by a repetition of the question those who do not reply, [17]in such a way that if the disciple remains silent at first he should not be held at fault, but it should be considered a mark of respect reserved for the master. [18]In this reverence the virtuous disciple is credited with hesitating to break the silence he maintains [19]in order not to overwhelm you with replies rushing from a glib tongue as soon as you state your question.

6. Lk 10:16
14. Gen 22:1

²⁰But as regards commands, if the master must repeat his order, however slow or negligent the hearers may be, when what was first said is repeated to them a second time, it is by all means proper that the second delay be interrupted by acts of obedience. ²¹If however there should be a third delay on the disciple's part—may it never happen!—it must be considered a fault, the perversity of contumacy.

²²It is right and proper to consider here the theme of the two ways, namely, the broad road which leads to perdition, and the narrow road which leads to life. ²³On these two roads proceed the various types of human obedience. ²⁴Thus, on the broad road go men of the world and sarabaite and gyrovague monks. ²⁵These live alone or two or three together, without a superior, on an equal footing and moving about as they please. ²⁶Alternating in authority, taking turns in commanding one another whatever each one wishes, safeguarding for themselves whatever they individually choose—²⁷since no one wants to be thwarted in his self-interest—such as these never banish dispute from themselves. ²⁸Right after a violent quarrel these evilly-assembled men break up and ²⁹wander off like a flock without a shepherd, dispersing in various directions, no doubt only to fall into the jaws of the wolf. ³⁰It is not God who provides cells for them once again, but their self-will. Individually, on their own authority, each one for himself alone, they assume the title of abbot. And you find that there are more monasteries than monks.

³¹One may be confident that such as these walk the broad road in that, while retaining the name monk, they live in the same way as do those in the world, distinguished from them only by having the tonsure. They give obedience to their desires instead of to God. ³²Trusting their own judgment they think that what is evil is allowed to them; ³³whatever they want they call holy, and whatever they do not want they consider forbidden. ³⁴They deem it proper to think about providing for their body rather than for their soul, ³⁵in other words, that they better than anyone else can be concerned

22. Mt 7:13–14
29. Cf. Mt 9:36, Ezech 34:5

about food, clothing, and footwear for themselves. [36]They recklessly fancy themselves so secure as regards the account they will have to give of their soul that, whereas they are living as monks according to their own judgment without the guidance of superiors, they think that in their cell they are perfectly observant of every law and all the justice of God. [37]If perchance some superior or other, in passing by, offers them some suggestions for their improvement and tells them that this solitary manner of living is not good for them, the advice as well as the very person of the teacher immediately displeases them. [38]Unmoved, they do not promise to reform by agreeing with him and heeding him, but reply that they must live all alone, [39]ignoring what the prophet said: 'Such are corrupt; they do abominable deeds', [40]and that testimony of Solomon which says: 'There are ways which men think right, but whose end plunges into the depth of hell'.

[41]Such as these therefore travel the broad way because wherever the foot of their desires leads them, they immediately consent to follow, [42]and most willing indulgence is unhesitatingly at the service of whatever their lust craves. [43]Breaking for themselves new paths of licentiousness and self-will without a master, they enlarge the way of their life by divers kinds of forbidden pleasures, [44]and toward whatever place their delights wish to go, they direct their wanton and criminal steps. [45]They never want to realize that for the creature man, death is stationed at the entrance of delight, [46]and they bypass with unhearing ears what is said to them: 'Do not follow your lusts; restrain your desires'.

[47]Those whom love urges on to eternal life, on the contrary, take the narrow way. [48]Not living according to their own discretion or obeying their own desires and pleasures, but walking by the judgment and command of another, [49]they not only exercise self-control in the aforesaid desires and pleasures and do not want to do their own will even if they

39. Ps 14:1
40. Cf. Pr 16:25
42. *Passio* 13
45. *Passio* 14
46. Sir 18:30

could, ⁵⁰but they also submit themselves to the authority of another. Living in monasteries, they wish to have an abbot over them and not bear this title themselves. ⁵¹Certainly such as these conform to what the Lord says: 'I have come not to do my own will, but to do the will of the one who sent me'. ⁵²And not doing their own will, denying themselves for the sake of Christ, they follow God whithersoever the command of the abbot leads them.

⁵³Furthermore, under the care of the abbot, not only are they not forced to worry about temporal necessities, that is, food, clothing and footwear, but ⁵⁴solely by rendering obedience in all things to the master, they are made secure about the account they will have to give of their soul and about whatever else is profitable for both body and soul. ⁵⁵This is so because, whether for good or for ill, what happens among the sheep is the responsibility of the shepherd, ⁵⁶and he who gave orders is the one who will have to render an account when inquiry is made at the judgment, not he who carried out the orders, whether good or bad.

⁵⁷Now, it may be said that such as these travel the narrow way, because their own desires are never put into effect at all and they do not do what they wish. ⁵⁸But bearing the yoke of another's judgment, they are restrained from going where their own pleasure would lead them, and what they themselves would choose to do or achieve is denied them by the master. ⁵⁹In the monastery their will is daily thwarted for the sake of the Lord, and in the spirit of martyrdom they patiently endure whatever commands they receive to test them. ⁶⁰In the monastery they will assuredly say to the Lord, with the prophet: 'For your sake we are being slain all the day; we are looked upon as sheep to be slaughtered'. ⁶¹And later on, at the judgment, they will likewise say to the lord: 'You tested us, God, you refined us like silver. ⁶²You let us fall into the net. You laid heavy burdens on our backs. ⁶³You have set men over our heads'. ⁶⁴Therefore when they say, 'You have set men over our heads', it is evident that they are

51. Jn 6:38
60. Ps 44:22
63. Ps 66:10–12

to have over them as God's representative a superior, whom they fear in the monastery. [65]And continuing with what is stated, they will rightly say to the Lord again, this time in the next world: 'But now the ordeal by fire and water is over, and you allow us once more to draw breath', [66]that is, 'We have gone through the thwarting of our own will and by serving in obedience we have come to the enjoyment of your love.'

[67]But obedience such as this will be acceptable to God and gratifying to men only if the thing commanded is done without fear, without apathy, without hesitation, without murmuring or protesting, [68]because obedience offered to superiors is given to God, as the Lord says to our teachers: 'Anyone who listens to you listens to me', [69]and elsewhere he says: 'No sooner do they hear than they obey me'. [70]Obedience is such, therefore, if it is given with good will, because 'God loves a cheerful giver'. [71]The disciple obeys with ill will if he reproaches not only us verbally but God inwardly about what he does in a bad mood. [72]And even though he does what he was commanded, still it will not be acceptable to God, who sees that he is murmuring in his heart. [73]To repeat, even though he does what he is told, but does it in a bad mood, [74]he will get no reward for doing it, for God is watching his heart right now and finds in it the wretched disposition of one who acts in this way.

Questions of the disciples:

VIII. What should be the mode and measure of the disciples' silence.

The Lord has replied through the master:

[1]The structure of the human race is our poor little body. [2]Although it is small in stature and in some of the taller men reaches a height of scarcely five feet from the ground—[3]oh,

65. Ps 66:12
68. Lk 10:16
69. Ps 18:44
70. 2 Cor 9:7

the emptiness of boasting, every man living!—[4]despite its littleness, it thinks that by its wisdom it can measure 'the height of the sky and the breadth of the earth'. [5]So, knowing we are weak vessels made of the earth's slime and, so to speak, clods of dirt thrown up from the earth for a short time only to fall back again into their furrow, let us as dust of the earth be made humble and admit what we are.

[6]Therefore the flesh of our poor little body is a sort of lodging for the soul, assigned to the service of life as a sheath serves for the sword. [7]We hold that the soul has its seat fixed in the root of the heart. [8]This root has two main branches in the body, and these are very susceptible to sin. [9]The one we may think of as a physical wall with windows through which the soul, with the eyes as the apertures, looks out, and we know that it is always inviting from within what it desires. [10]In the other branch the soul echoes in us what the heart has conceived and produced, bringing it by means of the tongue to the birth of speech, so that, issuing through the door of the mouth, it demands to be heard by others. [11]And whatever stirs and moves in us is the soul acting in the body.

[12]On the other hand, it follows that when the soul leaves its dwelling, everything that was done in the living man by the now-departed soul ceases in the dead man. [13]Soon its dead clod is returned to the earth, man's dust reverts to the nature of dust. Man is buried in a grave, the grave is filled in again, his dust takes on again the quality of a dirt road. [14]It is thus evident that this is the same dust that was in the man when he was alive, that it was held up by the firmness of the soul, and that it was temporarily transformed for transitory life. [15]Therefore when the soul's firmness in us departs, the dust of our body cannot remain erect; [16]falling back into its proper nature, the earth buries in its bosom the creature which it had engendered.

[17]So if this soul in us activates the seeing of the eyes, the speaking of the mouth, the hearing of the ears, and, [18]because it will some day be called to account by its maker, desires to obey the will of God and while in this life to serve

4. Sir 1:3

under his command, [19]it must close the windows of the eyes to its cravings and lower its gaze, fixing it on the ground. [20]It must do this so that it does not see evil; when our eyes are cast down, the soul will not yearn for whatever it sees.

[21]Thus our soul has in place its door the mouth, and its lock, the teeth, which it closes to depraved speech so the soul may not offer the excuse that its maker did not in any way provide it with defenses for its protection. [22]In other words, when some sin arises from the root of the heart and sees that its exit is blocked by the enclosure of the outside wall, namely, the mouth and the teeth, [23]returning again to the root of the heart it perishes there as a miscarriage and is dashed upon the rock while yet young instead of being born of the tongue and growing up to be punished.

[24]As to the other branches of our body which are subject to the rule of the heart, they are easily restrained from sin, that is, touching with the hands and walking with the feet, [25]because shackling in chains holds the thief in check, and fear of judgment the murderer, and hobbling restrains the fugitive.

[26]Therefore the three faculties we referred to above, that is, thought, speech and sight, must be very carefully kept under guard so that as soon as an evil thought takes hold of the mind, the brethren should immediately sign themselves on the forehead, and the breast too, and not delay in recalling the precepts of Christ. [28]And let the brother say to himself with the prophet: 'I remembered God and I was consoled'. [29]And again he says: 'By you I shall be delivered from temptation, and by the help of my God I shall leap over the wall'.

[30]But if negligence has put angry or depraved or vain speech into the mouth, the brother, immediately closing his mouth and sealing it with a sign of the cross, will say to himself in his heart, [31]speaking with the prophet: 'I said, "I will watch my ways, so as not to sin with my tongue; I will set a curb on my mouth". "I remained silent and was profoundly humbled, and I refrained from saying even good things"'. [32]In other words, the prophet shows that if at times one

23. Cf. Ps 137:9
28. Ps 77:3 & 119:52
29. Ps 18:29
31. Ps 39:1, cf. Ps 39:3

should refrain from good speech for the sake of silence, much more should one avoid evil words because of punishment for sin. ³³Therefore, although permission to engage in good and holy and edifying conversation may be granted to perfect disciples, ³⁴though rarely because of the dignity of silence, brothers who have not been asked anything should suppress in silence talk of any other kind until the curb on their muted mouth has been removed by a question from the abbot. ³⁵To repeat, silence must be most carefully kept by the brothers because 'Where words are many, sin is not wanting'. ³⁶Therefore 'death and life are in the power of the tongue'. ³⁸It befits the master to speak and to teach; the disciple should be silent and listen.

Question of the disciples:

IX. HOW THE DISCIPLES OBSERVING SILENCE ARE TO ASK THE ABBOT ANY QUESTION THEY MAY HAVE.

The Lord has replied through the master:

¹Since the disciples are restrained from both evil and good speech by the curb of silence, and since the avenues of their unrestricted freedom are kept under surveillance by the master who is present, ²when any necessary and advantageous questions arise, the disciples, ³with head bowed in humility, are to remain standing before the superior, their mouth closed and stamped with the seal of gravity, until with the key of *Benedicite* they open their mouth which has been closed in silence. ⁴If at the first *Benedicite* requesting leave to talk, the master's permission be not yet given, ⁵the disciple, again bowing his head and repeating only the *Benedicite*, is to ask permission of the abbot a second time. ⁶But if even so he gets no reply from him, let the disciple again bow in humility and at this point let him, the brother, withdraw, ⁷lest it seem to the abbot that he is too insistent or presumptuous. ⁸Having

35. Pr 10:19
36. Pr 19:21

returned to his work, let him continue to play his part as a man of silence, [9]in quiet humility thinking that in the abbot's judgment he was deemed unworthy to speak. [10]Or again, let the disciple think that perhaps the enclosure of silence was not opened for him in order to test and gauge his humility.

[11]The reason we have said that only the *Benedicite* should be repeated a second time is that, even when this is said alone with nothing added, silence is nevertheless maintained; [12]when it is repeated and departure follows quickly upon refusal, one should feel that humility thus tested has been preserved. [13]Now, the disciple's repetition is presented to the master [14]not solely to enable the master to remain silent for a long while as a spiritual test to gauge the humility of the disciple, [15]but so that, though physically present, he will not with deaf ears fail to pay attention to the voice of the disciple asking, because his mind is preoccupied and his regard averted because he is overwhelmed by other thoughts; [16]and so that the disciple may not, by his excessive and importunate humility, provoke the master to give way to the vice of anger, [17]thus making the humility of a troublesome person the occasion for offense.

[18]This is why we said that after the second *Benedicite* a third should not be added if the superior does not consent, [19]but the disciple should promptly withdraw and in silence finish the work he was doing.

[20]The disciples are to do such questioning by means of the *Benedicite*—the only relaxation of silence conceded, and this reluctantly—with head bowed in humility. [21]This applies everywhere and at all times, which means, in the monastery, in the fields, on the road, in the garden, and any place whatever, [22]so that the thought of God, for whose sake all this is done, may never be absent from our mind. [23]If someone not aware of the situation perchance asks his brother, 'Why are

---

20. What follows is a digression on the permanent attitude of humility which bowing the head was meant to develop. Silence is associated here with sorrow (=absence of laughter) and with a downcast face. A bow to the superior while at table was not possible and so was replaced with the sound of a knock.

you silent and sad, and going about with downcast face?' [24]he will reply, 'Because I flee from sin and fear God, and so that I may be on my guard against everything that God hates. This is why I always keep close watch over myself.' [25]When seated at table, however, if someone wishes to let the abbot know that he has questions, [26]before saying the *Benedicite* he should knock with his knife or spoon or bread to indicate to the master the disciple's desire to speak.

[27]We have prescribed that all this, necessary to the soul for God's sake, is to be observed with such a strict safeguarding of silence [28]in order that no one be too easily misled by forgetfulness and ever be quick with his tongue. [29]For when silence is hedged in by the enclosing wall of the mouth, what should be long-considered and cleansed in the heart can then issue pure and sinless from the mouth. [30]As the apostle says: 'Guard against foul talk; let your words be for the improvement of others'. [31]And it is likewise written: 'The wise man is known by the fewness of his words'. [32]So we must greatly fear and at all times guard against much talking [33]because where words are many it is impossible to prevent some that are sinful from coming out, [34]according to what is written: 'A flood of words is never without its fault'. [35]So the prophet too, giving us a norm, shows that he is careful in this matter and that silence must be kept whether the words are evil or good, [36]saying: 'I said, "I will watch my ways, so as not to sin with my tongue; I have set a curb on my mouth. I kept dumb and refrained even from good words"'. [37]Thus it is made clear to the perfect disciple that he must refrain from both evil and good words, [38]because even though what is to be said may be good, teaching belongs not to the disciples but to the master. [39]For, as Scripture again says: 'Life and death are in the power of the tongue'. [40]Therefore it must be very carefully and rightfully kept in check.

30. Eph 4:29
31. Sextus, *Enchiridion* 145
34. Pr 10:19
36. Ps 19:1–3, RB 6
39. Pr 18:21

[41]So it is with good reason that such strict custody and observance of silence is demanded of the perfect and the pure of heart and those cleansed from sin, who fear the everlasting fires of hell and seek the immortal treasures of eternal life. [42]Therefore when the abbot is present, only the disciples who have been asked may speak. [43]When the abbot is not present, they may converse if it is about the word of God, but quietly and humbly, not with a loud voice, for speaking quietly always proceeds from humility. [44]But if the disciples begin to speak about frivolous or worldly matters or anything that has no reference to God, their deans must immediately impose silence upon them. [45]Psalms and Scriptures the brothers may, however, be permitted to rehearse by heart to themselves while they are working, outside the three hours daily when there is reading and not work.

[46]Above we prescribed a very strict enclosure of silence in the abbot's presence for those who are perfect in the sight of God, [47]those who are never caught forgetful of God and who earnestly seek to guard against vices of the tongue, wholly pure as the angels, and who endeavor to refrain from good as well as evil speech for the Lord's sake. [48]But since grace in its diversity, granted according to the measure of faith, can be weakened especially in the negligent, we make this concession to the tepid and imperfect and to those unconcerned about themselves: [49]when they wish to inquire about profane matters which have nothing to do with spiritual edification, and provided no sin is involved, at most they may take the liberty of speaking only if permission is granted after a blessing has been asked. [50]If the question is about something spiritual, however, the disciple should speak immediately after asking a blessing. [51]But we condemn by total exclusion any buffoonery and idle talk and such as causes laughter, and we do not permit the disciple to open his mouth for such words.

41. Cf. Mt 5:8
43. The first mitigation of silence is granted to everyone. The second only to the imperfect.
44. deans=*praepositi*

Question of the disciples:

X. THE NATURE OF THE BROTHER'S HUMILITY, HOW IT IS ACQUIRED, AND HOW ONCE ACQUIRED IT IS MAINTAINED.

The Lord has replied through the master:

[1]Holy Scripture cries out to us, brothers, saying: 'Everyone who exalts himself will be humbled, and the man who humbles himself will be exalted'. [2]In saying this, therefore, it makes clear to us that all exaltation is a kind of pride. [3]The prophet shows that he was on his guard against this, saying: 'O Lord, my heart is not proud, nor are my eyes haughty'. And he continues in the same vein: 'I do not busy myself with great things, nor with things too sublime for me'. [4]But what 'if I was not humble minded, if I exalted my soul? Like a weaned child on its mother's lap, so will you requite my soul'. [5]So, brothers, if we wish to reach the summit of supreme humility and if we would arrive swiftly at that heavenly exaltation to which one rises by the humility of the present life, we must, [6]by our deeds mounting up, erect that ladder which, raised to heaven, appeared to Jacob in a dream and on which angels descending and ascending were shown to him. [7]We do not doubt that this going down and up has no other purpose than to show that exaltation descends and humility ascends. [8]Now, this ladder set up is our life in the world, and with heart and head made humble in this, its present time, it lifts up to heaven its last end, death, exalted by the Lord. [9]We hold as absolutely certain that the sides of this ladder are our body and soul, into which sides God's call has inserted various rungs of humility and discipline which must be climbed.

[10]The disciple, then, mounts the first rung of humility on the ladder of heaven if, having the fear of God always before his eyes, he at all times shuns forgetfulness and is ever

---

1. Lk 14:11, RB 7
3. Ps 131:1
4. Ps 131:2
6. Gen 28:12
10. Ps 36:1

mindful of all that God has commanded, [11]thus constantly pondering in his mind how hell burns because of their sins those who despise the Lord, and what eternal life has in store for those who fear God. [12]And at all times keeping himself from sins and vices, of thought, tongue, hands, feet and self-will, as also from the desires of the flesh, [13]let the disciple be sure that God is always, at every moment, looking at him from heaven and that his deeds are everywhere kept in view by the Divinity and are all reported day after day by the angels.

[14]The prophet makes this clear to us when he shows that God is thus always present to our thoughts, when he says: 'God searches hearts and souls'. [15]And again he says: 'The Lord knows the thoughts of men, and how empty they are'. [16]He also says: 'You have understood my thoughts from far away'. [17]Likewise: 'For the thought of man shall give you praise, [18]and 'the heart of the king is in the hand of God'. [19]So in order to be on his guard against the perverse thoughts of his heart, let the virtuous brother always tell himself this in his heart: 'Then shall I be spotless in his presence if I have kept myself from my iniquity'.

[20]We understand, moreover, that God is always present when the tongue speaks, since the voice of the Lord says through the prophet: 'He who speaks falsehood shall not stand before my eyes'. [21]And likewise the apostle says: 'You shall give account of every idle word', [22]because 'death and life are in the power of the tongue'.

[23]Furthermore, we understand that God is present at our

14. Ps 7:9
15. Ps 94:11
16. Ps 139:2
17. Ps 76:10 (Vulg.)
18. Pr 21:1
19. Ps 18:24
20. Ps 101:7
21. Mt 12:36
22. Pr 18:21—a poor illustration for his point. The Master had trouble finding suitable texts here. The attribution of Mt 12:36 to 'the Apostle' [=St Paul] is erroneous.
23. Ps 139:16

manual labor, since the prophet says: 'Your eyes have seen my unfinished work'.

²⁴Then as regards walking with our feet, we understand that God is always present, since the prophet says: 'Without iniquity have I run and directed my steps. ²⁵Rise up to meet me, and behold'. ²⁶And again he says: 'Where can I go from your spirit? From your presence where can I flee? ²⁷If I go up to the heavens, you are there; If I sink down to hell, you are present there. ²⁸If I take wing before dawn, if I settle at the furthest limits of the sea, ²⁹even there your hand shall guide me, and your right hand hold me up'.

³⁰And as to our own will, we are forbidden to do it in the Lord's presence, for Scripture tells us: 'Keep your desires in check'. ³¹And we also ask the Lord in the Our Father that his will be done in us. ³²So we are properly taught not to do our own will, when we take heed of what Holy Scripture says: 'There are ways which men think right, but whose end sinks into the depth of hell', ³³and likewise when we fear what is said of the negligent: 'They are corrupt and have become abominable in their desires'.

³⁴So too regarding desires of the flesh, we believe that God is always present, for the prophet says: 'O Lord, all my desire is before you'. ³⁵Therefore every evil desire must be shunned, because death is stationed at the entrance of delight. ³⁶So Scripture commands, saying: 'Do not go after your lusts'.

³⁷Consequently, if the eyes of the Lord keep watch over the good and the evil, and 'the Lord is always looking down from heaven upon the children of men, to see if there be one who is wise and seeks God', ³⁹and if whatever we do is reported to the Lord daily, day and night, by the angels assigned to us,

25. Ps 59:4–5
29. Ps 139:7–10
30. Sir 18:30
31. Mt 6:10
32. Cf. Pr 16:25
33. Ps 14:1
34. Ps 38:9
36. Sir 18:30
37. Pr 15:3
38. Ps 14:2

⁴⁰we must always be on our guard, brothers, as the prophet says in Psalm 13, lest the Lord sometime see us turning to evil and becoming perverse, and lest, ⁴¹sparing us in this present time because he is loving and waits for our conversion, he say to us in the judgment to come: 'You did these things, and I was silent'.

⁴²Then the disciple mounts the second rung of humility on the heavenly ladder if, not loving his own will, he does not delight in fulfilling his own desires, ⁴³but by his deeds he conforms to what the Lord says: 'I have come not to do my own will, but to do the will of the one who sent me'. ⁴⁴And it is likewise written: 'The will gets its own punishment, but constraint provides a crown'.

⁴⁵Then the disciple mounts the third rung of humility on the ladder of heaven if, having taken nothing on himself by his own judgment, he chooses what may not be to his advantage. ⁴⁶As Scripture says: 'There are ways which men think right, but whose end plunges into the depth of hell'. ⁴⁷And David likewise says: 'They are corrupt and have become abominable in their desires'. ⁴⁸The apostle too says: 'For me there are no forbidden things', perhaps not, but not everything does good. I agree there are no forbidden things for me, but I am not going to let anything dominate me. ⁴⁹Therefore the disciple must not only be on his guard against such things, but must submit in complete obedience to the superior, imitating the Lord, about whom the apostle says: 'He became obedient unto death'. ⁵⁰So too the voice of the Lord praises the gentiles for such obedience, saying: 'No sooner do they hear than they obey me'. ⁵¹The Lord as well shows that we obey him when we are subject to the abbot, for

40. Hebrew enum.=Ps 14:3
41. Ps 50:21
43. Jn 6:38
44. *Passio* 17, p. 234.
46. Pr 16:25
47. Ps 14:1
48. 1 Cor 6:12
49. Phil 2:8
50. Ps 18:44
51. Lk 10:16

he says to our teachers: 'Anyone who listens to you listens to me, and anyone who rejects you rejects me'.

[52]Then the disciple mounts the fourth rung of humility on the heavenly ladder if, in this obedience, even though difficulties and contradictions and all kinds of wrongs are inflicted upon him, [53]he clings in silence to the steadfastness of patience and in his endurance neither grows weary nor runs away. As Scripture says: 'The man who stands firm to the end will be saved'. [54]So also the prophet admonishes us in this regard, saying: 'Be stouthearted, and wait for the Lord'. [55]And showing that the faithful must bear with all things, even contradictions, the prophet says in the person of the suffering: 'For your sake we are being slain all the day; we are looked upon as sheep to be slaughtered'. [56]And confident in their expectation of a divine reward, they continue, rejoicing: 'These are the trials through which we triumph, by the power of him who loved us'. [57]Similarly elsewhere Scripture says in the person of these same: 'You have tested us, God, you have refined us like silver. You let us fall into the net. You laid heavy burdens on our backs'. [58]And to show that we are to be subject to a superior, the text continues: 'You have set men over our heads'. [59]Furthermore, fulfilling the Lord's command, through patience in adversities and wrongs, when struck on one cheek they offer the other, when robbed of their tunic they give up their cloak as well, when forced to go one mile they go two. [60]With the apostle Paul they bear with false brothers and suffer persecution, and those who curse them they bless in return.

[61]Then the disciple mounts the fifth rung of humility on the ladder of heaven if, making humble vocal confession, he does not conceal from his abbot any evil thoughts that come into

53. Mt 10:22
54. Ps 27:14
55. Ps 44:22
56. Rm 8:37
57. Ps 66:10–11
58. Ps 66:12
59. Mt 5:39–41
60. 2 Cor 11:26, 1 Cor 4:12
61. *Inst.* 4:39, 2

his heart or sins that he has secretly committed. [62]Scripture exhorts us in this regard, saying: 'Commit your way to the Lord and trust in him'. [63]And again it says: 'Give thanks to the Lord, for he is good, for his mercy endures forever'. [64]So also the prophet says to the Lord: 'I acknowledged my sin to you, my guilt I did not cover. [65]I said: "I will confess my faults to the Lord," and immediately you took away the guilt of my heart'.

[66]Then the disciple mounts the sixth rung of humility on the ladder of heaven if he is content with the meanest and worst of everything and considers himself a bad workman, unworthy of anything offered to him, [67]telling himself with the prophet: 'I was stupid and did not understand. I was like a brute beast in your presence. Yet I shall always be with you'.

[68]Then the disciple mounts the seventh rung of humility on the ladder of heaven if he not only declares aloud that he is lower and more worthless than everyone else, but also believes this in the depths of his heart, [69]humbling himself and saying: 'But I am a worm, not a man; the scorn of men, despised by the people. [70]I was exalted, only to be humbled and confounded'. [71]And a brother such as this should always say to the Lord: 'It is good for me, Lord, that you have humbled me, that I may learn your commandments'.

[72]Then the disciple mounts the eighth rung of humility on the ladder of heaven if he does nothing except what is sanctioned by the common rule of the monastery and the example of the superiors, [73]saying with Scripture: 'For I meditate on your law', [74]and 'When he asks his father, he will teach him, and his elders will speak to him', which means, the abbot by his teaching.

62. Ps 37:5
63. Ps 106:1
65. Ps 32:5
66. *Inst.* 4:39, 2
67. Ps 73:22–3
68. *Inst.* 4:39, 2
70. Ps 22:6–7, Ps 88:15
71. Ps 119:71
73. Ps 119:77
74. Deut 32:7

[75]Then the disciple mounts the ninth rung of humility on the ladder of heaven if he forbids his tongue to speak and keeps silence, saying nothing until he is asked. [76]For Scripture shows that 'where words are many, sin is not wanting', [77]and that 'a man full of words will not prosper on earth'.

[78]Then the disciple mounts the tenth rung of humility on the ladder of heaven if he does not easily and quickly laugh, for it is written: 'A fool laughs at the top of his voice', [79]and 'Like the crackling of thorns under a cauldron is the laughter of man'.

[80]Then the disciple mounts the eleventh rung of humility on the ladder of heaven if when he speaks he does it softly and without laughter, humbly, with dignity, saying few and holy words, and not in a loud voice. [81]It is written: 'The wise man is known by the fewness of his words'.

[82]Then the disciple goes up the twelfth rung of humility on the ladder of heaven if his humility is no longer only in his heart but always manifest even in his body to those who see him, [83]that is to say, at the Work of God, in the oratory, in the monastery, in the garden, on the road, in the fields and any place whatever, whether he is sitting, walking or standing still, with head always bowed, his gaze fixed on the ground, [84]at all times conscious that he is guilty because of his sins, imagining that he is already appearing at the fearful judgment. [85]Let him constantly say to himself in his heart what the publican, standing before the temple with his eyes fixed on the ground, said: 'Lord, I, a sinner, am not worthy to raise my eyes to heaven'. [86]And let a disciple such as this likewise tell himself with the prophet: 'I am bowed down and utterly humiliated'.

[87]Therefore when the disciple completes the ascent of all these rungs of humility he will, in the fear of God, success-

75. *Inst.* 4:39, 2
76. Pr 10:19
77. Ps 140:10
78. Sir 21:23
79. Eccl 7:7
81. Sextus, *Enchiridion* 145
85. Lk 18:13
86. Ps 38:6

fully scale the ladder of his life and [88]soon come to that love of the Lord which, when perfect, casts out fear, [89]whereby all that he previously observed not without fear, he will begin to keep without any effort, as though naturally out of habit, [90]no longer because of fear of hell, but out of very love for this good habit and because of delight in virtue. [91]The Lord will be pleased to make this manifest in his workman now cleansed by the Holy Spirit from vices and sins.

[92]A soul such as this, therefore, having gone up these rungs will, when life has ended, doubtlessly enter into the reward of the Lord to which the apostle refers when he says: 'What we suffer in this life can never be compared to the glory, as yet unrevealed, which is waiting for us'. [93]Such souls will receive that eternal life which abides in the rapture of everlasting joy and will nevermore know an end. [94]There 'the red roses flower without ever wilting. [95]There the lush groves retain forever the greenness of springtime. [95]There the verdant meadows ever abound with rivers of honey. [97]There the grass emits the fragrance of saffron flowers and the flourishing fields are rich in the most pleasing perfumes. [98]There breezes endowed with eternal life are wafted upon the nostrils. [99]There the light is without shadow, the clear sky without a cloud, and the eyes enjoy perpetual daytime without nocturnal darkness. [100]There no distraction impedes delights. [101]There no concern whatever troubles peace of mind. [102]There loud moaning, wailing, groaning, lamentations and cries of mourning are never heard, nor are they even named. [103]Absolutely nothing that is ugly, deformed, hideous, gloomy, horrible or sordid is ever seen there. [104]There is beauty in the charming groves, luster in the delightful air. The eyes, always open, feast upon the loveliness and all the grandeur, [105]and the ears hear nothing at all that would disturb the mind. [106]Rather, instruments are always playing there to accompany hymns sung by angels and archangels to the praise of the king. [107]Harshness and the animosity of rancor have no place there. [108]There thunder is never heard,

88. 1 Jn 4:18
90. *Inst.* 4:39, 3
92. Rm 8:18

lightning flashes are never seen. [109]There shrubs produce cinnamon and bushes burst with balsam. [110]The perfume of the air fills all members with delight. [111]There the food causes no excrement. [112]For just as the ears are sated with good tidings and the nostrils with fragrance and the eyes with visual perfection, and eating cannot result in indigestion', [113]because the banquet of love consists not of food and drink but of seeing, smelling and hearing, [114]'so the refreshments which the mouth takes there, like honey in flavor, have in each person's mouth the taste that pleases him. [115]Finally, whatever the soul desires is immediately at hand to serve his whim'. [116]In the midst of this happiness and joy there is no growing old to fear, no end of life to dread, and death is no longer in prospect for these delights. [117]In the enjoyment of these immortal riches there is no question of the possessor passing on and being succeeded by an heir, for death is now unknown to those who have once died and purchased eternal life with the coin of good deeds.

[118]This is the heavenly homeland of the saints. [119]Blessed are they who, by mounting the rungs of humility on the ladder of discipline in this present time, were given the possibility of being taken up [120]into this eternal realm which God has prepared for those who love him and keep his commandments and are pure of heart, to rejoice with God in everlasting bliss.

HERE ENDS TREATMENT OF THE HEART'S SERVICE:
HOW TO FLEE SIN THROUGH FEAR OF GOD.

112 & 115. *Passio* 13

HERE BEGINS THE ORGANIZATION OF THE MONASTERY: DELIMITATION, OBSERVANCE, STRUCTURE, CONTINUITY, SUPERVISION AND NORMS, WHICH GIVE THE NAME OF MONASTIC RULE TO THIS, THE LORD MAKING IT KNOWN TO US AND, HAVING MADE IT KNOWN, HOLDING US ACCOUNTABLE FOR IT.*

Question of the disciples:

XI. THE DEANS OF THE MONASTERY.

The Lord has replied through the master:

¹Brothers, in the preceding pages of this rule the Lord has prescribed for us the ways of holiness which, if followed to the full, procure eternal life and save from the heat and flames of hell. ²But so that the enemy of good deeds, the devil—who is the adversary of the human race because he cannot bear to have man rise, by doing well, to the place from which he himself was cast out because of his pride—³so that he may not with his poisonous wiles corrupt the morals of those who live a good life, and by various openings given him by forgetfulness perhaps take hold of our senses to turn them away from God, ⁴therefore, with the help of the Lord, this provision and arrangement is made, namely, that two brothers, chosen for their proven gravity, wisdom, moderation, vigilance and humility, as well as the perfection of their ways, be appointed deans to care for ten brothers.

⁵Now, as it is written, let things earthly teach you what is heavenly. ⁶Just as in a man's home the master of the house, to make sure that everything is in order, appoints overseers of the household whom the subordinates must respect as representatives of the master, ⁷such as the vice-master, the steward, the forester and the major-domo, ⁸so also in the houses of God, namely, churches and monasteries, God has set

---

*The six subjects listed in the title (the English translation of which may be disputed!) are enigmatic, even if one assumes that different parts of the RM to which they could refer have been displaced.

2. Rev 12:7–10

5. Source unknown

superiors over subordinates, the experienced over the inexperienced, the discerning over the simple. And for those who are learning the divine art he has appointed masters in the churches, [9]namely, bishops, priests, deacons, and clerics, to whom the people must listen and whom they must respect when, as representatives of God, they issue commands, and from them gain knowledge of the law of salvation. [10]In monasteries these are the abbots and deans who for the soul's salvation must be listened to, superiors who must be respected as representatives of God. [11]For to them, be they priests in the church or abbots and deans in the monastery, God said this: 'Anyone who listens to you listens to me, and anyone who rejects you rejects me'. [12]Again, the Lord tells us through the prophet Isaiah: 'I will give you shepherds and teachers after my own heart, and they shall feed you, nourishing you with discipline'. [13]Therefore, in comparison with a human household, how much more in a house of God must the gradations of teaching and respect be complied with for the sake of God! [14]Since deans are appointed to purge the vices and sins of the brethren, the abbot may to a certain degree be at ease regarding the account he will have to give of the souls of the brethren he has received into his charge.

[15]Therefore, let the conferring of this dignity take place as follows: when these ten brethren have been called together by the abbot in the oratory in the presence of the entire community, the deans are given charge of the ten by receiving a rod while the abbot says aloud these words [16]warranted by

---

10. 'Deans' here and throughout this translation renders the Latin *praepositus*, for the group of ten monks headed by two *praepositi* is quite evidently a 'deanery'. In RB 65 the *praepositus* is the prior, second to the abbot. RM rejects this office specifically and vehemently (Ch. 92). RB's term for dean is *decanus*. In Chapter 5 of *The Community and Abbot in the Rule of St Benedict* (Cistercian Studies Series, 5), Adalbert de Vogüé presents a philological study of the term *praepositus* in RM and RB, and of the term *decanus* in RB: the literary precedents, the significance of the substitution of *decanus* for *praepositus* by RB to designate the decurion or head of a deanery, the fact that in RB *praepositus* is never a synonym for *decanus*. Other translations of the RM *praepositus* include 'provost' or 'decurion'.

11. Lk 10:16
12. =Jeremiah 3:15. Cf. Eph 4:11
16. Ps 2:9

Scripture: 'You shall rule them with a rod', that is, with an energy [which insures] fear. [17]The apostle likewise says: 'What do you wish? Shall I come to you with a rod, or in love?' [18]So too it was with the rod of divine power that Moses showed the people entrusted to him the way of salvation through the depths of the sea. [19]He is seen championing God's cause before Pharaoh by using the rod as a sign when he threw it from his hands to the ground and it was changed into a beast, and when the beast, picked up again, became a rod in his holy hands.

[20]Therefore, according to this arrangement, if the community is large, in charge of every ten brothers are to be put two brothers, [21]appointed because of their worthiness, of course, as we have directed above. [22]The reason we have determined that ten, not more, are to be placed under the care of two deans is so that when the brethren are dispersed in various places of work they may have one of the deans with them to guard against vices. [23]With few charges, the guardian's supervision is more effective, [24]for when there are many, what is not noticed is passed over and neglected; [25]because with few brethren entrusted to him, the two deans' alternating supervision is more attentive, and it is easy to make a report to the abbot, when required, about a small number. [26]It is with reference to this small group that the Lord declares the caretaker praiseworthy, and increases what was entrusted to his diligent supervision, saying: 'Well done, good and faithful servant; you have shown you can be faithful in small things, I will trust you with greater'.

[27]Therefore when these deans take charge of a group of ten brothers, they must be so solicitous for them that day or night and at any work whatever [28]they are first of all present with them and work with them no matter what they are doing. [29]Thus whether they are sitting, walking, or standing still, by their careful supervision and alert vigilance they must ward off from them the devil's activity [30]when they want to indulge in vices and sins of the tongue, correct them immediately

17. 1 Cor 4:21
19. Ex 14:16–21
26. Mt 25:21

with admonitions, and eliminate in them everything that is contrary to the divine law. [31]They must do what St Eugenia did while presiding over her subjects in this way. It is written about her: [32]'Her ears were so alert to what all said that she would not tolerate it when anyone burst into swear words or babbled in any sort of idle talk'. [33]But St Eugenia admonished her subjects [34]and told them: 'We are made aware of the great reverence with which we must serve the Lord, as he commands, if we imagine that we have before our eyes a person none of whose orders may be scorned'.

[35]Now, we have said that two deans are to be appointed for every group of ten so that if the abbot assigns some brothers of one group to another task which separates them from the rest, they may be accompanied by one of the deans, [36]leaving the other one with the brothers from whom they have been separated. [37]If, however, one of the brothers is to be sent on a journey, let him set out forewarned by his dean's instructions about guarding against various vices. [38]But of the ten, the one sent should be such that his dean is certain he can carefully guard against his vices and, in the absence of his dean, [39]all the more keep in mind the presence of God, and that the brother, concerned about his soul, will feel bound to a greater degree than ever to fear the presence of God, who will be our inquisitor and judge, more than that of a man.

[40]Therefore let these deans—it is for this they are at all times present with the brothers—keep them from sin in word and act and suppress their various vices and faults. [41]Thus, if the dean hears a brother speak when no question has been asked him, he should reprove him, saying: [42]'Brother, why are you doing what the rule forbids?[43] You are to keep silence until you are asked a question. [44]Say to the Lord with the prophet: "O Lord, set a watch before my mouth, a guard at the door of my lips", and [45]"Be quick to listen but slow to speak"'.

[46]If permission to speak is given to the brother, the dean

---

32 *Passio Eug.*, p. 394, ll. 6–7
33. Ibid., ll. 7–10
44. Ps 141:3
45. Jm 1:19

should see to it that he does not talk too loudly, which is not seemly for the wise. [47]Very soon the dean should admonish him saying: 'Stop, brother. [48]Speaking in this way is foreign to humility, for it is written: "A talkative man will receive no guidance on earth"'.

[49]But even if he perhaps speaks softly to another, the dean should take care that he does not let escape from his mouth any word that is useless or apt to cause laughter and that has nothing to do with edification and holiness. [50]If he hears such, the dean should call his attention to it, saying: 'Brother, why are you speaking in a way the rule forbids? [51]For it is written: "You shall give an account of any useless word". [52]So also the apostle says: "Guard against foul talk; let your words be for the improvement of others, as occasion offers, and do good to your listeners"'. [53]For it is the abbot who is to offer edification of this kind, so that the disciple's listening in silence to the teaching given by the master may make its response in deeds. [54]So the dean is to admonish the disciple who uses improper language and say: 'Close your mouth to evil speech, brother. [55]What is good ought to issue from the source from which you are bringing forth evil, so that we who are listening may admire the good speech of your mouth instead of laughing with you about something bad or frivolous. [56]What causes laughter is good for nothing. [54]Therefore let wisdom hedge your mouth with the barrier of integrity and the fear of God, and let this open your lips for good speech and close them to evil speech. [58]For when a frivolous word issues from your mouth, brother, even though it causes laughter, it is nevertheless lost to you by our hearing it, [59]because once out of your mouth it cannot return. On the contrary, accounting for it is saved up for the appearance of the inquisitor, [60]and since it contributes nothing to good deeds, it burdens your case and injures the soul. [61]And as regards our talking, may it not be said to us on the day of judgment: "Everyone speaks falsehood to his neighbor". [62]As a wise

48. Ps 140:10
51. Mt 12:36
52. Eph 4:29
61. Ps 12:2
62. Sextus, *Enchir.* 152

saying of Origen has it: "It is better to throw a stone in vain than a word"'.

⁶³If he hears a brother lie, let him urge truthfulness, saying, 'Why are you lying, brother, ⁶⁴when you know that it is written: "You destroy all who speak falsehood", ⁶⁵and you likewise know that "all the ways of the Lord are kindness and truth"?'

⁶⁶If he hears a brother swearing a great deal, let the dean who is present reprove him, saying: 'Hold your tongue, brother. ⁶⁷Why are you swearing so much, when Scripture commands us not to swear at all, lest the taking of an oath occasion the breaking of it? ⁶⁸"All you need say is yes if you mean yes, no if you mean no", believe me if you mean believe me, and we shall immediately believe what you say.'

⁶⁹If he sees that a brother is angry at a brother, let the dean who is present reprove him, saying: 'What are you doing, brother? ⁷⁰Do your work in meekness and silence and charity, because it is written: "Enough of anger, leave rage aside". ⁷¹Again, "To hate your brother is to be a murderer". ⁷²So also: "If a man calls his brother a fool he will answer for it before the council", ⁷³and "God's righteousness is never served by man's anger". ⁷⁴No one is allowed to delay reconciliation with his enemy beyond the setting of the sun, for the Lord says through the apostle: "Never let the sun set on your anger"'.

⁷⁵If he sees that a brother is too ready to laugh, let the dean who is present reprove him, saying: 'What are you doing, brother? ⁷⁶Do with seriousness what you do, because the span of our conversion [to God] is not for gay laughter but a time of penance to bewail our sins, ⁷⁷as it is written: "Let us prostrate ourselves before the Lord, let us weep before God

64. Ps 5:6
65. Ps 25:10
68. Mt 5:37
70. Ps 37:8
71. 1 Jn 3:15
72. Mt 5:22
73. Jm 1:20
74. Eph 4:26
77. Cf. Ps 95:6

who made us", [78]and again: "Those that sow in tears shall reap in joy". [79]And Scripture likewise says: "Happy you who weep now: you shall laugh" in eternity. [80]For "a fool laughs at the top of his voice"'.

[81]If he sees one brother cursing another, let the dean who is present reprove him, saying: 'Bar your mouth to cursing, brother. [82]Be mindful of God, who has told us through the apostle: "Bless and do not curse". [83]And just as a fountain cannot issue bitter and sweet water together through one outlet, neither can we; [84]if we bless God with our tongue, how can we with the same tongue curse men who are made in the image and likeness of God?'

[85]Again, if he sees brothers physically unrestrained and spiritually undisciplined surrender themselves to frivolity of any kind, let the dean who is present reprove them, saying: [86]'Sitting, walking and standing, brothers, be serious, because from heaven the eyes of the Lord observe us always and everywhere whether we are good or evil, [87]as David says: "The Lord looks down from heaven upon the children of men, to see if there be any who are wise and seek God". [88]Let us therefore fear, brothers, lest he at any time see that we "have gone astray and become perverse, and there is not one who does good, not even one". [89]And the prophet says: "You hate those who serve worthless idols" [90]because whatever does not come from God comes from sin, and what does not build up destroys'.

[91]While they are daily, day and night, every moment, keeping solicitous watch over the brothers entrusted to them, the deans themselves progress by taking care of others, [92]and while they are ridding others of evils by their surveillance

78. Ps 126:5
79. Lk 6:21
80. Sir 21:23
82. Rm 12:14
83. Sf. Jm 3:11
84. Cf. Jm 3:9
86. Pr 15:3
87. Ps 14:2
88. Ps 14:3
89. Ps 31:6
90. 1 Jn 3:10, cf. Rm 14:23, 1 Jn 3:8

they are at all times occupied with what is good, ⁹³because the mouth is made blessed by the good issuing from it and entering the ears of those who hear it.

⁹⁴Therefore while the dean is carefully watching over the brothers in these matters, in any work assigned to him the abbot will not demand as much of him as of the other brothers, ⁹⁵because even though he is accomplishing less with his hands physically, he is working for the interests of God spiritually by his solicitous concern in giving reproof; ⁹⁶and the less he is working with his hands the more he is doing for souls. ⁹⁷The reason we have said that in work of any kind less is to be demanded of deans is because pressure to produce material results must not cause negligence on the part of the dean charged with spiritual care, ⁹⁸and because God's interests must not be nullified by the predominance of vice, should there be more pursuit of the body's gain than working for the soul's good. ⁹⁹Rather, relying on faith together with hope, we believe that the Lord God will supply all that is required for our use when our own hands are unable to do so for us. ¹⁰⁰We are reassured of all this by what is written in the holy gospel: ¹⁰¹'Do not worry about what you are to eat or what you are to drink or what you are to wear, ¹⁰²for it is the people who do not know God who are concerned about all these things'. ¹⁰³But 'set your hearts on his kingdom and on his righteousness, and all these other things will be given you as well. ¹⁰⁴For your Father who is in heaven knows you need them all. ¹⁰⁵Look at the birds in the sky; they do not plough or sow, yet your heavenly Father feeds them. ¹⁰⁶How much more you'.

¹⁰⁷The deans are to have charge of the brothers' clothes. The deans are to have beds near theirs so that during the night they may correct any vicious faults of theirs.

¹⁰⁹We prescribe that they are to sleep one to a bed, not two. ¹¹⁰And when a brother gets up and does not make his bed properly, as punishment he is not to receive any unmixed wine at the next meal. ¹¹¹In bed they are to sleep clothed and girded, namely, with cincture, cord, or belt. ¹¹²We forbid a

102. Mt 6:25, 32
103–6. Mt 6:33,32,26,30

brother to wear a knife-belt during the night lest when he turns over while fast asleep the point of the knife come out of the sheath and pierce his flesh. [113]During the day, however, let them be girded with knife-belts, as Scripture teaches about St John: 'He wore a leather belt round his waist'.

[114]The reason we have said the brethren are to sleep clothed and girded is that when the time comes for the Work of God and the oratory signal is sounded during the night, they may rise and be ready immediately, [115]as Scripture says in this regard: 'And my signal, when it sounds early in the morning, I shall recite accordingly'. [116]For the signal took its name from this, that by sounding it signals that the time for reciting the psalms has come. [117]Therefore the prophet says about this: 'When it has sounded, I shall recite accordingly', that is, when it indicates that the time for saying the psalms has arrived, 'I shall accordingly recite the praises of the Lord'.

[118]The brethren are to sleep clothed and girded so that a brother may not touch his naked members. [119]For thereby lustful impurities are brought into the soul. When a pleasurable touching of the members occurs, immediately the heart's desires for women are titillated, resulting in sordid defilement of the members during sleep.

[120]The principal reason the brethren are to sleep clothed and girded is so they do not miss some of the prayers or psalms because in the dark they were asking for their clothes and belt from orderly and dressed brethren entering the oratory, and now because of their negligence are still making their beds in the dark, turning them upside down and scattering them around.

[121]The deans are to have beds near theirs so that, as we have said, they can correct any vicious faults of theirs, and so that they may sleep with greater decorum because a superior is present. [122]They are to be present at their table to eat with them in silence and moderation. [123]If a brother leaves this group of ten, no matter where, without orders from the abbot as well as the dean, they are to look for him with great care.

113. Mt 3:4
115. Cf. Ps 73:14–15
117. Ps 73:15, Ps 78:4

Question of the disciples:

XII. ABOUT EXCOMMUNICATION FOR FAULTS.

The Lord has replied through the master:

[1]If, in all that has been said above, any brother frequently proves contumacious or proud or given to murmuring or disobedient to his deans, [2]and after having been warned and reprimanded once and a second and a third time, in accordance with the divine precept, does not amend, [3]the deans are to report this to the abbot. [4]The one in authority will make a judgment according to the nature and gravity of the fault and, [5]so that he will know that it is God he despises, will sentence him to the excommunication [6]he deserves to have pronounced for the contempt shown a superior, for the Lord himself says to our teachers: 'Anyone who listens to you listens to me; anyone who rejects you rejects me'. [7]Excommunication is to be appraised as follows:

Question of the disciples:

XIII. TREATMENT OF AN EXCOMMUNICATED BROTHER.

The Lord has replied through the master:

[1]When the deans have informed the abbot about the offense of the disobedient one—[2]no longer to be called a brother but a heretic, [3]no longer to be called a son of God but a servant of the devil, [4]one who by going counter to the way saints act has become so to say a sort of scab in the flock—[5]let the abbot summon him, with his deans present and the entire community standing round. [6]When the abbot has asked his deans how he has sinned and how often he has been warned about his vice without amending, [7]let him state what they

1. The penitential code, much more developed than that in Cassian, begins here. The Master seems to have drawn on Mt 18:15–16, fraternal correction first by one alone and then in the presence of one of two witnesses, to prescribe three warnings and reprimands.
6. Lk 10:16

accuse him of. [8]When the vice has been heard, let him listen to the voice of the abbot directed against him, as follows:

[9]'O wretched soul, what response are you going to give to God, whom you anger every day by disobedience, when you approach to adore him? [10]Why, with God as your master, do you prefer to serve mammon? [11]Why, as another Judas, do you lie to Christ? [12]Judas sold justice for the price of iniquity; you squander the name Christian by your wicked deeds. [13]Judas, by deceitful peace, brought about the downfall of the Lord; you, nominally in the holy service of the Lord, are instead a rebel. [14]Judas, the false disciple, betrayed his master; you, bearing the holy name of Christian, follow the devil instead.

[15]'Standing beside you at the judgment will be our warning and your spirit, which you resisted through self-will while in the flesh, and which will say before the tribunal of the fearful judgment: [16]Lord, "he did not want to understand how to do good. [17]He planned wickedness, he set out on every way that was not good, he did not hate evil [18]but on the contrary gloried in it. He was a champion of iniquity".

[19]'When you are accused of these things at the judgment, after what we say you will also hear the voice of the dread judge saying to you: [20]"It is you who hated discipline and cast my words behind you. [21]When you saw a thief, you kept pace with him, and with adulterers you threw in your lot. [22]To your mouth you gave free rein for evil and you harnessed your tongue to deceit. [23]You sat speaking against your brother and put stumbling blocks in his way. [24]With your tongue you plotted injustice all the day. Like a sharpened razor you practised deceit. [25]You loved evil rather than good, falsehood rather than honest speech. [26]You loved all that means ruin, you of the deceitful tongue! [27]You did all these

---

9. *Visio Pauli* 16
10. Mt 6:24
12. Like St Basil, the Master saw in the monk nothing more than a Christian.
18. Cf. Ps 36:4-5, Ps 52:3
24. Ps 50:17-20
26. Ps 52:3-4

things and I was silent. [28]You thought wickedly that I was like yourself. I will correct you by drawing them up before your eyes. [29]God himself shall demolish you; forever he shall break you. He shall pluck you from your tent, and uproot you from the land of the living".

[30]'Moreover all the just in their glory will then see you at the judgment, [31]when you have been separated from them and placed at the left among the goats, [32]and they will laugh at you, saying: [33]"This is the man who did not make God the source of his strength but put his trust in his own worthlessness. [34]There was no fear of God before his eyes, for he acted deceitfully in his sight, [35]and like a fool he said in his heart: [36]God will not avenge it. [37]He hides his face, he never sees". [38]And he did not realize that for enemies who are faithless to the Lord, there will come a time of eternal punishment.

[39]'What are you going to say to God about all this? [40]Wretched man, what excuses for your sins will you have to offer him when your own sins will be the first to accuse you and hell is waiting to burn you?'.

[41]After these words of the abbot rebuking him in front of the community, the order will be given immediately to have him taken from the oratory. [42]He will be excluded from the common table. [43]Since he is branded an enemy of God, from that moment he may no longer be a friend of the brothers. [44]Therefore from the moment of this excommunication he will be assigned by his dean, in order to preclude idleness, to some work where he will be alone and isolated. [45]At this work he may not be joined by any of the brethren to help him; he may not be consoled by anyone speaking to him. [46]All must pass by regarding him in silence. If he asks a blessing, no one may

28. Ps 50:21
29. Ps 52:7
30. Cf. Ps 52:6
31. Cf. Mt 25:33
33. Ps 52:7
34. Ps 36:1-2
35. Ps 53:1
36. Ps 10:13
37. Ps 10:11
38. Cf Ps 81:15

reply: 'God' [bless]. ⁴⁷Whatever is given may not be signed with the cross by anyone. ⁴⁸Whatever he does individually and on his own over and above the work assigned him is to be thrown aside and destroyed. ⁴⁹He is to be alone everywhere, with no comfort but his guilt.

⁵⁰Should the abbot not wish, because of the lightness of the fault, to impose a double fast on him, ⁵¹if the brethren take their meal at the sixth hour, let his dean, out of compassion, give him one dish and a piece of very coarse bread, and water, at the ninth hour. ⁵²If the faultless brothers take their meal at the ninth hour, let him have the aforesaid meal deferred till evening, ⁵³so that he may experience what evils his fault has brought upon him, what good things he has lost by his heedlessness.

⁵⁴If any brother either openly or secretly speaks or associates with him, nonetheless, he will immediately incur the penalty of excommunication along with him. ⁵⁵He will be held guilty by everyone and he too is to be isolated by his dean in work of some kind, ⁵⁶and he too is to be alone and segregated both from the other offender and from all, and from then on he too is to be excluded from conversation with anyone. ⁵⁷Furthermore, neither will he obtain the superior's pardon until both the one and the other have made the same satisfaction of penance, ⁵⁸the one because he was viciously and sinfully disobedient, ⁵⁹the other because he rewarded the doer of evil with consolation.

⁶⁰A brother who has committed a light fault and does not amend after a first, second and third reprimand for a vice of any kind is to be excommunicated from table, not from the oratory. ⁶¹This excommunication will continue uninterrupted until the offender has made humble satisfaction with [his]

---

49. This is major excommunication, from oratory and table. The monk's 'asking a blessing' could be the *Benedicite* before speaking (9:49–50), before eating and drinking (23:24–6 & 77:2–3), or before certain actions (19:8, 24:13, 93:37).

61. Someone excommunicated for lesser faults would be present in the oratory at community prayers, but only as a passive listener. He thus reverted to the status of a novice (Ch. 90).

head bowed down to his knees, and has promised to amend in the future.

[62]But if a brother has committed a grave fault, he is to be excommunicated from both, namely, from oratory and from table, [63]and is not to obtain the superior's pardon until he has made satisfaction to God and to everyone by prostrating himself before the entrance to the oratory and by promising amendment with tearful voice during the interval when the psalmody of the choir prayer ceases, [64]provided the abbot, under God's guidance, wishes to accord pardon more quickly because of the very heavy burden of guilt, [65]as the following page will explain.

[66]The brother who has been excommunicated from table but not from the oratory may intone neither antiphon nor verse nor lesson until, [67]kneeling before the abbot (if he is present) or before his deans, he has promised amendment and has made satisfaction for his fault.

[68]But if the excommunicated brothers show themselves so arrogant that they persist in the pride of their heart and refuse to make satisfaction to the abbot by the ninth hour of the third day, [69]they are to be confined and whipped with rods to the point of death and, [70]if the abbot so please, be expelled from the monastery, [71]because such a life has no corporeal ties, and the society of the brothers does not have them with those who in their proud soul are in death's grasp. [72]Rightly therefore are such to be punished with whipping and expelled, since they do not deserve to be with Christ, the Lord of humility. [73]Instead, may they be deprived of the eternal promises of God, together with the devil, their seducer, who was cast out of the kingdom of heaven because of his pride.

[74]Let us then continue with the treatment of excommunication and satisfaction, begun above. [75]We believe that God and the abbot will hold acceptable the mode of penance and satisfaction as here given:

---

72. Cassian (*Inst.* 4,16,3) assigns confinement and whipping—apparently one or the other—to enormous faults and not, as here, to the refusal to make satisfaction for any fault. 'To be with Christ' echoes St Paul's definition of happiness in heaven.

Question of the disciples:

XIV. How must one who is excommunicated do penance?

The Lord has replied through the master:

[1]This he does if, when an hour of the Divine Office is celebrated (that is to say, when at the end of a psalm all fall to prayer) [2]the one under excommunication, lying prostrate before the entrance to the oratory, cries out, with tears, as follows:

[3]'I have sinned, and I acknowledge my offense. [4]I have erred, I promise to amend, henceforth I shall sin no more. [5]Pray for me, O holy assemblies, from whom I have deserved to be separated because of my recklessness and the persuasion of the devil. [6]Pray for me, my erstwhile deans. [7]Forgive me, good shepherd and kind abbot. Leave the ninety-nine for the sake of the one. [8]Come, pick me up and carry me, the lost sheep, on your shoulders, as our Lord has given you the example by his passion, [9]for he came and died not for the just but for sinners, [10]so that we who have been struck down by our sins may be raised up again together with him and by his justification. [11]As the Lord himself said: "I was sent only to the lost sheep of the House of Israel", [12]and "It is not the healthy who need the doctor, but the sick". [13]Imitate the apostles' loving master, whom you represent in the monastery by your teaching, [14]because after the prophets and apostles he has constituted you too as shepherds and teachers of discipline, [15]because through the blessed apostle Peter he has made clear to you that, as he said, an offense against a brother must be forgiven not seven times, but seventy times seven. [16]By your salutary counsel, therefore, raise up one who has been struck down. [17]By your intercession to the Lord, free me from the bonds of my heedlessness. [18]I acknowledge that I have sinned, [19]I trust that I shall amend, in your admonition I find the way to do so.'

3. Ps 51:3
7. Cf. Jn 10:11, Lk 15:4
9. Mt 9:13, Rm 5:6–9
11. Mt 15:24
12. Mt 9:12
15. Mt 18:21–22

²⁰Once these words have been addressed by the prostrate offender to the brothers at each of the prayer periods interrupting the psalmody, when the Divine Office has been completed in the oratory, and while the culprit is still lying before the entrance, ²¹let the entire assembly of the brothers, including his deans, humbly bow over to the knees on his behalf in front of the abbot as he exits. ²²If the abbot chooses to grant pardon there and then when this has been done, because of the lesser gravity of the fault, ²³he will order the offender's dean to raise him up. ²⁴After he has rebuked him anew for his fault, and he in turn has replied that he will henceforth amend, ²⁵the abbot will immediately say to the entire community: 'Come, brethren, let us with one accord tearfully pray in the oratory for this sheep of your flock who acknowledges his sin and promises to amend henceforth, ²⁶and reconcile him also before the Lord, whom he has angered by his disobedience.'

²⁷Thereupon the abbot together with the brethren will re-enter the oratory, and (still outside before prayer) his deans, ²⁸holding him by his right and left hands, will bring him [the penitent] into the oratory, both saying this verse: 'Give thanks to the Lord, for he is good', ²⁹and the rest of the community will continue with the response: 'For his kindness endures forever'. ³⁰Thus when the deans, still outside, urge confession upon the penitent by this verse, a loving God will immediately give assurance of mercy through the mouth of the brothers making the response.

³¹Then when his deans have brought him into the oratory, they will direct him to prostrate himself at the foot of the altar. ³²Together with the abbot all [the brothers] will immediately prostrate themselves to pray for him. ³³Then, prostrate, he will pray to the Lord with tears, because of his guilt,

---

28. Ps 106:1—this verse is said by the deans, not by the penitent, who may not pronounce any liturgical text (Ch. 13:66).

33. The penitent prostrates himself first, then those do who pray for him. 'With tears pray to the Lord' is unusual, for ordinarily such a prayer would be silent except for the conclusion, which would be pronounced by the superior. Here, as in Chapter 14, silence is replaced by discourse by the person excommunicated. Note that the penitent is prostrate at the time—hardly an apt position for a declamation.

saying these words: [34]'I have sinned, Lord, I have sinned and I acknowledge my offense. [35]I ask, I beg of you, forgive me, Lord, forgive me. [36]Do not drag me away with my sins, [37]do not condemn me to the nether world, [38]do not forever charge me with my evil deeds, [39]for you are a God of repentance. [40]Show your goodness also to me according to your great mercy, [41]for you, Lord, have said: "I take pleasure, not in the death of a wicked man, but in the turning back of a wicked man who changes his ways to win life". So for our misdeeds you prefer to grant life day after day so we may amend, [42]as Scripture shows us, saying about your loving kindness: "Will he be angry every day? Unless you be converted...". [43]And your apostle Paul says: "Do you not know that the patience of God is leading you to repentance?" [44]Therefore "the Lord has brandished his sword, he has bent his bow and made it ready. And thereby he has prepared the weapons of death". [45]We fear these weapons, Lord, so we promise to amend quickly. [46]For at the judgment you will say to the sinner: "You did these things and I remained silent". Shall I always remain silent? [47]For you will set our iniquity before our face, [48]and we, made aware of it by our indictment, will rightly condemn ourselves.

[49]'For you, "Lord, give death and life, you bring down to hell and you draw up". [50]You raise up those who are struck down. You loose in heaven those who are bound on earth. [51]You enlighten the eyes of our heart for our correction. [52]By your grace and your assistance you direct the steps of the just, [53]as Scripture says: "By the Lord are the steps of a man

34. Ps 51:3,4
36. Ps 28:3
37. Cf. Job 10:2
39. Cf. Jer 18:8–10
40. Ps 51:1
41. Ezech 33:11
42. Ps 7:11
43. Rm 2:4
44. Cf. Ps 7:12–13
46-7. Ps 50:21
49. 1 Sam 2:6
50. Ps 146:8 & cf. Mt 18:18
53. Ps 37:23

made firm", [54]and "Unless you guard and build the house, they labor in vain who build and guard it", [55]because to will is ours, to do is yours, [56]and "it is not a question of someone willing or running, but of God showing mercy".

[57]'Nevertheless you encourage us to hope in you, saying, "Ask, and it will be given to you; seek and you will find; knock, and the door will be opened to you. [58]For anyone who asks receives; the one who seeks finds; to the one who knocks will the door be opened". [59]You have also said: "Return to me, and I will return to you", and "When you call, I will answer: Behold, I am here". [61]So also, loving and merciful as you are toward your creatures, you call us to your grace; although we are your unworthy servants, [62]you say: "Come to me, all you who labor and are overburdened, and I will give you rest".

[63]'Therefore, Lord, do not despise your servant who acknowledges his sin, [64]in accordance with what the prophet promises about your indulgence toward our guilt when he says: "God does not scorn a contrite and humbled heart", [65]for you "can raise children for Abraham from these stones", [66]and what our despair considers impossible, your grace declares possible.'

[67]When these tearful words are finished, the abbot will immediately raise him up by the hand, saying to him: [68]'See to it, brother, see to it that henceforth you sin no more so as to be obliged to do penance for this vice a second time, [69]for the obligation to do penance a second time would cut you off into heresy'. [70]Then the one time offender will recite this verse: 'I

54. Cf. Ps 127:1
55. Cf. Rm 7:18
56. Rm 9:16
58. Mt 7:7–8
59. Zach 1:3
60. Cf. Is 58:9
62. Mt 11:28
64. Ps 51:17
65. Mt 3:9
69. An allusion to the teaching in antiquity that an ecclesiastical penance could not be repeated. This dates the RM before the introduction of repeating penances by Celtic monks, who came to continental Europe toward the end

have gone astray like a lost sheep. Receive your servant back, Lord', and all will make response. [71]After this verse, and after calling his deans, the abbot will commit him to their charge again, saying: [72]'Take this sheep of yours, restore the full number, readmit him to table. [73]For he was dead and has come to life, he was lost and is found'.

[74]The same day let him, as a sign of recovered humility, pour water over the hands of the brothers as they enter for Communion, [75]and as he does so, let him kiss the hands first of the abbot, then of each of the brothers, [76]begging them individually, while he pours it, to promise to pray for him. [77]As soon as he himself has entered the oratory let him again entreat everyone, aloud, to promise to pray for him, and [78]when he leaves with the brothers after having done this, let him go to table as usual.

[78]Young boys up to the age of fifteen, we prescribe, are not to be excommunicated but whipped for their faults. [80]After the age of fifteen, however, it is proper not to whip but to excommunicate them, [81]because then they understand that they must do penance and correct what wrong they do as adults. [82]For it is right that one who sins should repent in his heart, and not be physically whipped for it, because we live under the soul's rule and not in the body's service. [83]Therefore, since the soul rules and the body serves, it is evident that a misdeed of the ruler is greater than that of the servant. [84]So where there is understanding of correction, the thorns of sin must be purged from the root of the heart by excommunication, [85]since the limbs of the body should not unjustly suffer punishment for a fault not its own when, [86]without its consent, sin has been imposed upon it by the heart's command. [87]Nevertheless, brothers beyond the age of fifteen are to be whipped if they have committed a very grave offense, such as stealing and fleeing, or some other crime.

of the sixth century. The reference here to heretic is obscure, though it doubtless means that a relapsed sinner would be excommunicated as a heretic.
70. Ps 119:176
73. Lk 15:32
82. Sallust, *De conjur. Catalinae* 1.2. Cf. Jerome, *Adv. Iovanianum* 2.10.
87. Adolescence succeeded infancy at fifteen, but was lowered to twelve on the question of fasting (28:24).

Question of the disciples:

XV. Subordinates revealing evil thoughts to the deans and to the abbot.

The Lord has replied through the master:

[1]Brothers, the limbs of a tree are unblemished only if its wood is made faultless from the root up. [2]Nor is it seemly that the door should be cleaned on the outside while the room within is defiled with filth. [3]Rather, the proper thing to do is to throw out the filth from inside, and only then ought the outside to be cleansed. [4]Entrenchments cannot be secure when the enemy is within. [5]So also a bolted door is its own captor when the walls do not hold the foe off but keep him enclosed. [6]Similarly, a wound will fester when it is full of putrefaction, and unless the pus is pressed out and eliminated from it on the outside, and the suppuration after being pressed out is cleaned away, it can imbed its infection deeper. [8]Now, this is also the way we should feel about our soul, namely, we ought first to expel from our heart what we do not want to bear in our body, [9]telling ourselves: 'Why are you silent, soul, [10]and why do you not cry out and expose what is aflame in your spirit? [11]Why do you not from within cast out the fire of malice and give relief to your exhausting suffering?'

[12]When an evil thought comes to the heart of one of the brothers and he feels that it is causing him to waver, therefore, let him immediately confess it to his deans, [13]and they will inform the abbot of this after quickly saying a prayer. [14]Moreover the deans themselves should on their own initiative interrogate their charges about this, [15]lest perhaps because of the simplicity of some of them or indeed for very shame brought on by what is evil the brother is too shy to confess depraved and obscene things. [16]But if, on the other hand, they have been encouraged by the superior's initiative, they will reveal their sinful thoughts without shame. [17]And if the deans themselves experience this same thing in themselves, let them make their own report to the abbot. [18]Should the superior himself experience this same thing in himself, let him in the oratory ask the whole community to pray for him.

[19]Therefore when the deans have reported this to the abbot about one of the brethren, let the abbot directly call together

the entire community ²⁰and say to all: 'Come, brothers, let us in love help one another before the Lord, ²¹as the apostle says: "Brothers, if one of you misbehaves, the more spiritual of you who set him right should do so in the spirit of gentleness—²²encourage the apprehensive—²³not forgetting that you may be tempted yourselves, ²⁴and you who think you are safe must be careful that you do not fall". ²⁵So let us with one heart pray to the Lord for this brother of ours that he may by the sign of his cross and the exercise of his power thwart the tempations of the devil in him.' ²⁶After everyone has prayed for him this way for a very long time, the abbot and all the others will rise, completing the prayer. ²⁷Then they will leave and everyone will resume the work he was doing.

²⁸Keeping with himself only the brother who is troubled with evil thoughts, the abbot will bring out books ²⁹and there will be reading to serve as divine medicine required by the wound. ³⁰Moreover, every day for as long as the brother when questioned by the abbot replies that the temptation has not gone away, ³¹at the times assigned to reading whether in winter or in summer, passages pertinent to the needs raised by such thoughts are to be read from books to the group of ten to which the brother belongs. ³²For example, if fornication is suggested, passages showing how God loves chastity will be read to them from various books. ³³If lying is frequently suggested, various passages in which God commands truthfulness will be read to him. ³⁴If the desire is for something worldly, passages in which the Lord commands that what is temporal be disdained and the eternal kingdom of heaven be sought will be read to him. ³⁵Hence the abbot must be well-versed in the law so that he himself may either teach all things by bringing witness to bear or else may assign readings pertinent to the occasion. ³⁶Thus when a sick disciple is restored by a potion of this kind, is it not true that he will not only recover his former strength ³⁷but will also acquire new strength against the enemy, and the adversary will lose what he thought he had in his possession?

³⁸Then the following morning the abbot will again ask the disciple whether or not the adverse thought has ceased. ³⁹If he replies that it has not ceased, let a fast be imposed on

everybody. [40]If the next day he likewise replies, when again asked, that it has not gone away, let wine be withdrawn from all those taking their meals at table. [41]But if on the third day—God forbid that this should even be said, lest we be deemed of little faith, lest we seem slow to believe that God can come to our assistance, [42]since in any case we know that he is most merciful and loving and ready to help, [43]for 'God does not forget pity, nor does he in anger withhold his compassion'—[44]if, to repeat, on the third day he is again questioned and replies that it has not gone away, in addition to wine let oil be withdrawn from the meals. [45]Thus through the hardship and the ordeal of abstinence by the many, no one will perish, but all will be set free. [46]Hence in the affliction of all, there is hope for the remedy of divine mercy, [47]and in this way the apostle's precept is complied with, when he says: 'You should bear each other's troubles and so fulfill the law of Christ' [Galatians 6:2].

[48]Furthermore, when a brother is to be sent on a journey, let his deans admonish him to be on his guard against the devil at all times and everywhere, [49]because for some of us he acts as guide on the road and wants the satisfaction of drawing us along with himself into hell, [50]for he cannot stand it that man by doing good goes up to heaven, from which he himself was cast out because of pride. [51]Therefore the servant of Christ must remain cautious everywhere even when a superior is not present, [52]and carefully stay on guard against evil deeds as well as depraved thoughts. [53]And the brother should be warned of this, that when some such thought comes to him he must immediately, [54]with knees and head down on the ground and tracing the sign of the cross on his forehead, take refuge in the Lord, begging him to defend his soldiers against the devil. [55]For if vices are not repressed while they are small, they cannot be curbed when they have grown large, [56]and once evil thoughts are translated into acts, sin committed brings final death.

Question of the disciples:

XVI. CHARACTERISTICS THE CELLARER OF THE MONASTERY SHOULD HAVE.

The Lord has replied through the master:

[1]Brothers, every work has its value, for 'wages are due the laborer who has earned them', and 'the ox treading out the grain is not to be muzzled'. [2]Moreover, fruitful labors give joy to him who eats what they provide, [3]because after man was created the Lord put all things under his feet, and for him he created everything. [4]Therefore if diverse created food is subject to the use of the unjust and the enemies of God, namely, unbelieving pagans and heretics and sinners of all sorts, and the whole world is at the service of people of every kind, [5]how much more is it right and proper that to those who believe in God and serve him well the Lord has given over for their sustenance the various creatures he brought into being. [6]And by providing all the necessities of life in this present time as a pledge of the future promise, so to say, [6]'the Lord does not forsake those who seek him' for 'the rich have been in want and have hungered, but those who seek the Lord will not lack anything good', [9]and the Lord 'has filled the hungry with good things and sent the rich away empty', [10]and this: 'As having nothing yet possessing everything'.

[11]Therefore the cellarer of the monastery is nothing but the dispenser of divine things. [12]They are divine in the sense that in the gospel the Lord makes a promise to his faithful servants when he says: 'Do not worry about what you are to eat or what you are to drink or what you are to wear'. [13]So also he admonishes that no one should fret about the morrow,

1. Lk 10:7, Deut 25:4
2. Cf. Ps 128:2
3. Ps 8:6
7. Ps 9:10
8. Ps 34:10
9. Lk 1:53
10. 2 Cor 6:10
12. Mt 6:25

[14]but instead he gives his exhortation, saying: 'Seek the kingdom and the righteousness of God, and all these things will be given you as well. [15]For your father who is in heaven knows you need them all'. [16]So if the Lord puts the necessities of life at the disposal of God's servants, and the Lord our heavenly father knows and provides what we need, [17]you see that our food too is the Lord's gift, for it is he who provides it for us. [18]For if the servant of a human master, merely another man, is concerned about giving service [19]only because he is sure that his master will take care of his needs for food, clothing and footwear, [20]how much more proper is it that our heavenly master should bid us not to be anxious about what is necessary to our life. [21]Now if a man serving another man is right to trust him to provide for his needs, [22]how much more can God, who created all things and is able to do all things, put all at our disposal when we trust and serve him. [23]For 'I have been young and now I am old, yet never have I seen a just man forsaken nor his descendants begging bread,' [24]but rather 'all the day he is kindly and lends'. [25]Therefore if we are concerned solely about performing our service in seeking his kingdom and righteousness, [26]let us trust the Lord to provide us with everything, because without being asked he promises to make available to us everything necessary.

[27]If then the monastery's provisions, the appointed allowance which the Lord dispenses to his workmen, [28]are badly and fraudulently distributed by the cellarer and go to waste, [29]let the aforesaid cellarer know that on the day of judgment he will be called to account before the divine tribunal, [30]for the Lord will see that his servants' rations were squandered through negligence. [31]For what the Lord in justice grants those who are worthy of it, he does not allow to be squandered unworthily by wastrels.

[32]Without orders from the abbot the cellarer may not give, disburse, or distribute anything, [33]nor may he offer anything even to the sick without authorization from the abbot when

14–15. Mt 6:33,32
23–4. Ps 37:25–6

he is present. ³⁴The cellarer is to give alms by order of the abbot when he is present. ³⁵When he is not present, however, he may give alms to a poor man asking for them, ³⁶because of the Lord's precept which says: 'Give to everyone who asks you', ³⁷and likewise: 'Give, lest the one you refuse be Christ himself'.

³⁸The cellarer, together with the weekly servers, is to receive Communion every day in the oratory with the community in the abbot's presence. ³⁹He is to assign the kitchen utensils to the servers when they enter upon their week. ⁴⁰At the end of the week he will receive them back, cleaned, from those who have finished their week, and will assign them to those who are beginning theirs. ⁴¹If any of the monastery's utensils are broken by anyone through carelessness, ⁴²the one who broke them is not to go to table until he has penitently made satisfaction to the abbot, going down on his knees in humility. ⁴³When everything necessary has been taken out of the cellars, the cellarer is to sit at table in silence and eat with the community. ⁴⁴If the cellarer gets up to fetch something, everyone at the table at which he is seated is to wait until he returns before eating.

⁴⁵The cellarer will be given some work to do at such times as he is not occupied with any official charge, business, or disbursement, ⁴⁶so that he is not idle at such times. ⁴⁷In the oratory, if the cellarer is absent because he is occupied, ⁴⁸the abbot will ask the brethren, in his name, to keep him in mind. ⁴⁹And if the cellars are near the oratory, let the cellarer himself with his own voice ask that he be remembered in the prayers. ⁵⁰Even so, when he is busy doing something, he too should softly recite the Work of God by himself, following the words and verses being said in the oratory. ⁵¹And it is right and proper that he be remembered by everyone in the oratory, because he is engaged in caring for the needs of all.

36. Lk 6:30
37. Cf. Mt 25:35-6
38. To receive communion in the abbot's presence (*ante abbatem*) would seem to indicate that the abbot distributed communion.
44. The cellarer did not have a regular place at table, because he did not belong to any deanery (16:54). He seems to have taken his meal with the weekly servers (23:20).

[52]Thus, just as the one looks after the general welfare of all, so the prayer of all should be shared with the one.

[53]Vices of his mouth and body must be guarded against by the abbot himself keeping watch on them, [54]for the cellarer does not belong to any group of ten under a dean. [55]Otherwise, the flesh loving its own as it does, God's interests may be passed over for some appetite and the satisfaction of gluttony, [56]and excommunication may be bought off for food and drink in a carnal transaction, instead of being exacted.

[57]Let him receive all the utensils of the monastery and assign them to the various users. [58]Of all the things in the monastery, let no one except the abbot regard anything as his own, [59]whether it be something he has brought or found or made or acquired; [60]let no one appropriate or keep anything exclusively for himself, [61]because this is the intent of the rule: the goods of the monastery belong to everyone and to no one.

[62]The brother appointed cellarer should be someone whom the abbot knows from experience to be faithful and temperate, who has never at any time fallen victim to gluttonous desires of any kind, [63]and who does not love to eat and drink a great deal, [64]lest 'the devil be given a foothold', [65]as Scripture says: 'Do not give opportunity to those looking for an opportunity', [66]and lest it seem that there is more catering to than curbing of the greedy gluttony of voracious and ravenous brethren.

Question of the disciples:

XVII. TOOLS AND GOODS OF THE MONASTERY.

The Lord has replied through the master:

[1]The iron tools of the monastery are to be kept in one room, [2]and the abbot should assign their custody to a brother whom he knows to be careful. [3]This brother will give them out to the brothers every day for their tasks, keeping check on the

---

58. The abbot was the owner of all the goods of the monastery and bequeathed them to his successor (89:31-5, 93:13).
64. Eph 4:27
65. 2 Cor 11:12

number, ⁴and when work is over he will likewise receive them and put them back, cleaned. ⁵The abbot is to keep an inventory of everything. ⁶If a brother brings back from the field an iron tool not cleaned of dirt, ⁷the custodian of the tools is to accuse him at table and, ⁸as punishment, he will receive his portion of bread less one piece at mealtime until he has made satisfaction and promised amendment, ⁹because an iron tool will rust if it is put away uncleaned.

¹⁰In like manner this brother will have charge of the skins and sponges for shoes, the face towels, the table napkins and the bath towels. ¹¹As well as of a chest containing the personal effects of the abbot, and the chests of the various deaneries containing the personal effects of the brothers, kept locked by the deans. ¹²Also the chest containing the curtains and hangings and the ornaments of the monastery, ¹³and also a chest with the various books, parchments, and papers of the monastery. ¹⁴Also a chest with the affairs of the brothers who have recently entered the monastery, ¹⁵and these shall be ordered to be kept in case they return to the world, which God forbid!

¹⁶All the products of the artisans which are to be sold and which the workers in the various crafts hand in day by day, ¹⁷this same brother will take in and put away when they are finished, ¹⁸and those that are unfinished he will give back to the respective workers on the following day. ¹⁹In the evening he will likewise take in the tools of all the crafts of whatever kind, and in the morning will give them out. ²⁰In the room he will also keep, under the abbot's seal and lock, a chest containing the personal effects, conferred as a gift, of those recently entering the monastery.

²¹By means of a statement of expenditures he will give the abbot a full account of the monastery's expenditures. ²²So it is this brother must be governed by divine faith that he may, in the fear of God and in his sight, faithfully take care of what is entrusted to him.

Question of the disciples:

XVIII. THE WEEKLY KITCHEN SERVERS.

The Lord has replied through the master:

¹We said above that two deans have charge of each group of ten brothers. These ten brothers, two at a time, will serve

in the kitchen for periods of seven days. ²And when the service of one deanery has been completed, another deanery will take over the work, the cellarer consigning to it all the utensils. ³After this one is finished, the others will take their turns a week at a time. Each of the two deans, moreover, will do the cooking with the help of whichever of their brothers they wish. ⁴The deans are to do the cooking one at a time with the help of one of the brothers, ⁵so that, if both of them together are not occupied in the kitchen service, one will stay outside with the brothers of their deanery to keep watch over their various faults and vices. ⁶If even in this case some of the brothers are taken from their group for other work, those separated should be the ones who are more capable of fearing God's presence, ⁷and while the one dean is busy in the kitchen, the dean not thus occupied will stay with the more negligent. ⁸Thus they will in turn have the honor of giving correction and of practicing humility in serving. ⁹When all the deaneries have had their turn in this way, they will begin over again.

¹⁰Now, each deanery will take care of the seven-day periods in this way: two brothers at a time will be appointed by their deans to service in the kitchen for a week, ¹¹and all the kitchen utensils will be consigned to them by the cellarer when they begin. ¹²Two brothers at a time, so that they may help each other. ¹³Given this arrangement, entry upon the week will take place as follows:

Question of the disciples:

XIX. How the brethren should enter upon the week's service in the kitchen.

The Lord has replied through the master:

¹After Prime has been said in the oratory, the brothers about to enter upon their week are brought before the abbot

---

1. After Prime on Sundays, when the brothers went back to bed between Matins and Prime. On weekdays the servers began their work after Matins. They were appointed by their deans, who presented them to the abbot. The two brothers' prostration for prayer contravened the injunction against genuflections on Sundays (45:12–13), though only at the Divine Office. There is also genuflection specified at the other ritual blessings on Sunday morning (24:10) and Saturday evening (25:5).

by their deans, and the superior's attention is directed to them by these words: [2]'Please, Lord Abbot, bid the whole community pray for these brothers who are entering upon their week in the kitchen, [3]so that by being recommended to your prayers they may deserve not to fear the devil's snares and to perform everything for the community of God without fault'. [4]After these words the two brothers prostrate for prayer in front of the abbot, and behind them the entire community does the same together with the abbot. [5]And after all have risen, the two say this verse: 'Guard us, O Lord, as the apple of your eye, protect us in the shadow of your wings'. [6]After all have prayed for them, the aforementioned two brothers rise, kiss the knees of the abbot, and give the sign of peace to their deans and to all the community. [7]After the sign of peace has been given, their deans say to them: 'Go, brothers, in the name of the Lord Jesus Christ, enter upon your week, [8]and do everything after asking a blessing, saying *Benedicite* before doing anything, so that whatever you do may be blessed, the accursed devil may then not have the power of hindering you.'

[9]Every day after Terce has been said, starting that same day, if the brothers are to take their meal at the sixth hour, when the weekly servers leave the oratory with the community, they together with the cellarer turn their eyes to the abbot and ask him what he orders to be prepared for the community meal. [10]They then begin their kitchen duties after Terce so that after Sext has been said everyone can go directly to table with everything ready. [11]But if the meal is to be prepared for the ninth hour, the weekly servers and the cellarer put this question to the abbot as he leaves after Sext has been said, [12]and immediately after Sext they start the fire so that everyone may go to table after None has been said.

[13]If it should happen that the weekly servers are not on time, let them incur the punishment of excommunication because by their laziness they have pained a community wearied by double labor, namely, that of fasting and that of

5. Ps 17:8
6. 'On the following day' is difficult to reconcile with 'the next seven meals' stated just before it. Perhaps the reference is to the day after the seven to ten days of punishment.

work. [14]This is to be the penalty of excommunication: if at the sixth hour, seven; if at the ninth hour, ten. [15]That is to say, if the servers transgressed and were not on time for the meal thus delayed at the sixth hour, they are to forfeit one piece of bread at each of the next seven meals; [16]if they delayed the meal at the ninth hour, one piece of bread will in the same way be withheld from them at each of the next ten meals, [17]This penalty of excommunication reducing their allowance of bread will continue for the excommunicated until, on the following day, satisfaction promised has given evidence of amendment.

[18]If the community is large, or if many guests have come, additional brothers are to assist and the cooking will begin after Prime has been said and the abbot has been asked about the meal, so that the meal will be ready at the appointed time.

[19]Moreover, throughout this same week these brothers serve at the community meals. They take care of the monastery's household affairs. [20]During this same week they take off the shoes of all the brothers, assisted by additional brothers from their deanery, [21]and with them remove the shoes and also repair them, and return them repaired in the morning to the brothers seated in order. [22]Likewise during the same week they clean the monastery, wash the rest places, chop the wood, bring water for the face. [23]They pour the water on the hands of the brothers as they go in for Communion. They wash the table napkins, bath towels, face towels and the brothers' soiled laundry during the time not devoted to cooking. [24]Every day they ignite and extinguish the monastery's lamps trimmed by the cellarer. [25]But the first task of their service as soon as they have entered upon their week after Prime on the first day, as we have said, is to clean the oratory and spread out the mats on the floor of the oratory. [26]On every one of the seven days of their week they do this in the oratory as the first task of their service after saying Matins.

[27]Furthermore, while on duty during their week in the kitchen, let them be prompt in asking the others to pray with them for themselves.

---

24. The monastery's lamps were lighted before compline (29:5, 95:13).

Question of the disciples:

XX. How those not present in the oratory should be
KEPT IN MIND.

The Lord has replied through the master:

[1]When the weekly servers are outside, occupied with kitchen duties and taking care of the whole community, [2]or the cellarer is busy in the storeroom, or the custodian of the iron tools and goods of the monastery is engaged in his charge, [3]their deans within the oratory will say to the entire community: 'Hold up before the Lord those who are outside, and pray for them'.

[4]But if others who are not present in the oratory are engaged in the interests of the monastery or are on a journey, it is the abbot who will tell the whole community to remember the absent ones in their prayers, [5]as one reads in the Acts of the Apostles that prayer was offered for one who was absent, that is, 'when Peter was in prison, prayer was offered for him in all the churches'. [6]Now if they who are busy are not kept in mind in the oratory, those outside will receive all the reward from God, and those inside will come out empty-handed, [7]for it was to free them for prayer that those inside were assured that the necessities of life would be prepared by those outside. [8]And it is right and proper that one who is absent should be remembered in prayer by everyone inside, because he is engaged in caring for everyone. [9]So just as the one procures the common good for all, so should the prayer of all be shared with the one.

[10]Moreover, he who is busy outside for the good of the monastery is to observe this practice: when those within the oratory prostrate themselves for prayer after the conclusion of the psalmody, [11]let him ask in a loud voice that he be kept in mind in the oratory, even though he has said the Work of God by himself in the place where he is occupied.

[12]As to the sick, the abbot will exhort everyone to keep them in mind at every prayer. [13]And when a visiting brother

---

3. Actually the request for prayer for the cellarer is made not by the deans, because he was not subject to them (16:54-6, 23:13) but by the abbot (16:48).
5. Cf. Ac 12:5

leaves the monastery, the abbot will tell the community at the next Work of God to keep him in mind, [14]because when he went away this brother asked this of everyone, saying: 'You have the Lord; pray for me and remember me through your angel'.

Question of the disciples

XXI. HOW ARE THE KITCHEN SERVERS AND THE CELLARER TO RECEIVE COMMUNION?

The Lord has replied through the master:

[1]When the brothers are standing before the abbot in the oratory for Communion, after all have been given the sign of peace and the abbot has received Communion, no one may as yet communicate after him, [2]but the deans of the weekly servers immediately ask leave to go out to summon these servers of theirs for Communion. [3]Outside, finishing their work for them, one of the deans who have gone out takes charge of the kitchen and the other one sets table.

[4]When these have come out, the weekly servers, after promptly washing their hands, enter, pray briefly, and after their prayer give the sign of peace only to the abbot; [5]to him only, lest if they give it to all they cause the community meal to be delayed, [6]and lest after leaving late they will not have made the necessary preparations, causing the abbot when he leaves with the community to give in to the vice of anger because they have not yet prepared what is required. [7]Therefore after a short prayer they at once communicate under both species, and after again praying briefly, say the verse in a low voice, the abbot concluding it, so that they may leave and send their deans back to the oratory. [8]As they leave, the abbot says to them: 'See to it, brothers, that you do not, at the devil's instigation, take any food or drink ahead of time, before the prayer in common at table. [9]Although we who are inside here do not see you outside, God, who is present everywhere and sees everything, to whom nothing is hidden,

---

7. *communicent et confirment: confirment* means to receive communion under the species of wine (*Ordo Rom.* XV:57, 58, 60).

does see you. [10][See to it, then], lest when he sees you eating ahead of time he subject your whim to reprobation, and at the judgment your theft be charged against you for punishment'.

[11]After this admonition they leave along with the cellarer; one of them returns to the kitchen and the other performs the services not finished by his dean, [12]that is, setting the tables, arranging the benches, putting on the tableware, wiping the cups, so that when the abbot comes out with the community he will find everything ready. [13]Soo too with the bread rations for all, placed in a basket hanging above the abbot's table, [14]so that when the abbot comes out and finds everything ready there will be no ground for indignation or occasion for anger and outcry, for the monastery should be a place of silence and of peace.

Question of the disciples:

XXII. AFTER ALL THE WEEKLY SERVERS HAVE DEPARTED, IN WHAT ORDER ARE THOSE REMAINING IN THE ORATORY TO RECEIVE COMMUNION AFTER THE ABBOT.

The Lord has replied through the master:

[1]After the abbot's Communion the dean whose turn it is to stand next to the abbot communicates, and each member of his deanery follows him. [2]After these are finished, the other dean communicates, and in the same manner each member of his deanery follows him. [3]If, by the grace of God, the community is larger, the rest then do likewise. [4]In the oratory all are to stand in the place and communicate in the order assigned.

[5]A brother who is haughty about Communion and does not wish to communicate is to be dismissed and allowed to abstain. [6]And if afterwards he wants to receive Communion, let him not be permitted to do so for a time. As long as he is puffed up without reason, so long will the abbot or the dean be angry with him for good reason.

10. Cf. Rm 1:28
5. i.e. wishes to keep fasting

⁷Likewise, if anyone is haughty and does not want to come to table, let him be dismissed and at the next meal not be permitted to eat; if he nevertheless sits down, he is to be removed from the table, ⁸because when the abbot wanted him to [come], he did not, and again when he wanted to [come], the abbot rightly did not wish it.

⁹In the oratory the deans and the other brothers are to take turns standing next to the abbot for a day at a time, so that second place remains always indefinite, ¹⁰lest anyone assured and proud of his rank cause the others to lose hope. ¹¹Rather, all will strive to please by the performance of good works and will compete with one another to attain the hoped-for honor by merit, not by pretense. ¹²Prompted by the Lord we shall again speak of this matter in detail.

¹³Furthermore, after the abbot and by his direction, the deans always intone the antiphons from one and then the other choir. ¹⁴After these have had their turn, the brothers of lower rank, likewise by direction of the abbot, intone from the opposite choirs, one after the other as they have been directed by name to do so, that is, now from this choir, then from the other.

Question of the disciples:

XXIII. HOW, AFTER THE ABBOT HAS LEFT THE ORATORY, THE WEEKLY SERVERS ARE TO SERVE AT TABLE AND EAT TOGETHER.

The Lord has replied through the master:

¹When the whole community along with its shepherd has come from the oratory, after the verses and prayer the abbot seats himself in his chair at table. ²The whole community immediately answers, 'Thanks be to God,' and while all remain standing at their tables the basket hanging over the abbot's table is lowered with the pulley cord, to give the impression that the provisions of God's workmen are coming down from heaven. ³As soon as the basket has come down, the abbot makes a sign of the cross over the bread, breaks it, and takes first his own portion, which as he raises his hand will be blessed by the Lord; ⁴he sets out the portion for those

who are standing before him at his table and who will eat with him, and distributes it to them. [5]Upon receiving it they kiss the abbot's hand and sit down in silence.

[6]Then he calls up the deans of the tables and gives them the portions for their whole table. [7]After these have been dismissed he calls up the others and gives them theirs. [8]If, by the grace of God, the community is numerous he does the same for all the tables. [9]Upon receiving the portions for themselves and their brothers, the deans kiss the abbot's hands to give honor to the superior. [10]Likewise when they themselves make distribution to the brothers at their tables, their hands are kissed by the brothers as a sign of humility, and after each one has received his portion he sits down in silence. [11]After all are seated, the weekly reader at table rises and receives his portion, kisses the hand of the one giving it, then hands it over to the cellarer and resumes his place with the book. [12]Then, together with the cellarer, the weekly kitchen servers enter, receive their portions from their deans and kiss their hands. [13]Meanwhile the cellarer, since he belongs to no deanery, receives his portion from the hand of the abbot. [14]When he receives it he too kisses the hand of the giver and places [the bread] on his table.

[15]Next they give out individual cups of unmixed wine, first to the abbot, then to everybody, and lastly to themselves. [16]Then the weekly servers go to wait on the abbot's table first, then the dishes of food for the various tables are brought in and presented to the abbot by the bearers for his blessing. [17]Everything, cooked or uncooked, placed on the tables is blessed this way: [18]he who makes the sign of the cross says these words out loud: 'Bless, O Lord, whatever we are to consume of this'. [19]What may be left over or be discarded or drops, hence does not come to be eaten, may be thrown to the ground unblessed and is trodden underfoot, yet it will not appear that something blessed is subjected to indignity. [20]The

12. The weekly kitchen servers enter, but the cellarer—as the previous sentence indicates—was already present. What is meant here is not entering but stepping forward to receive the portion of bread.

15. Unmixed wine (*merus*), into which three morsals of bread are dipped (27:3-4), was given primarily to rinse the mouth after receiving communion (24:18).

blessed food, then, is placed on each table, and when they have served it they sit down with the cellarer at their dean's table and eat together with the community.

²¹When the meal is finished, the servers rise. One removes the dishes, the other places a basin with water for the brothers to wash their hands themselves, beginning at the abbot's table. ²²Taken from there it is placed on each of the various tables, and when all have washed their hands it is set aside.

²³Next they prepare a warm beverage measured in one container of a size corresponding to the number at the first table, ²⁴and when the beverage has been cooled by airing it with a cup, the one who has prepared it asks a blessing, tastes the beverage to see whether it is of the right temperature, and then distributes it to everyone at the first table. ²⁵After these have been served, they go to the second table, prepare the beverage anew in the amount corresponding to the number there, ask the blessing as before, taste the beverage to determine the temperature, and then distribute it to these. ²⁶And when the servers come to the table where they and the cellarer were seated, they add their own portion to the amount, ask the blessing and take their drink last of all.

²⁷Whenever this bowl is prepared it is presented to the abbot to be blessed before the tasting and distribution. ²⁸If the abbot is not present, the deans at the successive tables shall bless the food brought in for their own table, and the beverage bowl with the drinks. ²⁹And when the warm drink is measured out in a cup for anyone, or indeed an additional amount is given him, when he is about to drink he says again *Benedicite* to ask that the supplement too be blessed by the Lord.

---

23. *caldus*: a hot drink

23 *in uno galletae vaso*: the *galleta* was a vessel for wine, most likely containing one to two gallons. The word occurs again in chapter 27, where the Latin has been retained in the present translation for want of a corresponding English word.

29. There was no 'second in command' or prior (92). Both deans blessed the food in this case because they were equal in rank. Not only is the container full of wine blessed, but each individual portion of wine is also blessed (23:26, 24:30, 27:2).

³⁰After the beverages have been served, the waiters go out to fetch the other dish of cooked food, and when they have brought it they sit down at their places in silence and eat. ³¹Then when this dish is finished, the servers rise and take it away. ³²Again, after the bowl has been blessed by the abbot and, with his blessing, has been tasted, they serve the beverage prepared in proportion to the number at each table and, as before, they themselves drink last. After this has been done, they at once wash the serving dishes. ³³Then the cellarer rises, takes them and uses them to bring in an uncooked course, whatever it may be, from the cellar. When the dishes have been brought in, blessed and placed on the tables, the waiters resume their places and eat. ³⁴As soon as these dishes have been taken away, the servers reverently gather up the crumbs of bread, first from the abbot's table and then from the several tables. ³⁵As the servers gather up and remove these crumbs from each table they say together, 'Thanks be to God'. ³⁶They hand over these crumbs collected every day and put into one container, as we have said, to the cellarer to be kept with reverence. ³⁷With these the servers will make a cooked dish at the end of their week, as a subsequent chapter will explain. ³⁸As soon as the crumbs have been gathered up, then, the servers distribute the customary measure of drink, as prescribed. ³⁹As before, they themselves drink last, after asking a blessing.

⁴⁰Now, the reason we have said that the weekly servers and the cellarer should be at table with the community is that no one may eat all by himself or outside in secret without self-control, but there is to be a common measure of temperance and sobriety for everyone, ⁴¹because if anything is eaten in secret it is done deceitfully, and to satisfy the appetite without measure is a sin.

⁴²As soon as everything that is done at table is finished, all rise as the abbot does so, and the whole community says along with the servers and the cellarer, 'Thanks be to God'. ⁴³Then after the verse has been said, all are to be present at the prayer giving thanks to the Lord. ⁴⁴And so that no one is

---

34. They 'reverently gather up the crumbs' out of respect for what has been blessed.

absent, the deans will call the role of their deaneries; as all were together at table, so also will it be seen that all are present at the prayer. [45]Let all eating and drinking, then, begin and end with a prayer and verses.

[46]If a brother is not present for the verse said before the meal, he may not sit down at table with the brothers but must eat by himself from a special dish with no blessing given and no sign of the cross. [47]He is to receive an unblessed mixed beverage, and until he rises no one may speak with him. [48]If indeed he is a spiritual person, it will grieve him to take his meal without God. [49]Anyone who is not present for the final verse after the meal is finished, too, will be excluded from table at the next meal and will get unblessed food and drink. [50]These excommunications will remain in effect for them until they have, with head bowed down to the knees in satisfaction, promised amendment to the superior.

[51]Now, if it should happen that the weekly servers performing their duties at table are unable to serve everyone, let them make this known to their deans, [53]who will then add a brother from the same deanery, assigning him to help them. [53]Whenever the table waiters serve at table in the performance of their duties in a negligent manner, the abbot will rise the following day at mealtime [54]and he and one of the deans, or both if the community is large, will themselves take over the service at all the tables [55]in order to teach them how what they cannot do should be done. [56]Thus all the brethren will blush to realize that in the one human nature and the same service of God they do not deserve to receive the grace of divine wisdom in equal measure with the helpful brothers.

Question of the disciples:

XXIV. THE WEEKLY READER IN THE REFECTORY.

The Lord has replied through the master:

[1]In both summer and winter, whether the meal is at the sixth or the ninth hour, each of the deans of all the deaneries will do the reading at table for a week at a time. [2]But a dean is not to read if the other dean of the group of ten is occupied in the kitchen service, lest while one is doing the reading and

the other the cooking, there be no one present to correct the faults of their brothers at table. ³When these deans have finished taking their turns reading at table a week apiece, they will appoint literate brothers to read for a week at a time, so that everyone in each deanery who is literate may read in turn. ⁴And after all the brothers have finished their weeks of reading, the deans will start over again one after the other. In this way divine food will never be wanting at a carnal meal; ⁵as Scripture says: 'Man does not live by bread alone, but by every word of God', and the brothers' meal will be double when they eat through the mouth and are nourished through the ears.

⁶Entry into each one's week is to take place as follows: ⁷on Sunday, the same day the kitchen servers enter upon their week, ⁸at the meal at the sixth hour, after the verse and prayer at table, when the abbot is seated on his chair, before the basket with the customary bread has come down by the pulley cord, ⁹this brother who is to read presents himself by saying aloud: 'Please, my lords, pray for me because I am entering upon my week of reading at table'. ¹⁰Then the abbot rises with the entire community, and kneeling down they pray for him. ¹¹And after they have risen, the new reader for the week says this verse: 'O Lord, open my lips, and my mouth shall proclaim your praise', and all respond together. ¹²As soon as this verse has been said and the abbot has finished, he gives the sign of peace first to the abbot, then to everyone. ¹³Then he provides a seat for himself in the center of the refectory, and after all are seated at table he asks a blessing and likewise sits down at his place with the book. ¹⁴After the abbot and all the others have received the first unmixed wine of the meal, he too in like manner receives his unmixed wine to prevent spitting out the sacrament, and then he begins to read.

¹⁵Every day he reads this Rule, marking the place to which he reads day after day, so that it is read in daily sequence yet in its entirety, and thus in successive weeks the reading of it

---

5. Lk 4:4
10. The abbot alone rises; the community is still standing (23:1–2).
11. Ps 51:15

can be finished and started over again. [16]When the respective reader has finished his week of reading, he shows his successor the mark where he left off, and the one starting his week continues from there. [17]He in like manner, perhaps finishing and beginning anew, shows the mark to his successor at the end of his week.

[18]Let him read distinctly, not rapidly, so that the hearers while occupied may clearly understand what they must put into practice, [19]and so that, should there be anything ambiguous or obscure that the brothers do not fully comprehend, the abbot may give explanations either on being questioned by the brothers or on his own initiative.

[20]If non-monks happen to come to the monastic meal, to avoid defamation afterwards in the world should a worldling learn the secrets of God, [21]let the reading be taken from some other book, if the abbot so please, so that the secret of the monastery and the established norms for leading a life of sanctity may not be learned by scoffers. [22]In this case let him read another text, first making a mark in the Rule. [23]If the non-monk admitted to the monastic meal is such that the abbot is certain he not only is capable of appreciating the divine ordinances but is even so religious that he could follow this manner of life and could be drawn to godly ways, [24]when such a one comes to table the reader will continue the Rule. [25]For those who are capable of observing it as it should be [observed] should hear the Rule of the monastery.

[26]The Rule is to be read in the refectory at mealtime, the entire community having been brought together for the meal, so that the reading of what is to be observed and amended then may enable all the hearers to put it into practice rightly and without excuse. [27]In this way all will hear the rule in its entirety and no one will miss anything, so that all must actually do what they have heard.

[28]While the brother is engaged in this duty during his week, the waiters will take for him platefuls from all the courses served at his table, [29]and the cellarer will reserve his portion of bread and the customary number of drinks, [30]so

---

19. RM has no other instance of a conference being given by the abbot.
20. *laici-saecularis*

that after all rise he himself may, after asking a blessing, take his meal.

³¹We have said that the Rule of the monastery is to be read every day at table so that no brother may plead ignorance as an excuse for not mending his ways—³²even though the Rule itself is daily put into practice, knowledge of it leads to better observance—³³lest a brother should say he does not know what in fact obedience could enable him to do.

³⁴Moreover, while the Rule is being read during the meal, let the abbot, in order to stimulate careful listening by all the brothers, ask any of the brothers at any of the tables, as he pleases, what was read. ³⁵When one of the brethren repeats what he heard, therefore, it will be evident that he was at that time paying closer attention to the reading than to his stomach, ³⁶and when one deaf through negligence does not tell what he heard, the presumption will be that he loved the flesh more than the spirit. ³⁷He must be scolded by his abbot then and there, and rightly so, for his inattention. So each and every brother, afraid of being embarrassed should he be questioned, will not let his mind wander elsewhere but will pay attention to what is being read.

³⁸The one appointed for the week will continue the reading at table as long as the abbot together with the brothers is seated at table. ³⁹When they rise he too, after making a mark in the rule, rises holding the book, and after the verse and prayer have been finished by all, he replies along with everyone else, 'Thanks be to God'. ⁴⁰Then he immediately sits down again at his table and receives all the food kept in reserve for him by the servers, and the due measure of drink, blessed either by the abbot or by the deans.

Question of the disciples:

XXV. THE SMALL DISH OF CRUMBS TO BE COOKED BY THE
WEEKLY SERVERS ON THE SEVENTH DAY.

The Lord has replied through the master:

[1]The crumbs of bread which, after having been gathered up
and removed from the tables every day, are kept in a container are taken away on Saturday evening, the seventh day
of their week, by the servers completing their week. [2]With
them is made a small cooked dish stiffened with either flour
or eggs, and this is placed on the abbot's table that evening
before the drinking of the last warm beverage. [3]Then when
the abbot and all the community are seated, the servers say
together: [4]'Please, lords, pray for us, for we have finished our
week of humble service.' [5]Thereupon all rise along with the
abbot, and kneeling down they pray for them and with them.
[6]And when they have risen, the servers say this verse: 'Let
those who hate us see, to their confusion, that you, O Lord,
have helped us and comforted us'. [7]Then, when the abbot
has concluded, they give the sign of peace to him, and
likewise to their deans and to the entire community. [8]And
when the abbot and the brothers are seated at table again, the
abbot makes a sign of the cross over the little dish; with a
spoon he first serves himself from what he has just blessed,
then places a spoonful into the mouth of each of those who
are sitting with him at his table. [9]And when he has made the
round of his table companions he calls up the waiters and
puts some into their mouths also. [10]Then the waiters hand
the abbot as many dishes as there are tables and into them he
dishes out whatever number of spoonfuls corresponds to the
number of brothers at each of the tables. [11]Their deans do the
distributing into the mouth of each of the brothers, so that
everyone receives some of what has been blessed. When this

---

1. As there was no meal Saturday evening, what the Master probably meant
here was that the crumbs were taken from the container. The crumbs,
gathered up at the end of each meal, symbolized the entire week's service
and showed that the servers had seen to it that nothing went to waste. The
ceremony took place between the two drinks served in summer (27:10) or
before the single serving of warm beverage in winter (27:31).
6. Ps 86:17

is finished, they take the last warm beverage, then rise, saying, 'Thanks be to God'.

¹²But if any weekly servers do not, through negligence, present this little dish on the seventh day, during the week following theirs they will each forfeit every day a piece of bread, withdrawn by the abbot, until they make satisfaction and promise to amend.

Question of the disciples:

XXVI. THE MEASURE OF FOOD.

The Lord has replied through the master:

¹We believe that two dishes of cooked food and a third of whatever uncooked food is available, with fruit, are sufficient for the daily meal at all the tables, whether at the sixth hour or the ninth. ²A half-loaf of bread weighing a pound will suffice for each of the brethren each day, according to the norm given by divine providence, because every day a crow supplied Paul, the servant of God, with a half-loaf of heavenly bread to eat.

³Therefore in summer and at other times when the meal is at the sixth hour, of the three pieces of this half-loaf of bread one from everyone's portion is retained in the cellar by the cellarer to be placed on the tables in the evening before the dish of uncooked food is brought in. ⁴The reason we have said that these pieces are to be withdrawn from everyone's portion beforehand in the cellar is this: should the entire portions be placed on the tables, ⁵perhaps a brother novice newly arrived, not yet aware of the amount determined by the Rule and thinking that more will be placed before him at supper again, may finish off the whole of it at dinner and in the evening have nothing to go with the fruit. ⁶Or a brother who is very fond of eating may choose to consume the entire por-

---

2. Jerome, *Vita Pauli* 10; PL 23:252BC.

3. During Eastertide and the summer, but not in winter or during Lent (27:28), there was an evening meal only on Thursdays and Sundays (28:1, 28, 40–42). 'At other times' probably refers to Christmastide, celebrated like Eastertide (45:2–7).

tion at that time, even though he knows the amount determined by the Rule, because he wants to satisfy the demands of his appetite, thinking that he will be quite content in the evening. [7]When all these pieces reserved in the cellar are brought out in the evening, [8]placed on the abbot's table and blessed by him, as custom prescribes, he first takes his own and those for his table, [9]and the rest is removed in a basket by the cellarer and placed on each of the tables for those there to take. [10]So only these pieces along with the dish of some kind of uncooked food mixed with fruit, and also whatever food served at dinner may be left over will suffice for the brothers' supper.

[11]However, on Sundays or other feast days, as also any day for the sake of guests who are present, the abbot may add to the fare whatever he wishes, as a superior is allowed to do, [12]even some sweets in accordance with the *Lives of the Fathers*, where one reads that on feast days they asked the Lord for tasty food, and then an angel with a honey-comb appeared to them. [13]Only let him keep moderation in mind and avoid excess which can be the source of corruption.

[14]But for those below the age of twelve less than a pound of bread a day will be sufficient.

Question of the disciples:

XXVII. THE MEASURE OF DRINK.

The Lord has replied through the master:

[1]As soon as the brothers are seated at table, before they eat, they each receive unmixed wine. [2]As each one receives this wine he presents it to the abbot to be blessed, and at the other tables the deans in turn bless it for their brothers. [3]At all the tables, every brother dips three morsels of his bread, not more, into his wine. [4]Not more than that, lest a brother use up a great deal of bread at this point and, when as a result of his greediness for his bread portion, he has none left for the food, he draw upon himself disparaging looks from the other brothers.

12. *Hist. monach.* 7; PL 21:416BC.

[5]After the first draught of unmixed wine at the meal in summer, whether at the sixth hour or the ninth, then, let four drinks of the warm beverage in addition to this wine suffice for all. [6]When during this season the meal is at the sixth hour, however, let three drinks apiece suffice in the evening for everyone. [7]After these are gone, whether at the meal at the sixth hour or at the ninth or at supper, the cellarer stands in the center of the refectory and says aloud: 'If anyone is thirsty, let him not hesitate to say so.' [8]As soon as this has been said, let anyone who is thirsty reply from his table, '*Benedic*'. [9]Then a drink of warm must, if the brethren so wish, with orach juice, is mixed in a container, and this beverage, which must always be available in addition to the food for those who are thirsty, is distributed to the thirsty ones with a large *galleta* or cup.

[10]On the days of summer when the meal is at the ninth hour, moreover, let two drinks apiece suffice for all before they say Compline in the evening, [11]seeing to it that they pray before they drink and again after they drink. [12]In like manner, when the meal is at the sixth hour on these summer days, every day after None has been said and the abbot has left the oratory and seated himself on his chair, [13]with everyone standing around in good order in front of him, [14]the cellarer brings in the wine and in the customary container the weekly servers mix the beverage for each member of each deanery at all the tables, according to the number of the community, themselves included. [15]Then the abbot rises and prays with all, [16]and before he sits down after the prayer, the vessel containing the mixed wine is presented to him and he blesses it. [17]Then he directs everyone to sit down at the tables as he does so, as usual, [18]and after he himself has drunk first, he has the mixed wine poured for all individually at each table. [19]Afterwards they again rise and pray, [20]and after the prayer all return to the work they were doing when interrupted. [21]Thus whoever is thirsty may take a drink im-

---

5. See below, l. 31.
9. 'warm must' translates *pusca calida*, a warm drink made of vinegar, water, and eggs.
11. Between the two drinks, the ceremony described in 27:43–5 took place.

mediately after None. [22]But once the tenth hour has begun, no one may drink any more until after Vespers.

[23]If, however, a brother gets thirsty during the ninth hour before the beginning of the tenth, as we have said, and wants a drink of water, he should not drink with one draught from the jug but should measure it with a cup or *galleta* or goblet, [24]because what goes beyond due measure is excessive and blameworthy and evidently satisfies desires which lead astray. [25]For according to the maxim which says 'Nothing in excess', even an excess of water can intoxicate the spirit, causing phantasies in dreams, and plague the body with troubles, [26]namely, throbbing of the veins, chills in the marrow, heaviness in the forehead, dizziness in the head, sleepiness in the eyes, continual sneezing in the nose.

[27]In winter, however, let three warm drinks apiece suffice for everyone at the meal at the sixth hour and at the ninth, because there is no heat to stimulate thirst. [28]On these winter days when they take their meal at the sixth hour there is to be no supper at all in the evening except one warm drink apiece, and this will suffice for everyone. [29]Let them see to it that they pray before taking the drink, and pray again after they have finished drinking. [30]But the drink which is brought from the cellar after None every day in summer for those who are thirsty is not given in winter, because not only does thirst not make itself felt but there is not much time between the meal and evening. [31]On the days when the meal is at the ninth hour in winter, however, after saying Vespers they receive not more than one cup of warm beverage, [32]seeing to it that they pray before taking the drink, and pray again after they have finished drinking.

[33]As to the days from Easter to Pentecost when the meal is at the sixth hour, on days other than Thursday and Sunday, they receive two cups of warm beverage apiece in the evening to celebrate these days, but nothing else, [34]except during the octave of octaves following Easter Sunday when they always take supper. [35]We have eliminated supper on the aforesaid days except Thursday and Sunday until Pentecost because, although the one meal retained on those days is not at the

25. Cf. Jerome, Ep 108:21

usual time, [36]still the principle of the ordinary fast is evidently preserved, since their suppers are exchanged for dinners— [37]on Thursday and Sunday they do take supper in the evening, however, as noted above where we treated of food— [38]but with the addition of one dish every day at dinner and a drink of whatever kind of beverage may be left over from Easter.

[39]The cup or *galleta* with which distribution is made on the various occasions should be such that a third of what is mixed in it will fill a *hemina*. [40]But two or three cups or *galletas* should be used to give out this uniform measure at the table service, so that by means of these several beakers distribution may more quickly be made to all.

[41]Children up to the age of twelve are to receive, in winter, two cupfuls of warm beverage apiece, and in the evening one. [42]In summer, however, they are to receive three cupfuls at the meal and two in the evening, on account of the summer heat.

[43]Now, as we have prescribed above concerning food, so we make this allowance concerning drink: [44]on Sundays and on feast days and because of the presence of guests, the abbot as superior may add whatever he considers suitable. [45]Moreover because of charity proper to joyful holy days and the coming of friends, he may add a beverage of any kind he wishes. [46]Only let him be mindful of sobriety and avoid drunkenness caused by wine, because if the body is not sober it cannot stay awake for the Work of God and the soul is not free of impure thoughts.

[47]Should one of the disciples wish to turn down part of the regular measure of drink or the bread he has left over, he is recognized as someone who loves the spirit more than the flesh, [48]and he puts the curb of chastity on dissipation. [49]When the abstinent brother turns this down, let him say in a low voice to the cellarer clearing the table: 'Take this too, and may what is denied the flesh redound to God'. [50]Then the cellarer puts this into a separate container to redound abundantly to God, [51]and let it be added as a gift to the

---

36. Jerome, Ep 22:35
39. Cf. RB 40:3. An unknown quantity.

monastery's aims and given by the cellarer into the hand of a poor beggar.

⁵²All this is an inventory of the monastery's supplies. ⁵³But if the Lord provides for his community something sent from outside, let the gift of the Lord that has been sent be gratefully accepted and, ⁵⁴if the abbot so wishes, let it be added to the meals, since it is clear that it would not have come except by the providence of the Lord.

Question of the disciples:

XXVIII. Days of fast and time of repast.

The Lord has replied through the master:

¹At all times let the meal be taken at the sixth hour on two days a week, namely, on Thursday and Sunday. ²On other days of the week the meal is to be taken at the ninth hour.

³For we should be ashamed, we who are spiritual, to want to get out of fasting until the ninth hour, ⁴for we know that in former times ancient custom knew no dinner but always assigned its meals to the evening, that is to say, supper. ⁵So true is this that the ration which was provided for workmen or soldiers is called *annona* up to the present day because it was given at the ninth hour of the day and thereafter eaten, and therefore has kept the name *annona* until today. ⁶Moreover, let us cite the more sacred witness of the Lord himself. We know that he took supper; we do not read that he took dinner, ⁷for the writings of the holy gospel say: 'When evening came Jesus was at table with the twelve apostles, and while they were supping he spoke to them'.

⁸Now, it is prescribed that the fast be broken at the ninth hour every day so that it may be extended a bit on the days of Lent, that is, until evening, which means, after Vespers. ⁹From Sexagesima on, moreover, let the meal always be taken after Vespers on Wednesday, Friday and Saturday, ¹⁰but on

---

54. Cf. *Vitae patrum* 7.1.4., *Hist. monach.* 7; PL 21:416D.
1. 'At all times' did not apply to the Thursdays of Lent (53:35).
5. *ad nonam horam*
7. Mt 26:20–21. Cf. Lk 22:14, Jn 13:2–4, 1 Cor 11:20

the other days until Lent let it be taken at the ninth hour, [11]so that what the Sundays of Lent subtract from the forty fast days may be made up by the prolongation of fasting until evening on Wednesday, Friday and Saturday from Sexagesima on, [12]and the number of forty fast days may be complete.

[13]The appointed fast is to be relaxed for the sick, however, and when the brothers eat at the sixth hour, let the sick be given nourishment at the third, [14]except those who are very weak, because no time is set for them if there is danger of death. [15]Therefore whenever perceived and proven need exists, these may be given nourishment. [16]So if the healthy brothers eat at the ninth hour, let the sick do so at the sixth. [17]The abbot must, however, make careful inquiry to ascertain and to be convinced by sure signs that someone is not pretending to be sick out of gluttony for a meal. [18]If we have said that the fast is to be relaxed for the sick, it is because of the body's weakness, which makes it impossible for them to do what they would like to do; as Scripture says: 'The spirit is willing, but the flesh is weak'.

[19]The children, however, are to fast on Wednesday, Friday and Saturday, but only on the shorter days, that is, in winter; [20]on other days let them take their meal at the sixth hour. [21]On the longer summer days, let the children take their meal at the sixth hour on Wednesday, Friday and Saturday, [22]but on other days let them eat at the third, [23]because at that age they lack strength on longer days, as also the proper understanding of endurance. [24]But we allow this relaxation only for children who are below the age of twelve. [25]Those who are older are bound by the regulation for adults. [26]For it is only right to decide that in mitigating meals, consideration should be the same for small children, those overcome by old age, and the sick.

[27]Furthermore, let brothers being sent on a journey receive this instruction from the abbot or their deans: [28]on Wednesdays, Fridays and Saturdays when the days are longer, that is, from Easter to 24 September, which is the winter equinox, they are not to fast when they are under way, on account of

18. Mt 26:41

the heat and thirst. [29]Then from the winter equinox until Easter, because the days are short, the brothers who are travelling are to prolong their fast until evening on Wednesday, Friday and Saturday. [30]Otherwise, while the brethren are busy taking a meal along the way at the ninth hour, the quick passage of the short day will prolong the brother's sojourn. [31]Then, too, since everything in the world is for mercenary gain, [32]once evening has come and they have already broken the day's fast—and the prohibition of a second meal eliminates the prospect of their buying anything at their stopping-place—[33]an inn may not wish to take in the brother once he has already had his meal, because there is no prospect of profiting from a sale. [34]And because of this refusal to take in the brothers for lack of profit, the brothers, to gain admission, are forced to pay out from their funds again [35]and to violate the fast by a second meal, which is not permitted. [36]However, on days other than Wednesday, Friday and Saturday when the days are shorter, they may interrupt their journey for a meal at the sixth hour, and may take supper in the evening because of the toils of travel.

[37]From Easter to Pentecost, except for those sent on a long journey, let the meal in the monastery or anywhere else always be taken at the sixth hour; [38]thus they exchange their suppers for dinners. [39]As holy Scripture says: 'You are not allowed to fast as long as the bridegroom is with you', [40]and there is to be no supper except on Thursday and Sunday. [41]The reason fasting is never permitted on Thursday is because the ascension of the Lord falls on that day every year, [42]and fasting is forbidden on Sunday because the resurrection of the Lord is identified with it; [43]St Sylvester in his books prohibits it. [44]It is forbidden to fast from Easter to Pentecost because Easter Saturday closes the fast of sadness and opens the alleluia of joy, [45]whereas Pentecost Saturday closes the alleluia and opens the fast. [46]But alleluia is closed for the churches, [47]but in the monastery the servants of God, de-

38. Jerome, Ep 22:35
39. Cf. Mt 9:15, Mk 2:19, Lk 5:34
43. *Vita Silvestri*, p. 510, ll. 14–29.
44. i.e. Easter Even

voted as they are to the divine service in a special way, sing the alleluia to the Lord in the manner set for the psalms until Epiphany.

Question of the disciples:

XXIX. TIME AND PLACE FOR SLEEP AND IN WHAT ORDER THEY ARE TO SLEEP.

The Lord has replied through the master:

[1]In summer, after Sext has been said, whether they are fasting or after the meal, let all take a rest, so that in those short nights the brethren may rise for the Work of God free of sleepiness and alert for prayer. [2]The beds are to be arranged in order in a circle within a single room, as is done in a dining room. [3]Let the abbot have his bed in the center of this circle, [4]so that by seeing to the silence and reverence of everyone around him he may, as a careful and solicitous shepherd, watch over the whole flock of his sheep gathered into one sheepfold. [5]There is to be a lamp hanging in this room. It is prepared by the cellarer, and the weekly servers light it every day in the evening before Compline so that everyone can see to go to bed. [6]When everyone has settled down, the aforesaid extinguish it, in case a shortage of oil should make itself felt in the monastery.

Question of the disciples:

XXX. NO ONE MAY SPEAK AFTER COMPLINE.

The Lord has replied through the master:

[1]In the evening after all have finished their warm drinks and the weekly servers have taken off everyone's shoes, [2]the abbot says to all the brothers: 'Now then, brothers, let everything be put away in its place, let all things be laid aside. [3]Servers, wash the brothers' feet'. [4]After the servers have

---

2. Cf. 24:13.

washed everyone's feet, [5]or while they are washing those of outsiders who are present, [6]both together say this verse, with all responding: 'You have commanded, Lord, that your precepts be diligently kept. [7]Oh, that my ways might be constant in keeping your statutes'!

[8]Then the abbot says to all: 'Now, brothers, bestir yourselves, so that, everything having been taken care of, there be no occasion requiring us to talk. [9]For it is now time to commend ourselves to the Lord, [10]and now that we have finished all the duties of the day and are entering upon the night, let our mouth be closed to rest from speech as also are our eyes for sleep'. [11]So when all this has been done, though permission to speak and give some order may still be granted, [12]when Compline is at an end let them say this verse: 'Set a watch, O Lord, before my mouth and a gate around my lips'. [13]Then let them begin the silence and go to bed, and let them keep so strict a silence that one would think not a single one of the brothers were there at all.

[14]We ought to keep silence after Compline so that we may rightfully say to the Lord at the very beginning of the night Office: 'O Lord, open my lips, and my mouth shall proclaim your praise', [15]that is, that we may ask the Lord to open for the night [Office] our lips which his protection closed at Compline. [16]You see, then, that whatever is opened is acknowledged first to have been closed.

[17]But should it happen that while silence is being kept some practical necessity urgently requires that a brother speak and one brother wishes to speak to another brother, [18]if the light of the candle or lamp is still burning, let him communicate with his hand or a nod of his head or a sign with his eyes; [19]but if there is no light, let the brother go to the brother he needs and tell him what he wants, but softly into his ear so

5. In the ceremony for receiving guests (65:1–9) there is no mention of washing the guests' feet, possibly because it was done not at their arrival but before they retired (30:26), to prevent their soiling the bed (cf. 81:29–31).

7. Ps 119:4–5

12. Ps 141:3

13. Compline was probably said in the dormitory.

14. Ps 51:15

that a third person does not hear him. ²⁰Likewise, if a brother is compelled by some necessity to say anything after the rest before the night office, ²¹let him first say quietly to himself the customary verse of the night Office, namely, 'O Lord open my lips, and my mouth shall proclaim your praise', ²²and then let him say what is necessary.

²³However, we grant permission to no brother to eat anything or to drink even water after Compline.

²⁴But if any outsiders arrive at the monastery after Compline is finished, let community members serve them refreshments in silence ²⁵and having washed their feet, and then concluded quietly to themselves, let these assign them to sleep in the beds for guests. ²⁷As soon as the porters have closed the doors, they themselves are to lie down on their beds and take their sleep during the hours of nightly silence.

²⁸If any brother is caught eating or even drinking water after Compline, he is to be punished with excommunication as follows: ²⁹after being accused on the following day he is to remain fasting, taking his meal only on the third day, because he presumed to do what was forbidden. ³⁰This punishment of excommunication will stay in force until he has made humble satisfaction, promised amendment, and asked pardon of the abbot if he is present, or of the deans.

Question of the disciples:

XXXI. The hebdomadaries of the Divine Office during the night.

The Lord has replied through the master:

¹Waking for the Divine Office at night is entrusted to the deans of the group of ten whose members are doing the cooking that week, and they are to take care of the waking ²as long as their ten brothers, two at a time (or three at a time because of the community's size), are having their turn at the week-long kitchen service. ³And when the turn of the deans them-

---

30. Accusation took place, no doubt, in the refectory, as in Chapter 17. The satisfaction required indicates that this was a minor excommunication, even though the fast prescribed was total.

selves to do the cooking comes, because they may be exhausted and heavy with sleepiness, their limbs tired out by service in the kitchen, ⁴let them choose from their deanery two of the more careful brothers to take over the responsibility of doing the waking during their week. ⁵So also as soon as the brothers of another deanery begin their kitchen service, it is their deans who by their vigilance take charge of waking the whole flock. ⁶Likewise during the week when these are on kitchen duty they are to get help from their more reliable brothers.

⁷Furthermore, those whose week it is to do the waking are to watch the clock carefully night and day ⁸and remind everyone, abbot and brothers, of the time for psalmody, lest because they are busy at work they forget ⁹and so let the appointed time pass by, and they are to announce that the time for the psalmody has now come.

¹⁰The waking is assigned to two so that they may take turns staying awake, ¹¹and if one through weakness of the flesh is overpowered by sleep, the other, vigilant, may perform the duty of his negligent companion at the appointed time. ¹²For with the Lord there is great reward for those who do the waking for the Divine Office, and it is to their honor that the Rule has called him vigilant cocks.

Question of the disciples:

XXXII. THE MANNER OF RISING FROM SLEEP.

The Lord has replied through the master:

¹During the night, when the time set for psalmody arrives, the one of these two who proves the more vigilant rises and quietly wakes up his more negligent companion of these weeks of theirs. ²And by rights quietly, because no one has as yet asked the Lord in the oratory to open the lips which were closed for the night at Compline. ³We have appointed two so that they may anticipate each other in their vigils. ⁴So both rise, go reverently to the abbot's bed and, after praying there, say softly to themselves this verse: 'O Lord, open my lips,

12. Cf. Gen 15:1, Wis 5:16

and my mouth shall proclaim your praise'. [5]As soon as they have finished saying this softly to themselves, they awaken the abbot by touching his feet. [6]When he wakes up they say together: 'Thanks be to God'.

[7]After hearing this the abbot rises, goes into the oratory, [8]strikes the signal, and prays until all the brethren who may have been attending to the needs of the body have entered. [9]But if anyone causes the abbot to prolong his prayer unduly, which should not be done, and comes to the oratory late, the blame falls upon their deans. [10]The reason we have said that during the abbot's first prayer all should be awaited and that they must hurry, is that after the abbot's intonation all may together with one voice ask the Lord to open their lips for the night Office, [11]just as at the request of all together the Lord closed them at Compline. [12]Then as soon as they have entered the oratory they say three times: 'O Lord, open my lips, and my mouth shall proclaim your praise'. [13]We have said that this verse should be recited three times by all so that none of the brothers who may arrive a bit late will be deprived of this verse's petition.

[14]After this verse has been said by all, the shepherd summons and rouses his flock to the praises of the Lord by means of a responsory, saying: 'Come, let us rejoice in the Lord: let us joyfully sing to God our Saviour'. [15]Let every bee that has not hastened to the sweetness of these words and to the divine honeycomb know that it will be devoid of the fruit of spiritual honey, and that by sleeping it produces only physical wax to be burned up in the future fire of hell.

Question of the disciples:

XXXIII. The Divine Office during the night.

The Lord has replied through the master:

[1]At the night Office during one season, winter, the nocturns are chanted before cockcrow; as the prophet says: 'At

14. Ps 95:1
1. Ps 119:62
2. Is 26:9 (LXX)

midnight I rose to give you praise'. ²And of summer he likewise says: 'At night my spirit keeps vigil for you, O God', that is, at some time after cockcrow during the night the signal for rising is given.

³But in winter those on watch must take care that the cock does not get ahead of or catch up with the nocturns, because nights are long in winter. ⁴Now cockcrow is the end of the waning light, since night gives birth to day; ⁵so too when the sun is in circuit one sees the day fading away already at the sixth hour ⁶and the sun hastening to descend in deference to night, just as it hurried in its circuit to ascend to midday. ⁷What is imperative in winter is that cockcrow follow after the nocturns are finished, because the nights are long. ⁸Thus the brethren, refreshed by sleep, inwardly alert and composed, will understand the Work of God they are reciting. ⁹And there is a set interval so that the long night may do away with the oppression of sleepiness.

¹⁰In spring and summer however, that is, from Easter to 24 September, which is the winter equinox, the brothers are to begin the nocturns at cockcrow ¹¹because of the shortness of the nights, ¹²and as soon as they have finished the set number of psalms they are to append Matins with its full number of psalms. ¹³We have prescribed that the nocturns in these short nights are to begin after cockcrow and are to be joined with Matins so that the brothers do not go back to bed after the nocturns, ¹⁴become drowsy and, overpowered by sweet morning sleep, not only miss Matins but be put to shame by saying even Prime late.

¹⁵Furthermore, we have said to join the nocturns with Matins after cockcrow so that the brothers, now refreshed by a long sleep, may go through both Offices attentively, ¹⁶then after paying the divine debt of Matins the brothers who so wish need have no qualms about going back to bed until Prime. ¹⁷Thus, rid entirely of drowsiness during these Hours and then fully restored, they may begin to work unencumbered after Prime, ¹⁸as we are shown by what is written about St Helenus when it says: 'He used to take a rest after Matins'. ¹⁹Indeed, should the brothers be forced to rise before

18. *Passio Eugeniae*, p. 392.

cockcrow on the short nights, still sluggish from sleep hardly begun, [20]while in the first surge of the veins blood and humors are boiling through them [21]and the organs, in the torpor of interrupted sleep, are digesting the food they have taken, the brothers would be not so much roused as killed when they start to get up in this heat of the unfinished cooking process. With head still heavy and belching from indigestion they put to flight the gifts of the Holy Spirit, [22]and because distress afflicts their body, which sometimes seeks its own interests in this life even though it is in God's service, [23]what is sweet for the sake of God will seem bitter, if not for all at least for some, [24]and in the psalmody the brother will not love God with his whole soul when he wants to satisfy his body with sleep. [25]For as the waning moon in its orbit gives less light in its service to the night, and when it is late in rising from the east enters on its tardy course only to set again in daytime, [26]so the shortness of nighttime relative to daytime requires, because of the weakness of human nature, that the psalmody of the Divine Office be curtailed and the daytime Office be joined to that of the night.

[27]Now, the psalms of the nocturns in winter, namely from the winter equinox to the vernal equinox, [28]that is, from 24 September to 25 March, or better still until Easter, because the nights are long, [29]are to be said with [thirteen] antiphons, always in the sequence of the psalter, plus three responsories, [30]so that there are sixteen intonations matching the number of the prophets, besides the lessons and the verse and the prayer to God. [31]Thus these sixteen intonations plus the eight intonations of Matins [32]make us bend our knees to the praise of God twenty-four times in the night in imitation of the twenty-four elders. [33]There must be more psalmody in the long nights for this reason: [34]as God has increased the time of repose for us during the night, so we should also increase the thanks to be given in praise of him.

21. Nicet. Remen., *De vigiliis* 10: PL 30:238C.

29. The number thirteen is conjectural, as is the nine in the next paragraph (where the manuscript has 'eight'), and the numbers in 44:2.

30. The exact nature of the 'prayer to God' is uncertain. It may have been a litany, or the Lord's Prayer, or the silent prayer prescribed in Chapters 55 and 56.

[35]But in summer, that is, from Easter to 24 September, [nine] antiphons are to be said, always in the sequence of the psalter as we have noted above, plus three responsories, besides the lessons and the verse and the prayer to God. [37]Thus the shortness of the night restricts the bending of our knees before God to twenty times at these twelve intonations of the nocturns added to the eight intonations of Matins. [38]For when sleep is brief it seems sweet to the flesh, when the human body, fatigued by a long day's work, gets less repose in a short night. [39]Therefore in summer, as we have determined above, because the nights are short, [40]nine antiphons and three responsories are to be said, so that there are twelve intonations matching the list of the apostles. [41]These nocturns in summertime, as we have said above, are to begin right after cockcrow, and as soon as they are finished they are to be followed by Matins because of the shortness of the nights. [42]But let care be taken at all times, in both summer and winter, during the day as well as the night and at the Vigils too, that in the psalmody the psalms be never combined, for this is forbidden. [43]On the contrary, each one of them must end with the *Glory be,* [44]lest the prayers to be said between them be lost and we seem to withhold the doxology from its praise of God when through a time-saving remissness the psalms are forcibly crammed together, [45]for the prophet who gave each psalm its beginning also determined its end.

[46]But should everyone in choir be constrained by some kind of necessity, they may not group together two psalms but three, each in turn with its own doxology however, [47]in order to finish more quickly without decreasing the number of psalms. [48]Now, the reason we have stated that they must be said either one by one or in groups of three is this: [49]just as we profess unity in Trinity and Trinity in unity, so we hold that the psalms must be said one by one or, if necessary, in groups of three but each with its own doxology. [50]It is, then, absolutely not allowed to group two together, because what is more or less than one and three is not proper for a Christian, [51]and we have the true faith if we acknowledge the Trinity in unity and unity in the Trinity.

[52]But if a very urgent necessity of some kind puts constraint

on those in choir, [53]let them recite one section of each of the psalms to be said, with one doxology, and then leave the oratory. [54]Thus, whatever the necessity may be, the Work of God will in any case not be openly skipped.

Question of the disciples:
XXXIV. THE DIVINE OFFICE DURING THE DAY.
The Lord has replied through the master:

[1]In the performance of the Divine Office, the order of the sacred service must above and before all be set, [2]and also the sequence to be followed in the correct course of its observance in accordance with ancient custom and the regulations sanctioned by the Fathers, which means, Matins, Prime, Terce, Sext, None, Vespers and Compline, [3]in order to comply with the schedule of the prophet who said to the Lord: 'Seven times a day I have praised you'.

[4]But the Office at the first hour is to be said analogously to that at the twelfth called Vespers. [5]For Prime must be said when the rays of the sun have already burst forth, and Vespers while its rays are still going down, [6]because just as the day is started with the Work of God at its very beginning, in the same way must it be brought to a close at its end, [7]in compliance with Scripture which says: 'From the rising of the sun to its setting'—it does not say *after* its setting—'praise the name of the Lord', [8]for the Lord 'takes delight in the coming of morning, and in the evening'. [9]At these times the Lord takes delight in the daily reports our angels make of the good deeds of the just; [10]as St Paul says in his revelation: 'Sons of men, bless the Lord unceasingly, but especially when the sun is setting'. [11]It is the sun that marks for us exactly the beginning and the end of the day, and by its departure it brings on the darkness of the night.

[12]In summer, because of the short nights, let Vespers begin when the position of the sun is still quite high, [13]so that the

3. Ps 119:164. Cf. Cassian, *Inst.* 3:1–4
7. Ps 113:3
8. Ps 65:8
10. *Visio Pauli* 7

brothers, their limbs tired from the long labor in the heat and from fasting, may get additional sleep for their weary repose while it is still daylight, to supplement the short nights.

Question of the disciples:

XXXV. THE MEASURE AND NUMBER OF PSALMS DURING THE DAY.

The Lord has replied through the master:

[1]At Matins six psalms are to be said at all times, one responsory, a verse, a reading from the apostle, and the gospel, which the abbot must always say, and the prayer to God.

[2]Three psalms are to be said at each of the daytime Hours listed above, namely, Prime, Terce, Sext, None, always in the sequence of the psalter, one responsory at each Hour, [3]a reading from the apostle, a reading from the gospel, which must always be said by the abbot or, if he is absent, by the deans in turn, and after this the prayer to God.

Question of the disciples:

XXXVI. THE VESPER PSALMS.

The Lord has replied through the master:

[1]At Vespers in winter six psalms are to be said, always in the sequence of the psalter, one responsory, a verse, a reading from the apostle, and the gospel, which the abbot must always say, and after this the prayer to God. [2]Thus these [eight] intonations of the psalmody plus the responsory and the gospel, not including the verse and the readings, together with the four intonations at each of the daytime Hours, [3]that is, three antiphons and one responsory apiece at the Hours of Prime, Terce, Sext, None, [4]all add up to sixteen, not counting the verses and the readings—a total making us bend our knees twenty-four times in the course of the psalmody [5]in imitation of the twenty-four elders who, adoring God in heaven unceasingly, cast their crowns and lie prostrate and, [6]praising the Lord day and night, give glory to God.

6. Rev 4:4, 5:8–9, 7:11–12

[7]In like manner in summer there must be eight intonations at Vespers, counting the responsory and the gospel but not the verse and the readings. [8]Thus these eight intonations, plus the sixteen during the day, [9]make us on earth too bend our knees in praise of God twenty-four times a day at all times, just as we said above that there must be twenty-four intonations every day corresponding to the number of the twenty-four elders in heaven.

[10]In this summer season Vespers must begin earlier because of the short nights during this season.

Question of the disciples:

XXXVII. The psalms of Compline.

The Lord has replied through the master:

[1]At Compline three psalms are to be said, a responsory, a reading from the apostle, a reading from the gospel, which must always be made by the abbot if he is present, the prayer to God, and the concluding verse.

Question of the disciples:

XXXVIII. The mealtime psalm.

The Lord has replied through the master:

[1]At mealtime one psalm is to be said, plus a verse. [2]Likewise another verse with doxology after the table has been cleared. [3]But this prayer at meals is a special act of thanksgiving and is not included in the number of the day's seven canonical praises.

Question of the disciples:

XXXIX. How are the psalms to be chanted at matins?

The Lord has replied through the master:

[1]The psalms at Matins must always be chanted with antiphons, that is, four are said without alleluia, after these four two with alleluia, the responsory, [2]the verse, the readings

and the gospel, which the abbot says without alleluia (but with alleluia on Sundays until Epiphany) [3]so that there are eight intonations, counting the gospel but not the verse and the readings. [4]Matins, however, is to consist of canticles except for Psalm 50 and the praises, [5]but on Sundays and other feasts and on anniversaries of saints the blessings are to be said. [6]After these have been said on Sundays there is to be no kneeling until the nocturns and, after the blessings have been said, [7]all the antiphons and responsories that day are to be said with alleluia until the following nocturns of Monday.

Question of the disciples:

XL. HOW ARE THE PSALMS TO BE CHANTED AT THE DAY HOURS?

The Lord has replied through the master:

[1]At the psalmody of Prime, Terce, Sext, None, all is chanted with antiphons, [2]but the third psalm is always intoned with alleluia except from Epiphany on, always in the sequence of the psalter, [3]a responsory each time, a reading from the apostle, a reading from the gospel, which is always made by the abbot or, if the abbot is absent, by the deans in turn, then a verse and the prayer to God.

Question of the disciples:

XLI. HOW ARE THE PSALMS TO BE CHANTED AT VESPERS?

The Lord has replied through the master:

[1]The psalms of Vespers are to be chanted with antiphons, [2]the last two with alleluia, always in the sequence of the psalter, [3]a responsory, a verse, a reading from the apostle, and the gospel, which the abbot always makes, without alleluia, but on Sundays with alleluia. [4]Moreover on that day, after the blessings have been said, all the antiphons are to be chanted with alleluia, and there is to be no kneeling until the following nocturns of Monday.

4. Hebrew Ps 51

Question of the disciples:

XLII. How are the psalms to be chanted at Compline?

The Lord has replied through the master:

¹The psalms of Compline are to be chanted at all times with antiphons, ²but the third psalm is to be intoned with alleluia, ³because the seven times a day the prophet says we must give praise to God are all sung in the same fashion ⁴because of the sevenfold Spirit, who is not divided in any way.

Question of the disciples:

XLIII. How is the mealtime psalm to be chanted?

The Lord has replied through the master:

²Because they are not included in the seven times of the canonical Hours but are offered separately to God to bless or express appreciation for the food by giving thanks, ¹the mealtime psalms when the table has been set and again when it has been cleared ³are said straight through without antiphon, but on Sundays and feast days with antiphon and alleluia.

Question of the disciples:

XLIV. How are the psalms to be chanted at night?

The Lord has replied through the master:

¹At the nocturns the abbot must say the opening verse, then the hortatory responsory. ²Then, in winter, [nine] antiphons without alleluia, then a responsory without alleluia, [then four antiphons with alleluia], in any case always in the sequence of the psalter, ³then another responsory this time with alleluia, so that there are sixteen intonations, ⁴a reading from the apostle, a reading from the gospel, which is always made by the abbot or, if he is absent, by the deans in turn, then a verse and the prayer to God.

⁵In summer, however, from Easter to the winter equinox, which is 24 September, ⁶after the opening verse and the responsory of the abbot, six antiphons without alleluia are to be said, then a responsory likewise without alleluia, ⁷then three antiphons with alleluia, always in the sequence of the psalter

as we have said above, then another responsory this time with alleluia, so that there are twelve intonations, [8]a reading from the apostle, a reading from the gospel, which is always made by the abbot or, if he is absent, by the deans in turn, then a verse and the prayer to God.

[9]Moreover, the one to whom the lesson has been assigned is to recite it by heart and not read it from a book, except only in Vigils. [10]We prescribe this so that the brothers will do more frequent studying and retain the Scriptures in their memory. [11]Thus when a book is lacking anywhere, the text of the lesson or of the page will be, if necessary, recited from memory.

[12]In the long nights, however, a light or lamp having been lit in the dormitory, the abbot may read if he so wishes, [13]or any brother of his own accord as he pleases may receive permission to read or listen [14]to or study something or do something of benefit to the monastery. [15]And if some wish to rest, let them similarly have permission to sleep, [16]because after what is due to the oratory is finished and paid off, the remaining hours of the night may be claimed for repose. [17]But if someone, so to say a spiritual person, wishes to give up some of his sleep in order to listen to the reader or he himself read or do some special work, [18]he is recognized as someone who of his own good free choice loves the spirit more than the flesh. [19]So the brothers are to have their beds all in one room in front of the abbot so that it may be known what each one chooses and what will be the character of the brother's way of life.

Question of the disciples:

XLV. How the psalms are to be chanted on feast days.

The Lord has replied through the master:

[1]From Easter to Pentecost all the antiphons and responsories, in both daytime and nighttime, are to be sung with alleluia, and there is no kneeling.

---

18. 'In the long nights' refers to winter, when the monks might go back to bed after nocturns (33:9). Although it may seem strange that in the same dormitory some brothers slept while others read aloud, this practice is attested to by canon 14 of the Second Council of Tours (567). See RB 48:5.

[2]Furthermore, from the Nativity of the Lord to Epiphany all the antiphons and responsories, in both daytime and night-time, are to be sung with alleluia, and during that time there is no kneeling, [3]nor is there either fast or abstinence. [4]But during the eight days preceding the Nativity of the Lord let the brothers, fasting and abstaining as in Lent, [5]similarly make official use of those prayers, unchanged, which are customary in Lent. [6]Thus, in the spirit of Lenten sorrow, as servants seeking reconciliation who give more service than daily duty requires, [7]let us then rejoice when the Nativity of our Lord has come with its rewards and gifts of gladness.

[8]At Epiphany, however, all the antiphons and responsories are to be sung with alleluia only in the night of its vigil and on the day itself—[9]and from that day onward the alleluia is to be locked up and the decoration of feast days immediately removed from the oratory—[10]and on Epiphany day itself there is no kneeling. [11]Now, we have said that alleluia is to be sung only on the day itself with its Vigils, and not until its octave, because as of that day the hundred days devoted to fasting and abstinence before Easter begin.

[12]But on all Sundays, after the blessings have been said, all the antiphons and responsories are to be said with alleluia until the following nocturns of Monday, [13]and there is no kneeling, because Sunday is reckoned as the paschal resurrection. [14]Furthermore, every Sunday from the saying of the blessings to the end of Mass in the church, let this verse always be said at the Work of God: 'The saints will exult in glory, they will rejoice upon their couches'. [15]In other words, wherever any saints have their chambers, that is, churches, Mass is celebrated with exultation.

[16]Whenever the feastday of saints occurs, there is no kneeling from the saying of the blessings until the saying of Prime. [17]Moreover, if it is the feastday of the saint in whose oratory the psalmody is being sung, there is no kneeling from the saying of the blessings until the procession for the Mass to be celebrated there that day by a priest and, [18]out of joy on his

14. Ps 149:5
15. An allusion to relics kept in the churches.
17. 'By a priest' seems to mean not the abbot (83:9) or a member of the community (77), but a guest (83) or a priest summoned from outside.

own oratory's festival, everything that whole day until the following Nocturns is to be sung with alleluia as on Sundays.

Question of the disciples:

XLVI. Intoning the psalms in the oratory at all times.

The Lord has replied through the master:

[1]After the abbot and by his order the deans in turn intone the antiphons, always in the sequence of the psalter, as we have said. [2]After the deans have had their turn, each of the brothers of every deanery does the intoning as ordered by the abbot when he is present.

[3]The deans in turn always say the lessons from the apostle. The abbot, if he is present, [4]always says the lessons from the gospel; if he is absent, the deans in turn do so. [5]Both at Matins and at Vespers, after the lesson from the apostle has been recited, the abbot always, if he is present, follows with the gospel, or the deans in turn if he is absent. [6]Thus, in the order in which Mass is celebrated by the clergy, that is, after a lower-ranking cleric has read the apostle, a deacon, higher in rank, follows with the reading of the holy gospel, [7]so too in monasteries there is compliance with the Lord's system of sequence in the order of dignity.

[8]At the nocturns and Matins and Vespers the responsorial psalms are said in full. [9]At Prime, Terce, Sext and None, however, two responsorial sections apiece are said, and then the doxology is said, [10]so that the brethren may leave the oratory more quickly and go back to the tasks they have to do.

Question of the disciples:

XLVII. The manner of chanting the psalms.

The Lord has replied through the master:

[1]So great must be the reverential seriousness and the manner of chanting the psalms that the Lord listens more lovingly than we say them; [2]as Scripture declares: 'You take delight in

2. Ps 65:8

the coming of the morning, and in the evening', [3]and again: 'Sing the psalms to him joyfully and skillfully, for direct is the word of the Lord', [4]and again: 'Exult in him with fear', [5]and again, 'Sing to the Lord wisely'. [6]Therefore if it commands the singing of psalms to be done wisely and with fear, the person singing them should stand with body motionless and head bowed, and should sing praises to the Lord with composure, [7]since he is indeed performing his service before the Godhead, [8]as the prophet teaches when he says: 'In the presence of the angels I will sing your praise'.

[9]So the singer of psalms must always be careful not to let his attention wander elsewhere, [10]lest God say to us when our mind has strayed to some other thought: 'This people honors me only with lip-service, while their hearts are far from me', [11]and lest it likewise be said of us: 'With their mouth they blessed and in their heart they cursed', [12]and lest when we praise God with the tongue alone, we admit God only to the doorway of our mouth while we bring in and lodge the devil in the dwelling of our heart. [13]For he who goes inside is held in higher esteem by the one who brought him in than is he who is left waiting outside. [14]Therefore for a duty so great and so important the heart should be in consonance with the tongue, in order to render with fear what is due to the Lord every day. [15]And in his heart let the singer of psalms pay attention to each and every verse he says, because if each verse is noted the soul derives profit for salvation [16]and therein finds all it seeks, for 'the psalm says everything for edification''; [17]as the prophet declares: 'I shall sing and understand in the way of integrity, when you come to me'. [18]Let him who resounds in the voice also be in the mind of the singer. [19]Let us therefore sing with voice and mind in unison;

3. Ps 33:3-4
4. Ps 2:11
5. Ps 47:7
8. Ps 138:1
10. Mt 15:8
11. Ps 62:4
16. 1 Cor 14:3, 26
17. Ps 101:2
19. 1 Cor 14:15

as the apostle says: 'I will sing with the spirit, but I will sing with the understanding also'. [20]We must cry out to God not only with our voices, but with our heart as well.

[21]Furthermore, care must be taken while singing that there is not a lot of frequent coughing or prolonged gasping or constant spitting out of saliva; [22]nor should the singer dispose in front of him of filth extracted from the nose, but the brother should get rid of it behind his back, [23]for the angels are instructed to stand before the singers of psalms, as the prophet says: 'In the presence of the angels I will sing your praise'. [24]Therefore when these distractions are presented to the singers by the devil, let him who is singing immediately trace the sign of the cross on his mouth.

Question of the disciples:

XLVIII. REVERENCE IN PRAYER.

The Lord has replied through the master:

[1]If to men in the flesh a petition is made with humility only when we ask them for some temporal favor, [2]how much more should we plead with Christ about our sins and crimes by praying as much as we can. [3]Therefore there must be no duplicity in prayer. [4]Let one person not be found in the mouth, yet another in the heart. [5]Prayer must not be protracted by an abundance of words; as the holy gospel says, those who do this become hypocrites.

[6]There should not be a great deal of frequent coughing or constant spitting or gasping, because the devil uses all these as a hindrance to prayers and psalms. [7]For what we have said above should be avoided also during the prayers, namely, if the one praying wishes to spit or dispose of filth from his nose, he should get rid of it not in front of him but behind him, because of the angels standing in front, [8]as the prophet indicates when he says: 'In the presence of the angels I will sing your praise; I will worship at your holy temple'. [9]So you

23. Ps 138:1
5. Mt 6:5–7, 23:14
8. Ps 138:1–2

see how evident it is that we pray and sing psalms in the presence of the angels.

[10]Now, the reason we have said that the prayer should be short is to avoid falling asleep because the prayer is drawn out, [11]or the devil might set various images before the eyes of those lying prostrate for a long time or insinuate something else into their heart. [12]So it is right and proper to pray suppliantly with fear, in such a way that he who is praying seems to be embracing the feet of Christ who is present. [13]And we must pray with a fear so great that we are conscious of speaking with God. [14]Therefore we must pray with full attention, as the apostle says: 'I will pray with both the mind and the spirit'.

Question of the disciples:

XLIX. THE NIGHT OFFICE OF THE MONASTERY.

The Lord has replied through the master:

[1]Every Saturday, in the monastery, Vigils are to be celebrated from evening until the second cockcrow is heard, with Matins then following. [2]The very name Vigils means that the brethren refrain from sleep, singing psalms and listening to those reading the lessons. [3]Then after Matins they take repose in their beds.

Question of the disciples:

L. DAILY LABOR AT VARIOUS TIMES ACCORDING TO THE SEASON.

The Lord has replied through the master:

[1]After the Divine Office has ceased during the day, we do not want these intervals when the psalmody of the Hours is suspended to be spent idly, [2]lest short-time idleness produce no long-term profit, because an idle man produces death and

11. Cf. Cassian, *Inst.* 2
12. Mt 28:9
14. 1 Cor 14:15
2. Pr 13:4 (LXX)

is always craving something. ³For while a brother is engaged in some task he fixes his eyes on his work and thereby occupies his attention with what he is doing ⁴and has no time to think about anything else, and is not submerged in a flood of desires. ⁵Absentmindedness does not bring blankness to his eyes when hand and attention are occupied doing something. ⁶Moreover, the apostle says: 'We gave you a rule when we were with you: that anyone who will not work, shall not eat'. ⁷Therefore after Divine Office there must be physical, that is, manual, labor so that when there is something to give to the poor good will be added to good works.

⁸Therefore various activities must fill in the periods between the several Hours, as follows: ⁹In winter from the winter equinox, which is 24 September, until Easter, because it is cold and the brothers cannot do any work in the morning, ¹⁰they are to devote the time from Prime to Terce to reading, with the various deaneries in places separated from one another to avoid having the entire community crowded together and disturbing one another with their voices; let one of the ten in each place do the reading while the rest of his group listen. ¹²During these three hours the boys, in their deanery, are to learn letters on their tablets from someone who is literate. ¹³Moreover, we also exhort illiterate adults up to the age of fifty to learn letters. ¹⁴Again, we wish it kept in mind that during these same periods the psalms are to be studied by those who do not know them, directed by the deans in their respective deanery. ¹⁵So during these three hours they are to read and listen to one another, and take turns teaching letters and the psalms to those who do not know them. ¹⁶Then after having spent the three hours in this work of the spirit and put away the tablets and books, let them rise for the divine praises at Terce, ¹⁷giving thanks to the Lord in the oratory for having been entitled to spend three hours of the day occupied in spiritual labors free from sin.

¹⁸As soon as they have come out from Terce, all the deans are to address themselves to the abbot, asking him what work he orders their deaneries to do. ¹⁹And when he has assigned

6. 2 Thes 3:10

its respective work to each deanery let them, obeying immediately and directly by their deans, do their assigned task, always in silence, [20]seeing to it that they pray before they begin to work and again after they have finished. [21]They are to work with their deans always present. [22]And when they have, with due decorum, completed these further three hours in silent labor, let them hasten to the divine praises at Sext, [23]giving thanks to the Lord in the oratory for having been entitled again to spend another three hours of the day occupied in silent labor free from sin.

[24]Now, the reason we say that the brethren must always observe silence is that sins of the tongue are not committed when the mouth is at all times kept from speaking. However, the brothers while working are to keep silence as follows: [25]They must refrain from uncontrolled chattering and from worldly matters and from idle words which are out of place. [26]But the brothers may have permission at any time, provided the abbot is not present, to rehearse the psalms and to repeat the Scriptures and to speak about God, if it is done humbly and quietly.

[27]Then as soon as they have come out from Sext they are to return to their places and finish their work. [28]And always when the number of brothers engaged in this work is rather large, let one who is literate read aloud from some book every day, and this provision must by made for the workers at all times in both seasons. [29]We have prescribed this reading to the workers every day so that while keeping silence about what is evil and listening to and speaking about what is good we may never sin. [30]And let the reading be done by a brother who the abbot knows cannot work because of some unavoidable impediment. [31]Furthermore, [if] this rather large group of brothers being read to is near the monastery, let the brothers engaged within the monastery in some handicraft which they can take along if they go to the readers, promptly join them [32]and listen with their ears even though working with their hands. [33]But if the workshop is in a set place or the work is such that the brothers cannot take it along if they go to the readers, let there also be reading for them the next day.

25. Cf. Eph 5:4, Mt 12:36

[34]Then when they have passed these further three hours in manual labor, let them hasten to the divine praises at None, [35]giving thanks to the Lord in the oratory for having been entitled again to spend another three hours of the day free from sin.

[36]After None, for whatever time remains until Vespers, let everyone do what work there happens to be, as the abbot orders and their deans direct. [37]The deans are to keep watch over the brothers at all times so that no brother is completely idle. [38]For when he is occupied in doing something he has no time to think of anything except what he is intent upon doing with his hands.

[39]In summer however, that is, from Easter to the winter equinox, which is 24 September, because it is cooler in the morning, [40]let them work instead from Prime to Terce in order to rid themselves of the fresh sleep, both pleasant and oppressive, of the short nights.

[41]After saying Terce let them again work until Sext, [42]but always keeping silent about worldly and useless matters and buffoonery, which have nothing to do with edification. [43]We do however grant the disciples permission for review and rehearsal of the psalms, and inquiry about divine precepts, and remarks about God for edification at any time, provided the abbot is not present. [44]But when he is present, work, humility, silence, and reverence are to prevail. [45]But when the abbot is absent, we permit them to speak of good and holy things so they never forget that custody of their mouth must be kept for the sake of serving God [46]and that what they say should deal with good rather than with evil.

[47]Furthermore, when they set about this work, whether it is work in the fields or some handicraft, let them begin with prayer beforehand and likewise always finish with prayer. [48]The purpose of their beginning with prayer beforehand is to ask God to be supported by his loving assistance [49]and at all times made secure by his protection during the hours when they are working, so that there may steal up on them no kind of sin whereby they could displease the Lord. [50]And they are to pray again after quitting work, in order to give thanks to God for having been supported by God's help. [51]So after working for these three hours let them hasten to the divine

praises at Terce, ⁵²giving thanks to the Lord in the oratory for
having been entitled to spend time occupied in manual labor
free from the offense of sins.

⁵³As soon as they have come out from Terce, let each one
return to his task, ⁵⁴and after having worked again during the
subsequent hours, let them hasten to the divine praises at
Sext, ⁵⁵giving thanks to the Lord in the oratory for having
been entitled to spend another three hours of the day again
occupied in manual labor free from sin.

⁵⁶Immediately after Sext has been said, whether it is after
dinner or during a fast, let everyone take a moderately long
nap on his bed. ⁵⁷Thus they will sleep through the midday
period and the burning heat, ⁵⁸and for their bodies fatigued
by fasting and labor the supplement of sleep at noontime will
compensate for the shortness of the nights in this season,
⁵⁹and the brother will then be alert when he rises during the
night in summertime since he has had some sleep during the
day. ⁶⁰So then, after lying on their beds following Sext and
having had a moderate rest, all the brothers are to be awak-
ened by their deans, and the deans themselves by the
'vigilant cock' of the week, and return again, ⁶¹for whatever
time remains until None, to their handicrafts and work, re-
fraining from idle talk.

⁶²And throughout this summer season, whether the meal is
at the sixth hour or at the ninth, for whatever time remains
after None until time for Vespers to begin, ⁶³the various
deaneries having been separated from one another in different places, ⁶⁴some as directed by their deans are to read,
others listen, others learn and teach letters, others study
psalms which they have transcribed. ⁶⁵When they have mastered and memorized them perfectly, let their deans take
them to the abbot to recite by heart the psalm or canticle or
lesson of any kind. ⁶⁶And as soon as he has recited it in its
entirety, let him ask prayers for himself. ⁶⁷Then when those
present have prayed for him, the abbot concludes and the one
who has done the reciting kisses the abbot's knees. ⁶⁸Either
the abbot or the deans immediately order something new to
be transcribed, ⁶⁹and after anything has been transcribed,

60. See 31:12

before he studies it, let him again ask those present to pray for him; and in this way the learning of it is to be undertaken.

⁷⁰At all times, but especially in summer, let Vespers begin somewhat early, while the sun is still above the horizon, for the prophet says: 'Until the setting', but did not say 'after the setting'. ⁷¹Hence we have said that Vespers should begin somewhat early especially in summer because of the short nights during that season.

⁷²Field work and missions requiring travel should be considered the province of those brothers who are not skilled in the arts and have neither the desire nor the ability to learn them. ⁷³The skilled craftsmen, on the other hand, are to stay at their respective craft every day, having their daily quota of work assigned and checked. ⁷⁴Should there be any urgent need for field work or travel in the interests of the monastery, however, they are to leave the crafts behind and occupy themselves in helping the brothers or in going on necessary trips.

⁷⁵Delicate and weak brothers should be assigned such work as will nourish them for the service of God, not kill them. ⁷⁶As to the hard of heart, as also the simple brothers and those who have neither the desire nor the ability to learn letters, let them be kept tied down by rough labor, ⁷⁷but in a measure consonant with justice lest they be the only ones continually oppressed by various kinds of work. ⁷⁸Little children, those already worn out by old age, and the sick are to be classed together and given equal consideration.

Question of the disciples:

HERE BEGINS THE RULE FOR LENT

LI. LENTEN PRAYERS DURING THE DAY.

The Lord has replied through the master:

¹Between Matins and Prime let simple prayer be said by all. ²Between Prime and Terce the same is to be done, likewise

---

70. Ps 113:3
1. Simple prayer (*pura oratio*): not preceded by a psalm as at the Divine Office.

between Terce and Sext, likewise between Sext and None, likewise between None and Vespers, ³likewise between Vespers and Compline, and this must be done throughout the days of Lent.

Questions of the disciples:

LII. PRAYERS WITHOUT PSALMS DURING THE NIGHT.

The Lord has replied through the master:

¹After the first period of sleep all are to rise and pray at their beds, the abbot concludes, and all lie down again. ²Likewise after the nocturns they go back to bed and, when the cock has crowed, all again rise and pray at their beds, the abbot concludes, and all lie down again. ³Hence the 'vigilant cocks' must be very vigilant during the nights and days of Lent, and during the day be careful to let the brethren know when the times for prayer have come. ⁴The reason all should sleep in the same room is so that all together may say these prayers in full at their beds and all hear the abbot conclude. ⁵Again they must rise and celebrate Matins because before Easter the recitation of Matins is still separated from the nocturns. ⁶Similarly there is to be simple prayer again between Matins and Prime.

Question of the disciples:

LIII. ABSTINENCE FROM FOOD AND DRINK DURING LENT.

The Lord has replied through the master:

¹Let one dish of cooked food suffice for all, and a second of whatever uncooked food is available, with fruit, and two pieces of barley bread. ²From the beginning of the forty-day period to that of thirty days the brethren are to receive, because of the work, two drinks apiece per day, not more, namely, one of unmixed wine and one of the warm beverage. ³From the thirty-day period to that of twenty days they are to receive only the unmixed wine. ⁴From the twenty-day period until Easter, however, the wine is to be withdrawn from everyone except the sick, children below the age of twelve,

and those worn out by old age. [5]But as regards the sick, let the abbot see to it that no one is lying and pretending to be sick. [6]For those who are well and those who abstain of their own accord, let a mixture of warm water and salt, with cumin and parsley seed, be prepared. [7]Oil is to be put not into the cooking pots but into the dishes, out of consideration for those who are abstaining. [8]Let these abstainers, nevertheless remaining at the table of their deanery, be directed to sit together, as many as there may be of their group at each table, as arranged by the superior, so that the abstainers at the same table may take their food from the one bowl. [9]Now, we have said that the abstainers are to sit together among the other brethren so that the voracious, though sharing the same nature, may blush for not being able in like manner to restrain the cravings of their appetite [10]and for being incapable of deserving divine grace along with the abstainers by choosing what is good.

[11]At the start of Lent, when they receive Communion after the first day of fasting, before Communion let permission be given by the abbot in the oratory as follows; [12]let the abbot say to all: 'Brothers, to him who wishes to engage in spiritual labor for his soul and abstain from something, we grant freedom of choice for this good work. [13]Let him, who does not so wish, however, accept what is prescribed by this chapter of the rule and be content with its measures for Lent'. [14]Then let those of the brothers who wish to abstain from something go and humbly kneel before the abbot there in the oratory, giving thanks for the granting of their desire to do good. [15]And after this manifestation of humility let them indicate to the abbot also by word of mouth what each one wishes to abstain from.

[16]Now, we have said that the abstainers are to be designated in the oratory so that when at table they are keeping this resolve to deny food to the body during Lent [17]they may not be persuaded by luke-warm and gluttonous brethren to go back on it again and eat with them, since no one wants to see anyone better than himself. [18]For this reason, then, let

18. The oratory was personified (cf. 44:16, 61:14) and associated with God, whom it symbolized.

such as these, with the oratory as witness, be as one chosen from among all in the sight of God and marked out as abstainers. [19]Moreover, it is right and proper that at Easter such as these should rejoice with Christ in the Lord's resurrection, for together with him they have crucified their body by abstinence during Lent, [20]as Scripture says concerning sorrow: 'Those that sow in tears shall reap in joy', [21]and 'Slight was their affliction, great will their blessings be'. [22]Lent is regarded as the symbol of this present short-lived world, whereas Easter proclaims, for the good, the eternal joy of the future life in that during the forty days there is abstinence from what may be eaten throughout the year. [24]Thus he who in the present life of this world denies something to his desires and the flesh will be free in the other world to let his soul feast abundantly and forever on the greater divine delights. [25]Because in this short time he chose to be distressed for the sake of the Lord, he will deserve to rejoice with him in the future.

[26]Then on Holy Thursday they are to tonsure their heads and wash themselves, and let them be given all they abstained from except the flesh and blood of land animals. [27]As to eating the flesh of birds, winged land animals and quadrupeds, let the abbot tell the brethren that it is good to want to eat it, but advise them that it is better to abstain. [28]Then let each one, depending on the grace proportionate to his faith, which he has deserved from God to find in his soul, choose whether he should eat or rather abstain. [29]Accordingly, after this announcement on Holy Thursday let the brethren, having been asked, declare by word of mouth what they wish and what they do not, [30]and let each one be

20. Ps 126:5
21. Wis 3:5
23. By 'abstinence from what may be eaten throughout the year' was meant the usual fare restricted during Lent, not meat, which was authorized only for Easter and Christmastimes (53:1–7,31).
26. In accordance with ancient tradition, RM considers the last three days of Holy Week as a separate period from Lent. But despite the concession made in this paragraph, Holy Thursday was still a fast day.
27. Eating meat was traditionally a test of orthodoxy against gnosticism.
28. Rm 12:3

granted freedom of choice because of the festive character of these days. If the abbot so please, let him set this norm for them about eating: [31]from Easter to Pentecost and from Christmas to Epiphany the eating of meat is allowed by free choice. [32]Nevertheless, let those brethren of a deanery who are going to eat meat be seated beside one another at their own tables, and let the specially cooked meat courses be brought to them in separate dishes, [33]lest the purity of the abstainers seem to be sullied, and in order that the eaters may notice how great the distance is between them, those who cater to their desires and those who master their stomach.

[34]But during Lent the fasting is to continue until evening, that is, the meal is taken after Vespers on all these forty days, with the exception of Sundays, because there is fasting on Thursday too. [35]On these Sundays they are to take no supper at all in the evening, so that there may be only one meal each day during that period. [36]Furthermore, the home brethren may not break the fast during Lent because of a visitor, [37]but only the visitor himself may be permitted to violate the time of fasting if he is known to be making a long journey.

[38]If any brothers wish to fast completely, they are not to be considered for work with the brothers on the day of their total fast. [39]Let them merely read to the brothers who are working so that they are not idle and may be nourished by the word of God instead of bread. [40]The reason they should engage in spiritual labor by reading is that, just as it is written: 'If any man will not work, let him not eat', so also it is right that he should not work who eats [41]only at that meal where he is nourished without bread, that is, at God's word. As Scripture says: 'Not by bread alone does man live, but by every word of God'.

[42]During these forty days the weekly servers do not wash the feet of the members of the monastery but only remove their shoes. [43]The feet of any visiting outsiders are to be

---

40. 2 Th 3:10
41. God's word (*eloquio dei*) cannot mean Holy Scripture here since the same terms were also used by the Master to refer to refectory reading, which was ordinarily not sacred scripture but the Rule (24:5,15).
41. Lk 4:4

washed because of the account of the woman who washed
the Saviour's feet while he was at supper and anointed them
from the alabaster jar. [44]But on Holy Thursday, in place of the
blessing, they take in hand the washing of the abbot's feet,
and afterwards the abbot, with the help of the brothers,
washes those of all the deans, but he himself starts it off.
[45]Furthermore the superior himself washes the feet of the
porters. When by this kindness he proves himself humble
toward them too, he will be judged worthy of higher honor
than all others. [46]Then the deans wash and dry the feet of all
the brothers in their deanery.

[47]At dawn on the Friday before Holy Saturday only the
nocturns are celebrated, since the nocturns are said before
cockcrow and still belong to Thursday, [48]and thereafter [no]
Matins and other Hours and regular Divine Office [will be
celebrated] until the Mass on Saturday [49]when the new alleluia of the joyful resurrection will, in the mouth of the
psalm-singers, break open the long silence clamped on the
psalms. [50]So while they sing no psalms from after the saying
of the nocturns on Thursday until Mass on Saturday, let them
nevertheless say in full the simple prayers of Lent, [51] and
during the day on Friday speak quietly to themselves about
the sorrow of the Lord's passion, not greeting one another
when they meet.

[52]Other than the sick and the children and those overcome
by old age, if any of the healthy want to eat, let them have
their meal without receiving a blessing and without a sign of
the cross over the food, so that, [53]partaking in gluttony by
themselves, they may blush for not being able to get through
one day of voluntary fasting with the others who are keeping
a total fast in the hope of divine reward, [54]when the exigency
of poverty sometimes demands that other people spend three
days in involuntary fasting. [55]And what front will he put up
when, during the coming octave of Easter, he wants to feast
because of the victory of the Lord's resurrection, yet did not

45. Cf. 95:14–16
50. The suspension of the Divine Office on Holy Thursday and Good Friday
conforms with ancient roman custom (Ordo Rom. XII, 17), which does however prescribe Nocturns and Matins. Nocturns on Thursday were actually
those of Friday, as the opening line of this paragraph states.

want to crucify his flesh with Christ a single day because of grief at his passion? [56]The sacrament of the altar, kept in the large glass vessel, is to be consumed in its entirety, so that when the Jews seek Christ on Friday to inflict his passion on him he will be hidden away in our souls that day, [57]and on Saturday will appear to us by his resurrection in a new Sacrament. [58]Accordingly, let those who are going to take a meal on Friday do so without Communion, to make it evident how wrong it is to have a meal without Christ.

[59]On this same day let provision be made for washing things and preparing for Easter. [60]On this Friday, too, the altar veil and all the oratory ornamentation are to be removed, [61]and at the same time the lights and lamps within the monastery are to be taken out of sight, [62]so that sorrow may have full possession of us on that day when the true light of the Lord, through his passion, departs from the present order of things; [63]and at dawn the following Saturday everything is restored to order in joy when the light of joy, through the resurrection of Christ, returns to us. [64]In general, the monastery should always be so well-appointed and clean that when viewed from all the entrances, themselves neatly kept and adorned with hangings, [65]it may everywhere have the appearance of a church, and thus no matter where any gathering occurs it will be in a place suitable and pleasant where prayer gives delight.

HERE ENDS THE RULE FOR LENT

LIV. WHEN IT IS TIME FOR THE DIVINE OFFICE, THE BRETHREN MUST HURRY TO THE ORATORY.

[1]When the signal struck in the oratory indicates that the time for Divine Office has come, let the workers immediately drop their work, the artificers lay aside their tools, and the copyists not finish their letter. [2]The hand of each brother must relinquish what it was doing. The foot must straightway, with gravity, hasten to the oratory and attention be directed to God, so that they may assemble without delay for the first prayer. [3]Like bees going for honey, let the brethren swarm into the oratory [4]in such a way that the holy oratory

which until then was a place of silence is suddenly filled with the sound of the psalms, and the silence of the holy place moves to the deserted shops and tasks.

⁵Moreover, whenever the signal is struck in the oratory, let all who hear it, make the sign of the cross on their forehead immediately, before hurrying off, and say in response: 'Thanks be to God'.

Question of the disciples:

LV. WHAT IS THE DISTANCE DETERMINING WHETHER A BROTHER MUST LEAVE HIS WORK AND GO TO THE ORATORY?

The Lord has replied through the master:

¹As soon as the signal struck by the abbot has sounded, let the brother who is working, whether alone or with others, let go of his iron tool and by a quick visual calculation determine whether or not he should hasten to the oratory. ²At a distance of fifty paces from the entrance of the monastery, his decision must be to hurry with gravity to the oratory. ³But if the place is at a greater distance than this, then they do not go; ⁴but having dropped the iron tool from their hands and bending their neck as the knees do in the oratory, they too recite the Work of God quietly by themselves there where they are.

⁵In case a brother must get some urgent work done, he may privately say the psalms in groups of three, but including their *Glory be,* ⁶because these doxologies said between them take the place of the prayers; and these doxologies should always be said with bowed head by the one saying the psalm. ⁷Moreover, he may say the psalms straight through because of the urgent work, as we have said above. ⁸After these together with the verse and the prayer are finished, he himself takes care of the conclusion and then promptly resumes what he was doing.

⁹We have said that if a brother is working in a place more than fifty paces away he should then not go to the oratory ¹⁰because otherwise the brothers running too quickly from a distance might make a speed contest out of it and run not

2. roughly 80 yards (74 meters)

with stateliness but for sport. [11]And entering the oratory late, out of breath from a long stretch, chest heaving after their trip, they would not have the strength to give voice to the psalms. [12]Again, someone might arrive from a distance, tired as he would be, only to find the Work of God already finished by the brothers who were present, [13]and then the spiritual brother would feel disheartened and personally hurt and profoundly saddened that it was not granted him to perform the Work of God either in the field or in the oratory, [14]and it would be the distance that caused him the loss of a canonical Hour.

[15]Let those inside the monastery, however, who are busy with what is urgently required for the service of the community, [16]ask aloud, when the psalmody ceases and there is prostration for prayer, to be kept in mind in the oratory. [17]Even so, let them perform the Work of God quietly to themselves right there where they are occupied, following along with the voices in the oratory. [18]Furthermore, wherever they are sitting or standing, let them bend their knees for the prayers at the completion of each of the psalms.

Question of the disciples:

LVI. How brothers on a journey are to perform the Work of God.

The Lord has replied through the master:

[1]When spiritual brothers are out travelling and no secular person is with them, let them draw together, go off the road a little way and kneel down, then after prayer return to the road. [2]Suppressing now, out of reverence for the Work of God, every word having nothing to do with God, and walking along thus, they proceed with the recitation of the psalm after a blessing has been asked. [3]When finished they make a short halt and pray briefly with head bowed. [4]After finishing

---

1. The brothers were to go off the road to pray with bowed head, i.e. without genuflection on the road itself because of the muddiness of the road or the ridicule of passers-by. The Master was concerned lest secular persons (*laici*) ridicule monastic rites (cf. 24:20–2, 58:5, 95:21).

this prayer, they start off again walking on the road, with a psalm. [5]This finished, they again stand still and pray. [6]When this prayer in turn is finished, as before they again take up a psalm while walking. [7]This finished, they again pray, bowing in humility. [8]When they have completed all that is customary for this particular Hour in this way, they go aside a little way and pray now on bended knee, themselves taking care of the conclusion alternately. [9]Only then do they return to the road and thereafter may engage in ordinary conversation if they wish. [10]But during the time they are performing the Work of God as they walk along, while engaged in the divine duty, let them take care not to mix into it any talk among themselves.

[11]If they are travelling in the company of seculars, however, they should withdraw from them to a place in the brush or, if the area is open, offering them no shelter, let them lag behind a bit. [12]Then on bended knee they say sections of three psalms and right after finish with a single *Glory be.* [13]Then they say the verse and after the verse they pray briefly, conclude, rise, and follow after their travelling companions.

[14]Now, we have stated that the brothers should say no more than one section apiece of three psalms together with a single *Glory be* because [15]otherwise their secular companions, caring nothing about what concerns God, might continue on their way and the spiritual brothers find the crossroads deserted, and perhaps not knowing the way the brothers might be separated from them by taking the wrong road. [16]And afterwards bitter sorrow might take hold of their soul and they would perhaps regret having tarried for the good of their soul. [17]So when the brothers leave the monastery they must be instructed by the abbot or by their deans to perform the Office in this way.

[18]On a cloudy day, when the sun hides its rays from earth, let the brothers, whether in the monastery or on the road or in the field, estimate elapsed time by careful calculation of the hours, [19]and no matter what time it may be, the usual Office is to be said. [20]And whether the regular Hour of the Office is said before or after the exact time, in no case may the Work of God be left out but it is to be performed, [21]because the lack of light caused by the clouds, with the sundial blind because of the sun's absence, serves as to excuse those who are performing the Office.

Question of the disciples:

LVII. How will brethren on a journey observe certain points of the rule?

The Lord has replied through the master:

[1]If a brother is sent out on monastery business in the morning and, because of the demands of the trip, does no reading between Prime and Terce in winter, or between None and Vespers in summer, [2]and returns to the monastery the same day, let him take his meal at whatever time he gets back, and let him do at least a little reading or memorizing, [3]to show that he is observing the rule that day too.

[4]But if he is sent on a longer journey, let him take with him from the monastery a small book containing some readings, [5]so that he can do at least a little reading whenever he takes a rest along the way. [6]But only if he knows the psalter.

[7]If he does not, let him take along tablets on which psalms have been transcribed by the superior, [8]so that when he stops to have his meal or take up lodging he may, insofar as he has opportunity, do at least a little memorizing, [9]in order to give the rule its due each day. [10]In like manner let a brother who is still learning letters take along from the monastery some tablets with transcriptions made by the superior. [11]Then if he is travelling with someone who is literate, when he stops for a meal or lodging he may, insofar as he has opportunity, do at least a little memorizing with the other's help. [12]Or if he is travelling alone he may practise by himself at least a little either at his meal or at his lodging, as we have said above, [13]to show that he is observing the customary rule every day.

[14]As for a brother who either does not want to go out on monastery business, or who would indeed go but murmurs about it and wants to delay his departure a while, let him now, [15]if the abbot so please, not be sent out. Furthermore, let him be immediately punished with excommunication, [16]and let him know that by clinging to pride he is rejecting a

---

2. Memorizing the lessons to be recited by heart during the Divine Office (44:9–11, cf. 50:65).
10. Learning to read was obligatory only for the children (50:12–13), but even they might be sent outside (59:10–11).
16. Lk 10:16

divine command—divine, because the Lord says to our teachers: 'Anyone who rejects you rejects me'.

[17]When brothers are on a journey, however, and come to where they will lodge, they should select to make their bed a place that is secluded and clean, [18]where during the night they may, on their bed, worthily and quietly commemorate the Lord to themselves.

[19]Furthermore, the brothers leaving on a journey are to receive from the abbot or the deans the instructions which follow. [20]Whenever they visit spiritual brothers at their place of residence, upon entering their cells or oratories let them, praying, say this verse: 'We have entered his dwelling, we have worshipped in the place where his feet have stood'. [21]Likewise when leaving there let them, praying, always say this verse: 'Make your ways known to me, O Lord, and teach me your paths. Lead me in your truth', [22]or perhaps this other verse instead if they prefer to say it: 'Hold my steps in your paths so that my feet do not falter'. [23]Moreover when brothers of ours are about to leave the monasteries and cells of the spirituals they should first bid farewell to the oratory, and also say a special prayer with reference to their going forth into the outside world. [24]Then too our travellers, when departing from them, should ask all whom they are leaving behind in their monasteries and cells to remember them at the next Work of God. And so let them be on their way.

[25]Again, when our brothers enter churches, after praying bowed down in humility before God, [26]let them stand erect and say this verse: 'The saints will exult in glory, they will rejoice on their couches', [27]saying it quietly, and after bowing and praying briefly they make their own conclusion, and then go forth into the outside world.

20. Ps 132:7
21. Ps 25:4–5
22. Ps 17:5
26. Ps 149:5

Question of the disciples:

LVIII. How many psalms are brothers on a journey to say at night in the various seasons?

The Lord has replied through the master:

[1]When they get out of bed at night to say the nocturns—whether the brother is alone or with another—[2]after the verse releasing from silence and then the first responsory, they are to say three psalms, then another responsory, then the lessons and the verse. [3]No more than that, because of the hardships of the travelling already done and still to come.

[4]Moreover, while on a journey at any time of year they are to continue with Matins immediately after finishing the nocturns. [5]Otherwise the light of morning may come upon them, and in the presence of seculars sitting there or more than likely making fun of our way of life, it may seem that the Office is being said without reverence in squalid, improper and filthy places at a hut or hostel. [6]Hence in the morning the brothers, now that they are free of concern about Matins already said, may start right off thinking only about getting under way, [7]and be concerned about putting together the animals' loads and packing the contents of their pouches.

Question of the disciples:

LIX. At what time brethren on a journey are to eat.

The Lord has replied through the master:

[1]Brothers who are making a long journey on a Wednesday, a Friday or a Saturday in winter, that is, from the winter equinox, which is 24 September, until Easter, [2]these travelling brothers are to take their meal in the evening and may not break this fast for any reason. [3]Now, we have specified the evening so that if they choose to take their meal at the ninth hour along the road, the lengthy stop, with hours already short occupied in eating, is a loss for them at the close of the short day. [4]Nevertheless they are to refrain from break-

---

3. 'No more than that' probably did not exclude the 'prayer to God' (44:8) or the final oration (55:8, 56:8-13).

ing this fast in winter only if they are not walking loaded with heavy packs on their backs.

⁵Furthermore, the abbot should have the travelling brothers take a meal if after very careful attention to considerations of time and necessity, whether in winter or summer, ⁶he has fears about the heavy frost of the plains or the burning heat of the roads or the precipitous heights of the mountains or the weight of the heavy packs, ⁷and has taken into account the weaknesses and incapacities of some brothers; ⁸in such case he should have them eat something before dispatching them from the monastery. ⁹So too he should send the brothers on their way warmed up in the severe cold of winter and refreshed in the heat of summer.

¹⁰Children below the age of twelve, however, must not only never fast while on a journey, but must not go outside the monastery fasting on any day, ¹¹unless they are sent out into the neighborhood and are expected back before Terce in summer or before Sext in winter, at which times they must, as prescribed, take their meal.

Question of the disciples:

LX. THE NUMBER OF PROVISIONS BROTHERS ARE TO RECEIVE FOR A JOURNEY.

The Lord has replied through the master:

¹Considering the daily ration due the brothers, as well as the length of the journey and the time required to do the business, ²while also taking into account the amount of the monastery's resources in money or in what can be taken uncooked, the abbot may add ⁴a little extra bread or wine as also other things and money, ³as much as he wishes, to the provisions sufficient for the normal ration, because of the hardship of the journey and even more for the sake of charity to someone perhaps joined as a road companion or partner.

Question of the disciples:

LXI. If a brother is sent from the monastery and is expected to return the same day, should he eat outside if someone urges him to do so, or should he keep fasting until he has returned to the oratory and receives Communion in the presence of the abbot?

The Lord has replied through the master:

¹A brother setting out from the monastery is to ask the abbot, saying: ²'What do you command, Lord Father? ³What if I should be kept at table, out of charity, by the one to whom I am being sent or by someone else, and he with an adjuration urges me to eat? ⁴Is the fast to be broken or not?'

⁵The abbot should reply, saying: 'If a spiritual brother, out of joy at your coming, invites you through charity to eat, provided it is with himself, ⁶refuse his first invitation, of course, if it is a Wednesday or a Friday or a Saturday, ⁷but then out of charity consent to his second invitation when it is repeated. ⁸On days other than these three weekdays, however, give your consent to the first such spiritual invitation to eat.

⁹'But if the invitation to share a meal is a secular one, we do not permit you to break the fast on Wednesday, Friday or Saturday. ¹⁰No matter how insistent the entreaties, refuse them, at least until an adjuration. ¹¹For should you be adjured by divine or holy things, then consent even on these three weekdays to show that you love the Lord, ¹²since you give your consent when adjured through him, and what for the sake of charity you willingly concede to the second invitation of a spiritual brother, you rightly accord, though unwillingly, to a layman when he adjures you by the divine name. ¹³But if on these three weekdays you are urged to break the fast without being adjured by the divine name, ¹⁴we do not permit the brothers to partake as guests of laymen, but let the oratory await your return to Communion.'

¹⁵If, however, the length of the trip is such that the brother will return in the evening but is nevertheless urged without

9. *saecularis*
12. *laicus*

adjuration by some lay person to break the fast on these three weekdays, as we have said, he may promise to take his meal, but at the ninth hour.

[16]Furthermore, if a brother is sent to a secular person who in all respects is already imitating the religious way of life, with the tonsure as yet the only discernible difference, [17]his urging may be given assent after the first invitation to take a meal on these three weekdays, as we have said, in consideration of his way of life and of charity.

[18]On other weekdays, however, if a brother sent out still needs considerable time for doing business with the one who is urging him to dine, the brother is permitted to eat either at the sixth or the ninth hour or in the evening, [19]so as not to bypass the regular hours for meals and outdo the ordinary norms of holy observance.

[20]But if there is no detainment and the brother is required to make the return trip the same day, let assent be given immediately to an invitation no matter when it may be urged upon such brothers while they are hurrying back, [21]for otherwise the regular mealtime may catch the brother still far away and without provisions from the monastery, [22]and when he returns late because of fatigue this brother may find no meal prepared for chance arrivals and the monastery meal already finished and cleared away, and on his return he would be doubly cheated. [23]Another reason why a brother hurrying along gives his consent to take a meal outside the regular time is to avoid grieving the heart of the host who is inviting him out of charity.

Question of the disciples:

LXII. WHETHER A BROTHER SHOULD EAT OR DRINK OTHER
THAN AT THE APPOINTED TIME.

The Lord has replied through the master:

[1]He may not eat any of his provisions ahead of the appointed hour, because these provisions were issued specifi-

---

18. The brother did not have the choice of eating meals at any of the three times, but had to conform to the hours prescribed for meals according to the day and the liturgical season (28).

cally and in the measure determined by the Rule. ²Therefore they are restricted to the hours set by the general regulations.

³If they are, however, importuned by some stranger to partake of provisions other than their own, the brothers may in charity consent because of fatigue from travelling, ⁴provided that before consenting they let the one urging them know that they have orders from Rule and abbot making it impossible for them to touch any of the monastery's holy provisions outside their due time. ⁵We have said that the well-instructed and spiritual brothers should make this disciplinary regulation known to their travelling companions who are ignorant of it ⁶because otherwise when they take nothing from their baskets to set out for the common meal at a wrong time, they will be thought to be doing this out of selfishness rather than discipline. ⁷But if those who are doing the urging counter this declaration of the brothers with the rejoinder that they are inviting them out of sheer good will toward them and for the sake of their company at the meal, in accordance with the charity enjoined by companionship in travel, and that, ⁸leaving their provisions intact, they want for charity's sake to use their own, ⁹then they may finally give in to them, and the discipline of keeping their provisions for the proper hour is nevertheless maintained. ¹⁰Then when the hour set in the trip's schedule arrives, it is our brothers who then properly take the initiative at the proper time and in their turn become the ones who do the inviting. ¹¹This time they set out some of their own provisions, and whereas those others anticipated the mealtime out of charity alone at the cost of propriety, these are now ministering both with reciprocated charity and with due regard for propriety, ¹²in such a way that what charity towards the former, who were unaware of what was proper, persuaded the latter to do, is for these latter a means of imparting their discipline to the former by making them aware of it.

¹³But if mealtime comes before the brothers have arrived at their destination, these brothers are to take their meal right

9. In ancient times the demands of hospitality were more stringent than they are now. It would have been unthinkable for some to eat while others did not. To refuse to partake would have been to oblige others to fast.

then and there, wherever the regular time catches them along the way, [14]lest it happen that when they arrive at their destination they get no invitation from the farmer to dine, [15]in which case the brother sent out would quite evidently miss his meal since the householder did not invite him to eat, [16]and afterwards he would be compelled by overpowering hunger to eat outside the proper time and at this irregular hour to desecrate the provisions given for a set time.

[17]Brethren on a journey are free before None to drink anything when they are thirsty.

Question of the disciples:

LXIII. OF WHAT KIND ARE THE BROTHERS WHO DEPART WITHOUT TAKING LEAVE OF THE BRETHREN.

The Lord has replied through the master:

[1]If spiritual brothers, while on a journey, separate without taking leave of one another and without offering prayer to the Lord together and without exchanging the sign of peace, [2]let them know that they are excommunicating themselves and are leaving charity behind until they meet again and tie anew the bond of mutual charity, [3]as is read in the Lives of the Fathers: a brother departed from the east, after arriving in the west and remembering that he had not taken leave of a brother, [4]because of this omission of charity retraced his steps in order to make up what he had failed to do in regard to the brother. [5]Wherefore the brethren must be concerned about this fraternal charity.

15. Meals might not be delayed any more than they might be anticipated!

Question of the disciples:

LXIV. HOW MANY TIMES SHOULD A BROTHER BE TAKEN BACK
WHO LEAVES THE MONASTERY AND THEN TURNS FROM HIS
ERROR?

The Lord has replied through the master:

[1]If a brother quits the monastery repeatedly, let him when
he returns be taken back up to three times, but then no more,
[2]because his fidelity to the divine service in the Lord's sight is
recognizable to the degree that the stability of his feet is discernible in men's sight. [3]And what need has the monastery
any longer of something that does not belong to God? [4]There-
fore after the third reproof let him be to the monastery, and
rightly so, 'as a heathen and a publican'.

Question of the disciples:

LXV. HOW SHOULD BROTHERS FROM ELSEWHERE BE GREETED BY
THOSE WHO BELONG TO THE COMMUNITY?

The Lord has replied through the master:

[1]When outside brothers chance to visit the monastery, [2]and
monastery brothers come to any place where these guests are
sitting or standing or lying or walking to and fro, [3]at the
moment of meeting let their voice first be heard giving the
greeting *Benedicite,* [4]then let them request prayer for themselves. [5]After the prayer the guest concludes, [6]and the community member with head bowed in humble salutation immediately goes to his knees, [7]and after this he rises to give the
other the sign of peace, [8]so as to put into practice the apostolic dictum which says: 'Anticipating one another with
honor'.

[9]Upon meeting outside brothers, after the prayer and before the conclusion, let the abbot say this verse with the
community members: 'We are receiving, O God, your mercies within your temple', with the *Glory be.*

---

4. Mt 18:17
8. Rm 12:10
9. Ps 48:9

Question of the disciples:

LXVI. DEPARTURE FROM THE MONASTERY BY BROTHERS WHO ARE GOING ON A JOURNEY.

The Lord has replied through the master:

¹When brothers leave to go on a journey, let them ask that prayer be offered for them then and there, ²saying the verse: 'Your ways, O Lord, make known to me and teach me your paths', ³or, if they wish, this other: 'Make my steps steadfast in your paths so that my feet do not falter'. ⁴Moreover, let them, whether they are leaving or returning, always conclude the verse with the *Glory be.*

⁵In like manner when they return let them ask that prayer be offered for them, ⁶saying this verse: 'We have entered his dwelling, we have worshipped in the place where his feet have stood' with the *Glory be.* ⁷And each time a brother, whether going or coming, crosses the outside threshold of the last portal of the monastery let him always ask, though without a verse, that prayer be offered for him.

LXVII. THE RETURN OF BROTHERS TO THE ORATORY AFTER HAVING BEEN ON A JOURNEY.

¹When brothers return to the monastery from a trip during any Hour of the Office and find the brothers at the psalmody in the oratory, ²let them say a prayer and immediately join in the psalmody with the others. ³Then let them too, after the psalm-singers have finished the psalm, voice the request that prayer be offered for them, ⁴so it may be seen that they are

---

1. 'Then and there' does not say where. At the door (66:7) or in the oratory (cf. 67, 57:23, RB 67:1)? This is not the prayer offered at each Hour for the absent (20:4).
2. Ps 25:4
3. Ps 17:5
6. Ps 132:7
4. During the Divine Office the gates were locked and the porters in choir (95:5), so brothers returning to the monastery no doubt entered by the oratory door, which was left open. Their request that prayer be offered (66:7) is directed to everyone in the oratory. At the gate this request would have been directed to the porters.

observing the rule about requesting prayer when they enter the outside threshold of the monastery's exterior portal. [5]And after the celebration of the sacred office in the oratory, let them receive first the abbot, then their deans and everyone for the sign of peace now that they have returned from their journey.

LXVIII. Immediately upon leaving the oratory they must keep complete silence.

[1]As soon as the brothers leave the oratory they are to keep silence [2]and not even repeat psalms as they come out, [3]lest what was said inside at the right time with reverence be sung over and over outside at the wrong time with disrespect. [4]Therefore let them keep quiet as soon as they leave the oratory, [5]because the time for the psalms is over with and that of silence has begun, [6]as Scripture says: 'A time for everything'.

LXIX. The sick brothers.

[1]Brothers who say they are ill and do not rise for the Work of God and stay lying down should not be called to task, [2]but for their meal let them receive only liquids and eggs or warm water, which the really sick can hardly get down, [3]so that if they are pretending, hunger at least will force them to get up.

[4]But if they rise after the [Work] of God let them be excommunicated [5]and not go to the body's meal because they were not present for that of the spirit in the oratory [6]and because they shirked the labor and despised the Work of God. [7]For in such as these it is evident that the devil is catering to the sloth of sleep under the pretext of sickness. [8]Let this therefore be the recompense they receive.

[9]Now, if a brother who is very tired, with aching limbs but no fever, does not want to incur the punishment of excom-

6. Eccl 3:1
5. The meal of the spirit could refer to communion, which preceded the meal (22) but more probably it refers to the morning Hour which followed the period of sleep (cf. 69:12–13). In this case the Divine Office was considered a spiritual meal nourishing the soul with Holy Scripture (15:36, 47:15).

munication mentioned above, let him at least go into the oratory with the brothers at the usual time. [10]And if he cannot stand, let him chant the psalms lying on a mat as if at prayer. [11]But let the brother standing next to him keep an eye on him so he does not go to sleep.

[12]If afterwards he does no work at all, moreover, let him receive one piece of bread less in his allowance and let two of the drinks be withheld, [13]and only this much because he got up at least for the Work of God. [14]For it is an injustice to equate an idle brother with a working brother, to whom recompense commensurate with his labor is due, [15]and 'the ox treading out the grain is not to be muzzled'. [16]And so if one does not work, even if his sense of justice does not eliminate eating altogether, he should at least, because of the very nature of sickness, not eat as much as one who works and is healthy. [17]Hence one who is weak and declares that he is unable to work should be considered likewise unable to eat—[18]because it is in accord with justice that the one impossibility includes the other and this shows that the distress is genuine; [19]for if we are incapable of working, we should consequently also be incapable of eating, [20]for it is evident that the laziness of an idle glutton makes him feign such sickness—[21]so when he himself declares that he cannot work and says nothing about not being able to eat, if he does not want to state this inability with his own tongue, let him very quickly hear from someone else that whether he likes it or not he is incapable of eating. [22]Now, it stands to reason that if, in an individual the soul, the stomach and the limbs are in a balanced relationship, [23]then one and the same distress ought to be felt alike in all three, in such a way that what these three are capable of together in health they should, on the other hand, manifestly be incapable of simultaneously in distress. [24]Why then should distress sanction impossibility in the one case and admit of possibility in the other, [25]when in one and the same body of an individual the soul, the stomach, and the

10. Normally the psalms were chanted standing and the other prayers said prostrate (cf. 47:6, 48:12). There was more than one mat in the oratory (19:25), perhaps one for each brother, as in the dormitory (81:31).
15. Deut 25:4

limbs cannot feel and suffer this distress disjunctively, [26]be-
cause in us it is still the soul that feels all pains and, once this
has departed, the dead body cannot feel what happens to it?
[27]Oh, the wickedness of dishonesty! The head is tortured
with pains when work is concerned and the stomach is not
tortured when eating is concerned, as if the stomach were
located in another body.

LXX. CHARITY TO THE SICK BY THE BRETHREN.

[1]Brothers who would show that they are filled with charity
should vie with one another in visiting, comforting and serving the sick brethren, [2]so that they may give proof of fraternal
charity where there is distress, [3]and put into practice the
word of the Lord saying: 'I was sick and you visited me'.

Question of the disciples:

LXXI. WHETHER SPIRITUAL BROTHERS ON MEETING ONE
ANOTHER SHOULD PRAY FIRST OR GIVE EACH OTHER THE SIGN OF
PEACE OR A GREETING.

The Lord has replied through the master:

[1]When brothers enter monasteries or meet spiritual
brothers on the road, [2]after greeting each other with the *Benedicite*, they should first pray and only then exchange the
sign of peace, [3]as we read was done when the hermits Paul
and Anthony met. As soon as they had caught sight of and
hastened toward each other, [4]after a mutual greeting by their
respective names, they immediately said a prayer and the
conclusion, and afterwards embraced each other in charity,
exchanging the kiss of peace.

[5]Therefore those who meet should pray before they give
each other the sign of peace—[6]for if prayer is not said first,
how will the brother know?—[7]lest a diabolical temptation
present itself in human guise, and in place of what appeared

---

3. Mt 25:36
3. *Vita Pauli* 9; PL 23:25B
7. *Hist. monach.* 1; PL 21:404A

to be a body, a diabolical phantasm suddenly disappear. [8]So we may deceive ourselves with our own sight if we trust human eyes for what we fail to test by means of divine prayers.

[9]Again, those who meet should pray before they give each other the sign of peace because it is proper first to thank the Lord by prayer that the meeting has taken place, [10]for it is he who granted that the two should become acquainted or meet again in accordance with their mutual desire. [11]Once the prayer to the Lord is finished, it is then right to give a man the gracious token of peace.

LXXII. A MEAL TAKEN FOR THE SAKE OF CHARITY TOWARD BROTHERS WHO VISIT.

[1]When outside brothers visit the monastery, [2]if it is a Wednesday, a Friday, or a Saturday, let them be asked by the abbot personally, if he is present, or by the cellarer in the abbot's absence, to stay for the meal at the ninth hour. [3]But if even at a third invitation they do not consent to stay until the ninth hour but adamantly insist that they must be on their way, all the brothers of the monastery may, [4]for the sake of the charity prompted by their coming, break the fast and share a meal with them at the sixth hour. [5]If, however, they insist on resuming their journey before the sixth hour, whatever may be the time of their hasty departure, [6]let them in this case eat alone, not with the members of the community. Nor let them be allowed to depart fasting from the monastery, [7]because of their travelling, for the charity of Christ came to be known in the breaking of bread, [8]and one reads in the Acts of the Apostles that the apostles Andrew and John departed after having broken and eaten the Eucharist.

---

9. *Vita Pauli* 9

2. Only the 'second' is authorized to substitute for the abbot (93:66), but since normally there was no 'second' the cellarer acted in the abbot's name here, as he did in giving alms when the abbot was away.

6. Cf. *Hist. monach.* 7; PL 21:419B

7. Lk 24:35

8. Ps-Gregory of Tours, *Liber de miraculis b. Andreae apostoli* 20, *Acta Iohannis* 109–111.

LXXIII. Brothers who come late to the Work of God.

[1]A brother who misses the first prayer or psalm of the nocturns, Matins or Vespers, at him the abbot shakes his head in the oratory to inspire fear, and then outside privately admonishes him to amend. [2]If he misses the second prayer or psalm, after the psalm is finished let him be sharply rebuked there in the oratory in the presence of the community. [3]But if he comes in after the third prayer or psalm, he and his deans together with him are to be excommunicated immediately and expelled from the oratory [4]and may not return for pardoning until and unless they have all equally made humble satisfaction before the threshold of the oratory. [5]But this is to be in accordance with what we said in a previous chapter about a distance of less than fifty paces.

[6]At Prime, Terce, Sext and None, however, anyone who does not arrive for the first prayer and the first psalm after the signal has been struck is to be sharply rebuked in the oratory in the presence of all. [7]But anyone who comes after the second prayer or the second psalm is to be excommunicated forthwith and he with his deans must leave.

[8]Whoever is not present for the antiphon or the verse preceding the meal must eat and drink by himself and be deprived of the sign of the cross, [9]without a blessing being given or received, without a word from anyone until they rise. [10]And it is right that one who before the meal did not speak with God should have to eat without a word from any man. [11]Anyone who is not present at table for the verse afterwards to give thanks to God after the meal is to receive at the next meal the same punishment of being segregated as he who before the meal did not speak with God.

[12]But these rebukes and excommunications are prescribed only for those who are late because of willful negligence and are not occupied with the interests of the monastery. [13]Even if they call out in their own voice that they should be remembered as absent ones in the prayers in the oratory, they are to be ignored by the brothers, [14]and let them know that they are excommunicated because it was not the concerns of the

---

2. 'If he misses the second prayer' means the prayer that followed the first psalm; the third prayer followed the second psalm. The Divine Office was interrupted for the reprimand. Cf. interventions in Chh. 14, 21.

monastery but their unconcern that detained them. [15]On the other hand, those who are absent because occupied in the interests of the monastery deserve to be remembered by those who are present in the oratory, [16]even though those thus occupied are also saying the Work of God by themselves there where they are.

[17]The brother who was rebuked in the oratory, even though he was not ordered to leave the oratory, may on no account intone a psalm or a responsory or a lesson or a verse [18]until he has made satisfaction for his fault in the oratory itself, bowed down to the knees, and has humbly asked aloud for prayers for himself.

[19]A brother who is occupied in the interests of the monastery is to be kept in mind in the oratory as one who is absent. [20]Those who are detained by unconcern or slowness are to be silently ignored because what they get instead is guilt for not wanting to be mindful of God in prayer.

LXXIV. THE BROTHERS' FREE WILL MUST BE HELD IN CHECK.

[1]A brother who has made a resolution to go beyond the established norm in fasting or in going all day without eating or in abstaining, [2]and without orders from the abbot wants to do something by the decision of his own will, [3]would best not be permitted to do so, because the devil is deluding him even by means of what is good in itself, in that he is impelling the brother to do his own will, [4]whereas in the monastery a brother is not allowed to do what he wants by his own will.

LXXV. THE SUNDAY REST.

[1]On Saturdays in summer, from the ninth hour on, after the meal, they should no longer do any reading. [2]On Saturdays in winter, from None on, they do not work, as has been

---

4. Going all day without eating (*superponere*) was permitted in Lent (53:38–41) and was sometimes imposed on the whole community (15:39). Here it is a matter of caprice condemned in 22:7–8. What a brother was not allowed to do of his own choice, he might of course do with the authorization of the Rule or of the abbot (26:47–51, 44:13, 53:12–14, 75:5).

prescribed above. [3]Then too on the next day, Sunday, let them refrain from all manual labor [4]and even from the daily memorizing normally done for three hours a day in both seasons, winter and summer. [5]Instead, after Mass in the church everyone may, according to his preference, read what he wishes or what affords him pleasure as he chooses, [6]and they also have complete freedom to go back to bed. [7]Thus they should rejoice in having Sunday assigned them for resting.

Question of the disciples:

LXXVI. HOW SHOULD THE BLESSED BREAD SENT BY A PRIEST BE RECEIVED IN THE MONASTERY?

The Lord has replied through the master:

[1]When blessed bread comes to the monastery from a bishop or from priests next in rank, [2]let the abbot immediately kiss the eulogia sent as a gift, then rising together with all who are there present, [3]let them pray, saying this verse: 'We are receiving your mercies, O God, within your temple', with the *Glory be*. [4]After the conclusion he sits down again.

LXXVII. THE PRIESTS' BLESSING AND SIGN OF THE CROSS.

[1]When priests are detained in the monastery for a meal, however, it is they who make the sign of the cross over all the food and the mixed drinks, as also over the first serving of unmixed wine at their table; [2]and let them give a blessing in response to those who ask for it. [3]When the priests themselves, however, ask others for a blessing in eating or drinking, those of lesser rank are not allowed to respond to them [4]because what they themselves give, the ordained cannot receive from the unordained.

6. The freedom to go back to bed is quite understandable as there were only two hours of sleep at the end of the night (49).
1. The Latin for bishop here is *summus pontifex*, now used only of the pope. Other terms for bishop in chapters 93 and 94 are *praesul ecclesiae, episcopus, pontifex, summus sacerdos*, and *sacerdos*.
3. Ps 48:9

[5]Furthermore, if there are clerics present at meals of the servants of God, making the sign of the cross should be deferred to them too. [6]So also giving the conclusion after the prayer should be deferred to them.

LXXVIII. A VISITOR, BE HE A BROTHER OR A LAYMAN, SHOULD NOT BE FED MORE THAN TWO DAYS WITHOUT WORKING.

[1]When any brother comes to the monastery as a guest, [2]out of respect for his status as a guest and because of the fatigue of travel let him, if he wishes to remain unoccupied, be seated at table in common with the brothers at the regular time for two days. [3]But after Prime has been said on the third day, when the abbot leaves the oratory, let the weekly servers and the cellarer detain the guest within the oratory and [4]say to him: 'Would you please work with the brothers at whatever the abbot assigns either in the field or at a craft. [5]If you do not so please, be on your way, because the rule limits your stay as a guest to two days.' [6]And if he consents to work, let some task with the brothers be assigned to him immediately. [7]If he does not wish to do this, he is to take his leave, [8]and let his bed be stripped at once [9]until it is made up afresh at the arrival of another stranger, when perhaps it will be some spiritual person who comes.

[10]Therefore, if he does not want to work let the weekly servers and the cellarer tell him to depart, [11]lest the brothers working for their monastery have good reason to resent hospitality given to parasites and loafers and, [12]resorting to murmuring and criticizing, they begin to detest such strangers who, [13]because of their wretched laziness, do not settle down anywhere but visit monasteries under the pretext of religion and remain idle while devouring the bread due to workers. [14]They neither betake themselves to monasteries to stay there as declared members nor do they declare frankly by begging that they are weaklings. [15]Indeed, as we have said above, almsgiving to such as these for more than two days is loss for the giver, whereas in the case of a poor beggar whose

---

5. Weekly servers and the cellarer detained the guest because they needed to know about preparing meals for him.

neediness is evident this is gain for the giver and calls for reward. [16]So if after two days such as these do not want to work, let them be honest enough to acknowledge [17]that their being received and fed for two days while they remained idle, out of consideration for the hardship of their long journey, was in accord with the apostolic precept which says: 'You should make hospitality your special care'. [18]So also to impel them to do manual labor with the brothers there is likewise a precept of his which says: [19]'You yourselves know how you ought to imitate us; for we were not unruly while with you, [20]neither did we eat any man's bread at his cost, but we worked night and day in labor and toil, so that we might not burden any of you. [21]Not that we did not have the right to do so, but that we might make ourselves an example for you to imitate us. [22]For indeed when we were with you we used to charge you: if any man will not work, let him not eat. [23]For we have heard that some among you are living irregularly, doing no work but busy at meddling. [24]Now such persons we charge and exhort in the Lord Jesus Christ that with quietness they work and eat their own bread'.

[25]Now guests who are spiritual men, though they may not be able because of the exhausting hardship of travel to do any work the day they arrive, [26]will at least the next day of their own accord join the brothers in what they see them doing, [27]lest those who are working consider them not only loafers but worse.

Question of the disciples:

LXXIX. The lodging for strangers.

The Lord has replied through the master:

[1]The guest quarters should be set apart in the monastery, with beds made up, [2]where the brothers who come, especially those who are unknown, may sleep and deposit their bags. [3]Things belonging to the monastery, whether iron tools or utensils, should not be put into this room, [4]lest it happen

---

17. Rm 12:13
24. 2 Th 3:7–12. Cf. Cassian, *Inst.* 10:7–14

that guests who were thought to be spiritual men are suddenly and with consequent loss found to be thieves.

⁵Moreover, for the purpose of precautionary surveillance let two brothers from the same deanery ⁶as those who are doing the kitchen service be assigned in turn out of this deanery by their deans to keep an eye on strange brothers without their being aware of it, and this until all the members of the same deanery have had their turn a week at a time. ⁷Then when members of another deanery take over the cooking and strangers arrive during the course of their weeks, ⁸those from this same deanery appointed by their deans to keep an eye on visiting brethren without their being aware of it are to do so until another deanery succeeds them. ⁹So all the deaneries, by going through them in this way and beginning over again, are to keep watch at all times over the strangers who come.

¹⁰When strangers arrive, therefore, the two brothers whose turn it is to keep watch are to make up beds for themselves as well in the same place, ¹¹so that should one of the guests wish to go to the oratory during the night and the other perhaps not want to get up because of fatigue, or should they wish to go outside one after the other, ¹²each of the two would have his own watchman without realizing it. ¹³In this way the one who leaves for the oratory or to go outside is to be guided by the community member through the exits and entrances of the monastery, not easily found during the night, and at the same time is kept under guard, while the other watchman remains with the one who stays behind. ¹⁴In this way they will manifestly be fulfilling the requirements of charity toward guests by accompanying them, while protecting the goods of the monastery from persons who are not trusted though they are not aware of this.

¹⁵Furthermore, during the day these same are also to make it their business to keep an eye on them within the monastery so they do no mischief. ¹⁶And this charge is committed to two so that during the night they may take turns watching over the strangers, ¹⁷and if during the day one of them is perhaps occupied with something else, the other may look out for the stranger, watching him from a distance.

¹⁸This room is to be locked from the inside as well as from

the outside. [19]After shutting in the guests together by themselves at night, the bolts having been put in place on the inside, they are to remove the key and hide it in a place known to them. [20]Then should a guest want to go outside, he will have to wake up his own guards, since he needs the key, [21]and accompanied by one of them he will set off and go outside to the place of refreshment, not knowing where it is. [22]These same brothers again are to take their pouches and their staffs and keep them in the same room, properly secured by an outside lock.

[23]Now, should it be found that there are guests who by faithfully persevering for a long time and working with a will show signs of staying permanently in the monastery, let their custodians bring this to the attention of the abbot. [24]Then after the Rule has been read to them, let the number of days they have already spent in the monastery be taken into account and [25]let the remaining days of the period of deferment be given them for thinking it over. [26]And when the days of the set period of deferment are finished, if these men are pleased with their experience of the life and the discipline of the rule, [28]only then may they give themselves to the monastery to persevere there until death, [27]in accordance with what is prescribed in a subsequent chapter about settling brothers into the monastery.

[29]If they, however, do not want to commit themselves permanently but would like to remain at the monastery working with the brothers every day in this way and [30]are agreed to supply their own clothing and things while working for someone else, [31]let the monastery at least provide the community meals and the necessities of life for them, but nothing more. [32]There is to be no supplying of the other necessities, because although all things must be provided for permanent members, the monastic fare alone must suffice for those who are doubtful about commitment—[33]and this only because he has wanted to stay and work with the brothers. [34]At any rate they are to be watched by those brothers day and night, every day.

26. Phil 2:8, Caesarius, *Reg. monach.* 1

Question of the disciples:

LXXX. WHETHER BROTHERS WHO HAVE SUFFERED POLLUTION DURING SLEEP SHOULD RECEIVE COMMUNION OR NOT.

The Lord has replied through the master:

[1]Brothers who are aware that they have defiled themselves during sleep [2]are to confess this secretly to the abbot at the door of the oratory, bowed down to the knees, before they enter for that Hour of the psalmody at which they customarily receive Communion. [3]And then let the abbot ask them what impure thoughts they could have had the previous day that consent to lust should have occurred during the night. [4]And if the brother is indeed spiritual he should not blush to confess this evil, as we have said in a previous chapter—[5]and if he wishes to save his soul from death—[6]so the abbot can provide the remedy for it by admonitions. [7]Nevertheless let them abstain from receiving Communion for two days, and then communicate again, cleansed, on the third day.

[8]Now should there be brothers who are in this situation frequently, let them know that it is not by accident but by their own choice that they are incurring excommunication. [9]They are the ones estranging themselves from the body of God because by their thoughts they feed their own lust and are responsible for defiling their body through impure desires. [10]For 'as a moth in clothing and a worm in wood corrupts and devours', [11]so also does impurity in thought contaminate and undo the undefiled soul. [12]So it is taken for granted that these persons are present to God in spirit in just that condition in which through guilt they actually are in bed. [13]For Holy Scripture says: 'Perverse thoughts separate from God'.

4. Cf. Gal 6:1, Jm 5:16
5. Jm 5:20
7. This is the only passage in which excommunication is given explicit reference to Holy Communion.
10. Pr 25:20
13. Wis 1:3

LXXXI. The clothing and shoes of the brethren.

[1]For daytime in winter the brothers must have a garment of thick stuff and for nighttime another tunic, [2]which they are to delouse after the nocturns because during the day they are busy at various tasks. [3]Furthermore, in winter they are to have also a cloak made of cloth, drawers of woollen cloth, and leggings or fabric footgear.

[4]But in summer they are to have a garment of linsey-woolsey, not very thick because of work and sweat, [5]and they are to have light cloaks of linsey-woolsey, not very thick because of sweating in the heat, and drawers of linsey-woolsey. [6]We forbid the men of God, however, to wear linen drawers, so that there may be some difference between monk and cleric. [7]And everyone is to have a rather light garment of linsey-woolsey to wear only at divine services on feast days. [8]Furthermore, in summer each one is to have a linen handkerchief because of perspiration, and there are to be face towels for each deanery.

[9]All these things are to be kept in separate chests in each deanery, with the deans having the key for them. [10]The chests are to be placed in the vestiary, where also the iron tools and all articles of the monastery are kept. [11]We have above already treated of the custodian of this room. [12]Now, we have said that all these changes of clothing of one deanery are to be stored in the same chest with the deans holding the key, [13]so that the individual brother, not having a chest at his disposal, will not have any place to hide anything of his own, [14]and all deaneries are to observe this regulation. [15]But if it is seen that any brother is dressing up and taking too much pleasure in his appearance, [16]let what he has be immediately taken from him by his deans and given to another, and that of the other to him. [17]And this is so that self-will will not assert itself in the brother, [18]for whatever his soul seeks to obtain for him must instead be denied to him. [19]For the spirit opposes

---

4. Linsey-woolsey is a coarse cloth made of linen and wool, or cotton and wool, and was no doubt the traditional mantle of monks.
6. Linen drawers were a sacerdotal article of clothing in the Old Testament (Ex 28:42, 39:27).
19. Gal 5:16–17

the desires of the flesh; [20]wherefore the man of God is spiritual, not carnal.

[21]Those entering upon their week of service in the kitchen are to have tunics of sackcloth and cowls of matting. [22]Such materials may, especially within the monastery, without embarrassment endure the indignity of dirtiness, [23]as well as the grime of the cooking pots, cauldrons and tar, as well as the heat of the fire and the various soilings of the kitchen. [24]At the end of the week, therefore, on the evening of the last day, the servers are to wash these items of clothing and turn them over to others who are entering upon their week.

[25]Now as to footwear: the brothers ought to have hobnailed shoes [26]to be worn in winter, not for futility but for utility, [27]but in summer they are to be oiled and put away, and everyone is to have nailed clogs in the monastery as well as on the road. [28]Thus the shoes stored for a long time will be kept intact and the brothers' feet will be kept cool in the clogs. [29]Furthermore, let them wear wooden sandals at the nocturns in summer so that they do not return to their beds with dirty feet and soil the bed coverings. [30]But at the nocturns in winter they are to wear footgear made of fur for their cold feet.

[31]On their beds in winter they are to have individual mattresses and heavy quilts and blankets—[32]but in summer they are to use coverlets instead of blankets on account of the heat—[33]and in front of each bed a pelt on which to wipe their feet clean before climbing into their beds.

Question of the disciples:

LXXXII. IN THE MONASTERY THE BRETHREN MAY HAVE NOTHING OF THEIR OWN.

The Lord has replied through the master:

[1]In the life of this world three things spur every man on and he works for and pursues them. [2]The traveller on the

---

25-6. Hobnailed shoes translated *viclinas*, which is otherwise unknown and which no one has tried to translate. 'Not for futility but utility' is a whimsical attempt to reproduce the rhymed Latin *non ad lusum sed ad usum*. One definition of 'futile' given by Webster is 'frivolous'; the noise of hobnailed shoes could in fact occasion frivolity.

road, the soldier in battle, the emperor in his palace, the farmer in the field, the merchant in his business, [3]all have as their incentive, and work in order to have as long as they are alive, the means to be clothed, shod and fed. [4]But the Lord has made clear to those upon whom he has bestowed the gift of serving him that they should not be much concerned about the present world—[5]for all this passes away, [6]and all these things that we see and use are at our disposal for only a few days [7]and being of brief duration last no longer than the period of our life, [8]then when this world's light is extinguished in us by the death of the body and our eyes are closed to life, all that we have is left behind to the world—[9]but should always think about the things of eternity which, once they have come, admit of no further transition but remain as they are, [10]whether it is the good things of eternal life for the just or the pains of hell for sinners. [11]Therefore in this life we should always keep our minds occupied with heavenly thoughts concerning a desire for the good things and a fear of the evil, as if we saw ourselves already confronting them. [12]Accordingly the Lord has given his servants the rule that no one must be anxious about the necessities of this life, [13]and those who believe in him he admonishes not to worry about the morrow but to desire only his kingdom and justice, [14]as he says in the holy gospel: 'Do not worry about what you are to eat or what you are to drink or what you are to wear' [15]but 'seek the kingdom and the justice of God, and all these other things will be given you as well'.

[16]Therefore since the Lord provides us with all these necessities and it is the concern of the abbot alone, with God, to supply everything, [17]why should the disciple dare to do or to have or to demand anything for himself? [18]Now, it is forbidden to have anything of one's own in the monastery because 'no one in the service of God entangles himself in worldly affairs, that he may please him whose approval he has secured'. [19]Thus, when he has subjected himself and everything that belonged to him to the dominion of another, nothing is left to activate his self-will, which is the enemy of

12. Cf. Mt 6:25-33
18. 2 Tim 2:4

God's will. [20]Indeed, Ananias and Sapphira did not succeed in getting the apostles to believe their fraud concerning their property. [21]When they laid all they had at the feet of the apostles, they were judged and condemned to sudden death for the fraudulent withholding of some of their possessions, [22]because it is impossible to deceive God since 'nothing is hidden which will not be revealed' by him. [23]Therefore if for each and every brother the abbot takes care of food for the table, clothing for the body, footwear for the feet, [24]why should anyone need to have anything of his own, whether an article of clothing or gold or coins or any necessity, [25]since God, through the monastery, provides him with everything that needs to be bought or had?

[26]Therefore if any private property is found in anyone's possession, the abbot is to condemn him to a major and long-lasting excommunication, [27]so that with this chastisement serving as an example, no one will dare to do likewise. [28]To ensure no one having anything, let there be frequent general inspection by the deans, [29]and if it is seen that a brother is well satisfied with himself or takes a great deal of pleasure in some article of clothing, [30]let it be taken from him and given to another, [31]and that of the other to him, whatever it may be, so that self-will does not assert itself in him.

Question of the disciples:

LXXXIII. How should priests be received in the monastery?

The Lord has replied through the master:

[1]Priests are to be considered outsiders in the monastery, [2]especially those who retain and exercise their presidency and preferment in churches. [3]If their choice is to live in monasteries for the love of God and for the sake of discipline and the pattern of a holy life, [4]even so it is only in name that they are called fathers of the monastery, [5]and nothing is to be permitted them in the monasteries other than praying the

20. Ac 5:1 ff
22. Mt 10:26

collects, saying the conclusion, and giving the blessing. [6]Let them not presume or be allowed anything else, nor may they lay claim to any part in God's organization or government or administration, [7]but it is the abbot, set over the whole flock by the Rule, who is to adjudge and reserve to himself every kind of authority and ruling power over the monastery. [8]So if we have prescribed that they be called fathers of the monastery, but solely as a title of honor, it is because of their sacerdotal consecration [9]and not that they may use this very honor as a pretext to oust the abbots, because they are laymen, from the management and government of the monastery.

[10]Now, if these priests choose to use the monastery's fare, clothing, and footwear every day, [11]they must also work in common with the brothers, in compliance with the apostle's precept, [12]though the abbot should not unduly force them by way of command but respectfully urge them to do so. [13]For if they are spiritual men they will impose upon themselves what others could force upon them, [14]and will always keep in mind the example St Paul gave in himself, saying: 'We did not eat your bread at your cost'. [15]And he likewise says: 'We worked with our own hands so as not to burden any of you'. [16]And it is he again who says: 'If any man will not work, neither let him eat'.

[17]Therefore if they remain idle for a very long period and do not want to earn their keep by the labor of their hands, [18]let the abbot respectfully present the matter to them with a large number of religious persons as witnesses, and then let them return to their churches. [19]But if, God forbid, they do not want to leave peacefully but instead make a scene, [20]let them be held and stripped of clothing that belongs to the monastery, provided there is no serious injury, then let them

---

9. This makes explicit that the abbot was not a priest. The abbot distributed communion (16) at the Hour preceding the meal (21, 22), hence at Sext, None, or Vespers depending upon meal time.

13. Cf. Gal 6:1

14. 2 Th 3:8

15. Ibid., 1 Cor 4:12

16. 2 Th 3:10

be ousted and the door closed. ²¹For they themselves ought by all means to do what they preach to others: ²²it is a universal precept of God that the workers' bread must be refused to the idle.

LXXXIV. WHO SHOULD EAT WITH THE ABBOT.

¹To be seated at the abbot's table are the seniors, visiting outsiders and, ²taking turns as the abbot wishes, those who know the psalter; ³but not the deans, because they are required to be present at their deanery tables in order to tend to God's business, namely, silence and decorum among their charges. ⁴Now, we have said that both are to preside at the table of their deanery so that while alternately exercising vigilance they may vie with each other in keeping from all vices the ten brothers committed to them.

Question of the disciples:

LXXXV. HOW AND FOR HOW MUCH THINGS MADE IN THE MONASTERY SHOULD BE SOLD.

The Lord has replied through the master:

¹When any of the crafts has some finished product left over which is useless for the monastery or for sending out as eulogia, ²let inquiry be made about the price for which seculars could sell it, then let it always be sold at a lower evaluation and for sufficiently less money ³to make it evident that in this regard spiritual men are distinguished from seculars by the difference in what they do, ⁴since they are not, out of commercialism which is the enemy of the soul, seeking profit beyond what is just ⁵but are even benevolently agreeing to accept a price lower than what is just. ⁶Thus people will believe that they are engaged in the arts and crafts not out of greed and avarice ⁷but so that the hand which should provide for its own sustenance by charging honest prices cannot find time for idleness and spend the hours of a workday uselessly. ⁸The payment received must, however, be faithfully handed

---

1. Seniors=porters (95:1)

over to the abbot by the artificers themselves. [9]This reduction in price should be set for the artificers by the abbot's decision [10]so they will in turn know what amount they should ask of purchasers, [11]and to make it impossible to trick the abbot about the price received since he already knows how much it is.

LXXXVI. The domains of the monastery.

[1]All the lands of the monastery should be rented out [2]so that a secular lessee is burdened with all the field work, the care of the estate, the clamors of the tenants, the quarrels with neighbors—[3]a man who does not know how to be concerned exclusively about his soul and whose interests in the present life are limited to love of this world. [4]And thinking only of this life they so love things of the present and imagine they are going to remain in the light of this world for a long time [5]that while loving the present they never in consequence desire or learn to know what is to come. [6]And while during this time they are taking delight in transitory goods they neither desire everlasting life nor fear eternal punishment, [7]since the cherished 'shackles of the world day after day make them, miserable ones', unwilling to depart from this life without their possessions, 'taking with them nothing but their sins'.

[8]On the contrary, those who have become spiritual men 'do not entangle themselves in worldly affairs, so that they may please him whose approval they have secured'. [9]Moreover, concerned not about things which at death remain in the world, but about their soul, which alone with the record of its deeds passes on after death, [10]they choose rather to think about what really matters; [12]as is proper while we are living we should not occupy our thoughts [11]with things which remain in the world after we depart from this life and which cannot follow our soul after death, [13]but always desiring what is on high and setting all our hope on the future we should let it be seen that we are still waiting for the life of happiness rather than enjoying it already.

7. *Visio Pauli* 10 & 40, *Passio Sebastiani* 11
8. 2 Tim 2:4

[14]Therefore the lands of the monastery should be rented out so that a secular workman may be busy with secular matters, [15]but then we, to whom the priest cries out: 'Lift up your heart,' and we assure him with the response: 'We have lifted it up to the Lord', [16]we should not let it wander off in earthly thoughts. [17]So also the Lord himself cries out to us in the gospel, saying: 'None of you can be my disciple unless he gives up all his possessions'.

[18]But since the life of our body cannot be maintained without the food that sustains it, [19]and especially in view of a possibly numerous community and the necessity of providing for the needs of visiting strangers, and also because we do not want to be stingy to anyone asking alms, [20]for these reasons we are seen not to renounce worldly possessions, [21]but we openly and legitimately retain monastic property for the benefit of God's workmen.

[23]With all this taken into consideration, if these possessions are tended with concern and care on our part, while they benefit the body they are definitely a burden for the soul. [24]It is therefore better to own them under someone else's management and to be sure of receiving annual rents, while we take care of nothing except our soul. [25]For if we want them to be under the active care of spiritual brothers, we enjoin heavy labor upon them and they lose the habit of fasting. [26]Again, it is not when strength is subjected to fasting that there should be discussion about whether a man ought to work more for his stomach than for his soul and God. [27]Wherefore let the crafts alone together with the garden suffice as work in the monastery.

16. Cf. Cyprian, *De orat.* 31, Augustine, *Sermo Denis* 6.3
17. Lk 14:33

Question of the disciples:

LXXXVII. How a brother, whether already turned to God or still of the world, is to enter the monastery, commit himself, and be received.

The Lord has replied through the master:

¹When a new member enters the monastery, whether he has already turned to God or is still of the world, and asks the favor of being accepted into the monastery, ²let the abbot at first tell him that he may not be able to keep the prescriptions of the Rule. ³But if he says that he can be obedient in all things, then let this Rule of the monastery be read to him. ⁴When the reading of the Rule is finished and the abbot has explained the prerequisites in his own words, and the new brother has replied that he is ready to put it all into practice, ⁵let the abbot then go on, saying: 'What about your possessions which you have the liberty of using? ⁶It is not expedient for you to be settled here for the sake of God while your possessions remain elsewhere. ⁷Rather, as Scripture says: " 'Let your treasure too be there where your heart is' ". ⁸It is not expedient because, through your craving for them, your possessions located outside might possibly entice you, seduced by the devil, out of the monastery. ⁹Then having deserted from service in the holy school you would go back to do service according to your own will ¹⁰and be pleased to return like a dog to your vomit, ¹¹and reswallow with dirt the spittle you had spit out on the ground.

¹²'But because perseverance wants to remain oblivious of any chance to go elsewhere, we offer the salutary advice

---

1. *conversus sive laicus. Conversi* lived in the world in the manner of religious. They entered upon this life of penance and chastity by a commitment till death. They wore simple clothing, similar to that of monks, and were tonsured, at least according to Caesarius of Arles. This may be the reason why the Master did not provide for their clothing and tonsure when they became postulants (90:83–4). On the other hand, these *conversi* in the world were not subject to a set rule of life and could retain what they possessed. So on these two points they were treated as 'lay' postulants.
7. Mt 6:21
10. Pr 26:11, 2 Pet 2:22
12. Mt 19:21, Lk 18:22

[13]that you listen instead to the voice of the Lord saying to you: "Go, sell everything and give to the poor, and come, follow me". [14]So if you wish to comply with this voice, go, sell what you have and bring here to me the entire sum received, [15]so that in your presence I may distribute it to the poor and you may have nothing left as a pledge to the world to go back to it again. [16]Indeed it is for this very reason that as long as your admission into the monastery has not been made permanent, you are still allowed free disposition of your possessions, [17]because after admission has been made permanent, a disciple is forbidden by the Rule to have anything of his own whether in the monastery or out of it, [18]so that there may be no occasion for his self-will to assert itself.

[19]'But if you find it hard to sell everything, and the things are such that they, with you, can be of service to the monastery, [21]be honest in bringing everything with you to the monastery [20]so that in any case nothing is left behind as a commitment to return to the world. [22]Conceal nothing from God to whose service you are submitting yourself together with all that you possess, [23]for he sees everything everywhere and nothing escapes him who reveals what is hidden. [24]Remember the double-dealing of Ananias and Sapphira who, having offered their possessions to God, wanted to conceal even some of that, and instead of trust met eternal death.'

[25]If after the new brother has heard all this, in accordance with the first divine proposal he sells everything and distributes it through the hands of the abbot—[26]if he firmly resolves to sell everything and not reserve anything for the monastery, [27]let no pressure be put on him, but let him do so only if he wants to of his own accord—[28]so then, when he has distributed everything through the hands of the abbot and then wishes to become a permanent member of the monastery, let no document of perseverance be demanded of him [29]because by disposing of all his possessions as alms he gave the pledge of his fidelity before God. [30]For it is evident that by making total distribution of his goods he is capable of remaining with

23. Mt 10:26
24. Cf. Ac 5:1–11

God faithfully, because for his sake he does not desire to keep what he owns. [31]Let him merely give his word that nothing at all remains hidden away from him outside. [32]The abbot gives this option to the entrants so that when they are being admitted they do not get the idea that he wants what a man possesses rather than his soul.

[33]But if the brother chooses to give himself along with his possessions to the monastery and does not wish to sell them, in case he should ever want to leave, [34]subverted and backed by the devil, and make trouble for the monastery by demanding his things, [35]let him first with his own hand draw up a pledge of stability, adding an inventory of his goods. Then let him offer every thing with his soul as a gift to God and to the oratory of the monastery, [36]with religious persons—bishop, priest and deacon, and the clergy of that area—signing as witnesses. [37]In the document itself let him make this declaration, that should he ever want to quit the monastery he will depart from the monastery without his goods and from God without forgiveness of his sins. [38]If the abbot sees that anything of the things now put at his disposal is superfluous, over and above what is needed for the monastery's use, [39]let him sell this superfluous item and give the proceeds from it to the poor for this brother's soul, because of the aforesaid precept about following the Lord through almsgiving. [40]In this way, what this inexperienced brother could not do well, the abbot as a skilled manager can perform for him.

[41]As to a brother who declares that he has nothing at all, first let inquiry be made of the neighbors in the area where he lived, [42]and if his poverty is found to be really total, [43]then let him give a guaranty of perseverance, with a penalty stipulated at the end of the document, provided of course that he is known by this time. Only then should he be received into the monastery, [44]because otherwise it may turn out that he has stored some of his things outside for a time, feigning poverty in the monastery, [45]and not only does he give nothing to God as alms or to the monastery as a gift, [46]but he also leaves for any reason that suits him, enticed by his possessions waiting for him outside. [47]For only when he has provided the safeguard of a guaranty with a penalty [48]may the goods of the monastery or purchase funds and draft ani-

mals be safely and without suspicion entrusted to him for monastery business.

⁴⁹But if a brother comes to the monastery who is unknown in his own country and is recognized by no one at all, and wants to become a member of the monastic community, ⁵⁰let only his sworn promise be demanded of him, ⁵¹that should he ever wish to quit the monastery he will leave with the knowledge of the abbot and of everyone else. ⁵²And when he does want to go, let him first swear that he has stolen nothing belonging to the monastery, either by having stored anything outside ahead of time or by secretly taking anything with him, ⁵³unless the abbot out of kindness wishes to give him something. ⁵⁴Then if he has perjured himself, he will bear in his soul what physically he could not bring himself to do. ⁵⁵In any case let him give back to the abbot the clothing and shoes that belong to the monastery, ⁵⁶so that what is taken from those who depart may benefit a brother who perseveres, ⁵⁷and that one who lives in the monastery may, as is right, have the things that belong to the monastery, ⁵⁸whereas they are justifiably taken back from one who unjustifiably withdraws his heart from perseverance in the monastery. ⁵⁹For giving these things to one who is displeased with the discipline corresponding to them should not be acceptable.

⁶⁰If, however, he takes an oath to remain for a time but not to become a member, ⁶¹let him merely certify that he will not depart without notifying and taking leave of the abbot, or with anything stolen, ⁶²and from then on let him be kept under surveillance without his being aware of it. ⁶³He must have nothing in his control and must be compelled to work in common with the brethren in order to live by his labor. ⁶⁴But if he has no clothing and the abbot wishes to give him some, he may use it for as long as he is in residence there, ⁶⁵knowing that he must give it all back when he wants to leave. ⁶⁶Now, it may happen that someone who entered without giving the monastery any sworn assurance, ⁶⁷and as one unknown furnished the abbot no bond of fidelity for security, ⁶⁸whether he has given nothing to God in alms ⁶⁹or has bequeathed none of his possessions to the monastery as a gift through a guaranteed pledge, ⁷⁰or whether, as an unknown, he has found no guarantor ⁷¹or he is bound by no promise

under oath, [72]if this brother of doubtful stability is sent out with animal-drawn vehicles and funds for purchasing things he may, some fine day, [73]under the devil's guidance, finding himself with funds and vehicles, suddenly set out for foreign lands while in charge of the monastery's goods. [74]And those who felt sure of him will daily await his return, because they were deceived, and will go after him only after a long time or belatedly or not at all.

LXXXVIII. Delaying the admission of brothers so that they may deliberate about committing themselves to stability.

[1]When there has been presented to the new brother by the Rule through the abbot all the foregoing about committing himself to stability, [2]whether by disposing of his possessions as alms or as a gift to the monastery, or by a document of guaranty under penalty or, if he is unknown, by a sworn promise, [3]let such still be granted a period of two months to deliberate with themselves, [4]meanwhile working with the brothers, content with the common measure of food and the discipline of excommunications according to the Rule, [5]so that such a one may make a trial of the monastery's way of life and himself be tested by the monastery. [6]Let him deliberate with himself whether he should stand fast with God or freely go back to the devil. [7]During these two months they are to be in the custody of the brothers who watch over strangers, and they too are to be kept under surveillance without their being aware of it [8]and are to sleep in the place assigned to guests [9]so that the presence of the custodians will ensure supervision of their coming and going in the monastery, [10]and if at any time and anywhere they absent themselves from the community of the brothers, the custodians will take care to look for them lest they perhaps get a head start, making off without taking leave but taking something stolen.

[11]Then if at the end of the two months they are dissatisfied

---

3. Cf. Ambrose, *De virginitate* 5; PL 16:267C, *De officiis* 3.81; PL 16:168–9

14. The departure of a postulant was equated with that of an apostate (90:85–7).

with the discipline and with those who are at the monastery and would like to go, ¹²let it be with the knowledge of the abbot and of everyone else. After giving his word that he has committed no theft and returning what monastery belongings he may have received for temporary use, ¹³let him next give the sign of peace to everyone and then receive a staff into his hand and provisions for the road. After a prayer, a verse is said and then the sign of peace is given to him. ¹⁴If he wishes it, let him depart as a guest, and let the devil reclaim this citizen of his, whom Christ unwillingly received as a guest.

LXXXIX. How a new brother is to confirm his admission into the monastery.

¹If the discipline pleases them and they instead choose stability after completing the two months' delay for deliberation, and would like to commit themselves to perseverance after having promised anew their steadfast adherence to the Rule read to them, ²let the abbot again question the new brother to learn what he has decided during the period of delay granted him. To his response that he promises to practice obedience in all things, the abbot shall reply, 'Thanks be to God'.

³The next day, when the prayers after Prime has been said are finished, and the abbott is at the threshold of the oratory on his way out with the community, the new brother with neck bowed down to his knees ⁴begs him and all his community to remain a little while longer in the oratory and pray for him. ⁵Then they pray for him at great length, and the abbot concludes in the name of all. Then when he goes to leave, the new disciple in all humility will take hold of his garment and with his hand detain him. ⁶He will present this petition to him: 'I have something to propose, first to God and this holy oratory, then to you and the community.' ⁷When the abbot replies: 'Make known what it is,' ⁸the petitioner continues, saying: 'I wish to serve God in your monastery through the discipline of the Rule read to me.' ⁹When the abbot says in reply: 'And this is your pleasure?' ¹⁰the future disciple continues: 'First it is God's, so then also mine.' ¹¹Then the abbot says: 'Mark well, brother, you are not promising anything to me, but to God and to this oratory and to this holy altar. ¹²If

in all things you obey the divine precepts and my admonitions, on the day of judgment you will receive the crown of your good deeds, [13]and I myself shall gain some remission of my sins for having encouraged you to conquer the devil along with the world. [14]But if you refuse to obey me in anything at all, see, I am calling the Lord to witness, [15]and this community will also give testimony in my favor on the day of judgment that, [16]as I said before, if you do not obey me in anything at all, I shall go free in the judgment of God and you will have to answer for your soul and for your contempt.'

[17]After these words, if he is entering with his possessions, the donor himself with his own hand then places upon the altar the inventory of his possessions and the deed of their donation to God through the monastery. [18]While so doing, the brother says: 'Behold, Lord, whatever you have given me I am returning to you, offering it together with my soul and in my poverty, [19]and I want my possessions to be there where my heart and my soul are, [20]but in the power of the monastery and of the abbot whom you, Lord, are setting over me to fear as your representative, since you say to them: "Any one who listens to you listens to me; anyone who rejects you rejects me". [21]Consequently, because through him you keep our needs in mind, we ought to have nothing of our own, [22]for you are our surety for everything and in all things you alone suffice. [23]So from now on, for us to live is Christ himself and to die is gain'.

[24]After these words, this same new brother says this responsory: 'Sustain me, Lord, according to your word, that I may live; do not disappoint me in my hope'. [25]After this responsory, the abbot says this verse: 'Confirm, O God, what you have wrought in us'. [26]As soon as this verse has been said, everyone gives him the sign of peace, and the abbot concludes. [27]Then, after taking the inventory from the altar, [28]he immediately assigns the new disciple to a dean, and

19. Mt 6:21
20. Lk 10:16
23. Phil 1:21
24. Ps 119:116
25. Ps 68:28
28. 'from the ceremony'=a guess at the meaning of *exeat disciplinae,* a curious phrase which occurs again in 93:36.

placed in their charge he goes out with the rest of the brothers from the ceremony.

²⁹Moreover, that same day it is he who, in token of humility, pours the water on the hands of the brothers as they enter for Communion, ³⁰and while he is doing so he kisses the hands of all and asks each to pray for him.

³¹As to the inventories of donations made by the brothers, the abbot at the time of his death includes in his last will what is left over after expenditures for the needs of the monastery, ³²as also the names of those whose gifts are recorded, ³³so that after his death no one chancing to quit the monastery will have the effrontery to demand the return of his possessions, ³⁴cutting short his stability in the monastery and breaking his word to the deceased, ³⁵or claim that something belonging to him is being kept in the monastery without having been given to it.

Question of the disciples:

XC. WHEN SOMEONE ENTERS THE MONASTERY FROM THE WORLD*, HE IS NOT TO CHANGE HIS GARB OR RECEIVE THE RELIGIOUS TONSURE FOR A YEAR.

The Lord has replied through the master:

¹When some new man comes fleeing from the world to the service of God in the monastery and declares that he wishes to become a monk, let him not be too readily believed. ²Indeed, let the abbot pretend to refuse him residence in the monastery, though only verbally, not actually. ³To test him let difficulties be made, and to ascertain his obedience let him be told in advance about things contrary and repugnant to his will. ⁴Let daily fasting be held up to him. ⁵Furthermore, from the reading of the Rule and from what the abbot says let him understand this: that to say: 'I want this and I reject that, I like this and I hate that,' is allowed to no one in the monastery, so that self-will be not chosen and indulged. ⁶And let him know that whoever wishes to live the religious life perfectly in the

---

*'lay' postulants
6. *conversi*

monastery will more than likely not be permitted what he desires according to his own will. [7]Why? Because 'there are ways which men think right, but whose end plunges into the depth of hell'. [8]And what he does not want, this will be enforced, in order to root out his self-will, which is the enemy of God. [9]Accordingly, he who wishes to live the religious life perfectly should be denied whatever he loves and desires, and whatever he hates should be imposed on him; [10]as the Lord says: 'If anyone wants to be a follower of mine, let him renounce himself and follow me', [11]that is, let him not do his own will but God's. [12]Indeed, whoever wants to serve in his school must endure all things for the Lord's sake. [13]Even so, what can we endure for the Lord that is worthy, when the apostle says: 'The sufferings of the present time do not deserve to be compared with the glory to come'? [14]So if a persecutor should subject the servant of Christ to fire, the heat, being transitory, is no longer felt once the suffering is finished, and is quite unlike that other fire which is unquenchable; [15]nor does it burn like the punishment of everlasting hell stored up, never to cease, for the sinful soul. [16]If he inflicts the tortures of the claw or of the rack or of scourging, the endurance of a little pain quickly gives way to a crown of eternal joy. [17]If for the sake of God a dark dungeon imprisons us, in its stead the eternal Jerusalem, built of gold and adorned with precious stones and pearls, awaits us. [18]If for the sake of God the dungeon's darkness makes us blind, it can deprive us of sight for the moment, but afterwards we shall be received into eternal life by that other light [19]which shines not with the brightness of the sun or of the moon, not of the stars of heaven or of lamps, but with the everlasting majesty of God himself. [20]If by dying for the sake of God we deserve to quit this earth which in the present life we tread under foot, we shall immediately be delivered to walk forever on that other land which is 'seven times brighter than silver'.

7. Pr 16:25
10. Mt 16:24
13. Rm 8:18
17. Cf. *Visio Pauli* 20, Rev 21:18–21
19. Cf. Rev 21:23
20. *Visio Pauli* 21

²¹If for the sake of God, moreover, we despise what are considered this world's delights, which defile rather than nourish our viscera, we are immediately for all eternity given access ²²to those rivers which never cease to flow and are swollen with an abundance of 'honey and milk, wine and oil,' ²³as also to all and sundry fruits which the trees there produce twelve times a year', not by human cultivation but through divine exuberance. ²⁴It is not hunger that makes the eating of them delightful, nor appetite that avidly desires to consume them, ²⁵but after the eyes of the saints are sated by the very sight, in addition each one has in his mouth the taste which gives him pleasure.

²⁶It is right and proper therefore that fasting and abstinence should make us suffer for a short time for the sake of the Lord, so that we may deserve to be forever filled to satiety with the good things he has prepared there. ²⁷For the sake of God we are kept in the darkness of a dungeon by the persecutor, so that in the perpetual light 'we may shine like sparks darting about through stubble'. ²⁸For the sake of God we embrace death for the moment, so that we may be forever freed from the eternal death of hell. ²⁹Finally, even when there is no persecution, even when Christianity is in peace, we serve in the school of the monastery under the abbot's command through testing and thwarting of the will, so that when, ³⁰after the pilgrimage of life in this world, our Lord summons us to his judgment ³¹we may present to him our seemly works, offering him the patience with which [we submitted to] all the diverse and difficult things that the abbot commanded us and we cheerfully endured for the sake of his name, ³²as also the various frustrations of our wills which we very willingly bore for the sake of God's name and the salvation of our soul, ³³saying to the Lord: 'For your sake we are being slain all the day; we are looked upon as sheep to be slaughtered'. ³⁴And when all this came upon us we did not forget you, and by practising obedience we were not disloyal

23. Ibid. 22–3
25. *Passio Sebastiani* 13
26. Cf. 1 Cor 2:9
27. Wis 3:7
33. Ps 44:22

to your covenant, [35]neither did our hearts shrink back from perseverance in well-doing nor from the desire for what hope had in store, because our steps did not turn aside from your paths. [36]In these paths you put us to the test, O God, you subjected us to fire, as silver is refined with fire. [37]You let us fall into the net of testing, you burdened our back, our humility, with the anguish of frustration, [38]so that we should not be permitted to do our own will but be forced to do yours. [39]So 'you set men over our heads', [40]for you made it clear that we must be subjected to testing under the abbot as teacher and the dean as disciplinarian. [41]Such as these, therefore, following the Lord, now say in that other world: 'We have passed through the fire and the water, and you have led us into a place of rest,' [42]that is, 'We have passed through the bitter thwarting of our own will, [43]and by serving in holy obedience we have come to the refreshment of your fatherly love.' [44]And likewise we say to him: 'We are glad for the days when you afflicted us, for the years when we saw evil'—[45]so that the fire of hell may have nothing in us to which it can lay claim, since the devil, who must burn there, has had no success in us.

[46]Indeed, he who desires to serve in the Lord's school must endure all things for his sake. [47]And like gold, he who is to enrich the diadem of God and the Lord's crown must be put to the test with file, hammers, and the fire of the furnace, [48]because when one does not do his own will he is bound to do his to whom daily we say in prayer: [49]'Thy will be done on earth as it is in heaven'. [50]Now, our body is earth; to it the Lord has said: 'Earth you are and to the earth you shall return'. [51]Because all self-will is carnal and issues from the body, its seductiveness leads us to commit what is wrong,

35. Ps 44:17–18
36. Ps 66:10
38. Cf. Ps 66:11
39. Ps 66:12
41. Ibid.
44. Ps 90:15
47. *Passio Juliani* 36
49. Mt 6:10
50. Gen 3:19

⁵²and during the short span of this life it seems to the flesh sweet through its desires, ⁵³only to be more bitter than gall afterwards and forever. ⁵⁴Therefore it is right that our tongue should be under compulsion to cry out daily to the Lord: 'Thy will be done on earth', our body. ⁵⁵If in the monastic school this will is communicated to us by the superiors, and we fulfill it every day through obedience, ⁵⁶we have a right to believe that the Lord will spare us in the time to come. Furthermore, we are confident that his grace can win us a crown, ⁵⁷because we always did his will, not ours, ⁵⁸and we never preferred ourselves and the desires of the flesh to his love. ⁵⁹And for his sake we are ready even to lose our lives in this present time so that we may deserve to find them with him in the time to come.

⁶⁰So when someone, drawing near the fear of God, desires to live the monastic life and wants to be a disciple, ⁶¹let his future master in the Lord's name explain to him, as we have said above, ⁶²that whatever he at any time tries to get by his own will's desire may, he should know, be refused him, and whatever he does not want may, let him hear, be imposed on him. ⁶³Personal possessions are to be denied him in advance. ⁶⁴Let the entire Rule be read to him, and let him promise to put it into practice. ⁶⁵Let him know that henceforth his parental home is foreign to him. Let him make up his mind that now he no longer has access to its threshold, for unless one leaves father or mother or brothers or home he cannot be a disciple of Christ. ⁶⁶Let him know that he may not go outside the monastery without orders from the superior.

⁶⁷If after the abbot has told him all the aforesaid he promises to obey in every regard and to be always ready to put into practice all his admonitions and those of the Rule, then let him be received into the monastery. ⁶⁸Let him not, however, be so quickly clothed with the religious habit, for fear that he may give his word at the time but afterwards take it back, and thus enter as a wolf in sheep's guise. ⁶⁹When he was a man of the world the devil did not tempt him because as long as he was working for him he always did his will openly, ⁷⁰but as soon as he turned from the suggestions of the devil and ser-

65. Mt 19:29

vice to the world and gave himself to the fear of God, in the service of Christ, he may be absolutely sure that from that day on he made the devil his enemy for having deserted him and his world because of fear of the Lord.

[71]Therefore anyone entering should not be so readily trusted, unless it be to see whether he translates into deeds what he promised in words, as Scripture says: 'Do not trust every spirit but test them' first, [72]and again: 'Many come to you clothed as sheep but within they are ravenous wolves'. [73]So you see that Scripture commands us to act cautiously in what concerns God so that 'what is holy is not thrown to the dogs, nor precious pearls before pigs'. [74]But let the abbot keep reminding him day after day, saying: 'My son, the clothing you are wearing in the monastery for the time being in no way anticipates our judgment concerning you, [75]but only when you have first cleansed worldly ways from the depths of your heart in the divine service will you finally change your garments as well, [76]so that in your body it may from then on be apparent to all, and rightly so, that in your spirit you belong to God. [77]And after cutting malice out of your heart it is quite proper that you should also cut your hair. [78]Then when you, still in your own clothes, have perfectly put into practice all that is contained in the Rule of the monastery, you will remain steadfast, holier still, after receiving our habit.'

[79]When for a whole year from that day, then, he has faultlessly lived the full life of the monastery together with the rest of the brethren, let him finally be tonsured with no further hesitation, [80]and let his clothing be exchanged for that of his holy intention. [81]He is tonsured thus: this brother kneels in the middle of the oratory and, with everyone round about chanting psalms, the abbot tonsures him.

[82]During this year of probation he may not intone any antiphonal psalm or responsory or verse. As long as they are still earning the habit of their holy intention they shall not presume to eat with the abbot.

71. 1 Jn 4:1
72. Mt 7:15
73. Mt 7:6

[83]The secular clothes of which he was divested when he made the exchange are to be carefully put away and kept, those of nonreligious as well as of one who is already a full-fledged religious. [84]Should it ever be—and may this never happen in the case of religious!—that he wants to return to his vomit and decides to go the way of the world again, and cannot be restrained by any bonds of the Scriptures or of exhortations, let him give back to Christ what is His. [85]In other words, divested of the holy garments and the sacred habit, clothed again with his own garments in which he came, conformed again to the world, let him go back to the devil his counsellor, [86]and let the garb of Christ not be carried off and contaminated in the world by the fugitive. [87]Let the world take him back as he was when it sent him, since Christ has retaken that which belongs to Him and which He had given to one unworthy of it, for the Lord could not find in him what He sought.

[88]Furthermore, whatever he at any time acquired or made or contributed while in the monastery may absolutely not be given back to him when he leaves, because perseverance is required of everything that makes its way to God in the monastery. [89]For that reason permission to depart is refused. [90]Only that entity which has free will is not kept back involuntarily, that is, body and soul, [91]which says that it is endowed with the power of decision and thinks it is permitted what is evil, with the consequence that it is made captive by the devil in what it wills and desires. [92]The reason why the Fathers ordain that the belongings and contributions of apostates may not be returned to them from the monastery is this: [93]aside from the fact that they cannot in any case be disgorged and restored because they have been distributed and used up

83. *de laicis . . . de firmato converso.* The full-fledged religious is the *conversus* of Chapter 87. Here he is equated with the 'lay' postulant because the clothing he was wearing as a religious living in the world was different from that of the monastery.

84. Cf. Pr 26:11, 2 Pet 2:22

85. Cf Ch. 88:14.

92. The reference is probably to the *Regula Macarii* 25. The case does not occur in Cassian as he did not allow the postulant to give away anything (*Inst.* 4,4).

for the needs of the saints, they are primarily very definitely refused so that their very belongings may provide the disciples with a reason to restrain themselves and remain steadfast in the discipline of God in the monastery. ⁹⁴Therefore something offered to God must not be recalled to the world by man. ⁹⁵Indeed, such is the threefold intent of this Rule: in the monastery, work feeds the brothers; perseverance shoes and clothes them; departure restores things belonging to the monastery, and if he so wishes he goes.

Question of the disciples:

XCI. How THE SON OF A NOBLE IS TO BE ACCEPTED INTO THE MONASTERY.

The Lord has replied through the master:

¹Should the son of a nobleman want to flee to the monastery for the service of God, let him not be accepted before he has promised to practise obedience in all things, as we said above. ²Then let his parents be consulted to learn what is their wish for him. ³If, when this is done, they prove to be so opposed that they would do violence to the Lord to get him back, let him be claimed for the enclosure of the monastery, for the Lord has the power to defend him in his own interest, ⁴for his right arm is stronger to protect him than is the wickedness of the devil to harm him. ⁵But if, on the contrary, his parents consent to his wish, let the abbot ask them to come to the monastery and question their son about his desire for the religious life ⁶so that, as is right, it will be seen that they who gave him life are themselves pledging and offering him. ⁷In this case, accordingly, when the parents declare in response that they are happy to accede to what he wishes, let the abbot say to them:

⁸'Certainly for all of us God alone suffices in all things. ⁹But because worldly expectations are first cut off from those who come to the divine service and enter the monastery, ¹⁰let him, relieved of the burden of his fortune, no longer entangled in

4. Cf. *Passio Juliani* 11
8. Cf. Julius Pomerius, *De vita contempl.* 2.16.2

the world's snares, go to the Lord secure and alone, [11]because "no one serving God entangles himself in worldly affairs, that he may please him whose approval he has secured", [12]because a man "burdened with gold cannot follow Christ", [13]since "he cannot serve two masters"; [14]but he serves God well who desires to possess with him in heaven that treasure which "the moth does not consume nor thieves break in and steal". [15]As the Lord says in the gospel: "He who does not renounce all he possesses cannot follow me and be my disciple", [16]because, as we have said, a man burdened with gold cannot follow Christ, [17]and so true is this that in the gospel the Lord gives this admonition to anyone following in his footsteps, saying to him: [18]"If you wish to be perfect, go, sell all you have, and come, follow me". [19]This man became sad because of his great wealth and deserved to hear the Lord's voice declare that [20]"it is easier for a camel to pass through the eye of a needle than for a rich man to enter the kingdom of heaven". [21]The apostle too condemns them by what he says: "But those who seek to become rich fall into temptation and snares and many desires, which plunge men into destruction and damnation. [22]Covetousness is the root of all evils, and some in their eagerness to get rich have strayed from the faith and have involved themselves in many troubles". [23]You see then that he who does not want to give up his possessions in the world cannot follow God, nor can he who does not want to hate his riches love God; [24]the fact is that what the Lord knows how to give in return to those who make themselves poor for his sake cannot be compared with what they are spurning for God's sake, [25]and over and above this he grants them the eternal life they will enjoy forever.

[26]Indeed, God is seeking to deprive you of your possessions not in order thereby to gain anything for himself,

11. 2 Tim 2:4
12. Jerome, Ep 14.6
13. Mt 6:24
14. Mt 6:20
15. Cf. Lk 14:33
18. Mt 19:21
20. Mt 19:24
22. 1 Tim 6:9-10

²⁷for he does not take pleasure in your poverty or rejoice in your indigence, ²⁸but so that while you are on your way to him and desire his eternal riches, ²⁹the very short-lived encumbrances of this world [may not] so occupy your thoughts that you never think about your soul, ³⁰and that you may be concerned about death, ³¹ [lest] having passed your days carelessly until the very end of your life, leaving to the world all that filled your thoughts, death's final accounting at the judgment catch you with only your sins. ³²You would thereafter have nothing but eternal punishment and would begin then to repent forever when you could no longer find this repentance a remedy. ³³Therefore it is with good reason that Scripture cries out to us: "Run while you still have the light permitting you to take care of your future, lest the darkness of death overtake you and put your negligence on trial". ³⁴So if anyone approaches the Lord without having stepped back from love of his riches, he is one of those who, as the apostle said above, cannot remain steadfast in their expectations of God, and all too easily can stray from the faith since there is always something worldly that they love.

³⁵'Now, taking all this into account, O parents, it is right that we should, in accord with God, give you this advice about your son: if you wish to offer your son to God properly, first rid him of the world. ³⁶If you keep anything of the world with you to save for him, some day he will feel the itch of diabolical desire, ³⁷as a dog delights to return to its vomit, ³⁸so that, looking back after having put his hand to the plow, he is no longer fit for the kingdom of heaven. ³⁹Eventually quitting the monastery, assured of his portion held in reserve for him by you, desiring to return to your home in the world, wishing to be coheir with his brothers, ⁴⁰he will make up his mind to go back as suitor and master of his possessions. ⁴¹Restored to his former pleasures and splendors, he will crave nothing but marriage.

⁴²'Therefore, as we said before, if you wish to offer him to

29. *Visio Pauli* 10 & 40
33. Cf. Jn 12:35
37. Pr 26:11
38. Lk 9:62

God properly, think of removing his encumbrance before thinking of his soul. [43]So listen to the voice of that Lord whom your son says he is following, telling him: [44]"Sell all you have and give to the poor, and come follow me, and you will have treasure in heaven". [45]But because his portion is still in your power, and even more because it is evident that he is being offered to God with your consent and permission, it behooves you to dispose of it according to the word of the Lord. [46]If you are willing to listen [to it] in your son's place, you yourselves must make the arrangements called for. [47]What is important is that nothing remain with you in the world for your son, except God.

[48]'But if, because of the greatness of your wealth and your love for your family reared at home, this divine precept strikes you as hard and less than sweet, listen to our Rule's salutary advice set down by the Fathers. [49]Let his portion be equally divided into three parts. [50]Let one be sold and distributed to the poor and needy through the hands of the abbot. [51]Let him, as he departs for the court of the saints, leave the second to you and his brothers as a gift in the form of a bequest. [52]But the third part let him bring with him to the monastery as his travel funds, to be used for the benefit of the saints, [53]because just as your son contributes his portion to all the brothers in the monastery for their livelihood in accordance with what the apostle says about making distribution: "Especially to those who are of the household of the faith"; [54]so also every one of the brothers of the monastery, one after the other, bring what each of them has upon entering the monastery, in conformity with this practice, to benefit your son along with all the others.

[55]'But if you find both these suggestions so difficult that you will not listen either to God by sharing with the poor and ransoming the soul of your son, or to our advice by dividing his worldly substance into parts and taking it away from him, [56]at least give your son to God stripped of everything and completely alone, in such a way that you promise him under

---

44. Mt 19:21
51. Cf. *Passio Sebastiani* 12
53. Gal 6:10

oath on the sacred gospels that henceforth he will have nothing of your patrimonial fortune. ⁵⁷Thus, from now on going
to God with steadfast perseverance, he will know that there is
nothing to hope for from the world, for he will see himself a
stranger to you and to it. ⁵⁸He will desire only the things
above, because that sets free his soul. Consequently either he
will go to the Lord under arrangements made by you or,
better yet, disinherited by you for the sake of God, he will
make his way to him, ⁵⁹crying out to God whom he is following stripped of everything: ⁶⁰"It is you, O Lord, who will
restore my heritage to me". ⁶¹What is important is that he
have nothing worldly any more to hope for from your means,
while you are living or after your death, ⁶²because one "to
whom the world is once crucified" ought never again to take
delight in it. ⁶³Now, if you are unwilling to make any arrangements at all for him, I think his case will be reserved
for you at the divine judgment, ⁶⁴but as for him, know with
utmost certainty that he will receive from the Lord more than
he spurned, for he has made the Lord his debtor, having
followed him stripped of everything. ⁶⁵Indeed, your son will
undoubtedly receive much in heaven, as the Lord promises
him when he says: ⁶⁶"There is no one who has left gold or
silver or possessions or houses for my sake ⁶⁷who will not
receive a hundredfold in the kingdom of God and, over and
above, eternal life". ⁶⁸Hearing all this, your son is ready. ⁶⁹If
you wish, he may surrender everything to you so that he can
find the hundredfold with God, because our Lord is sufficient
for us in every regard. ⁷⁰What then does suffice for one whom
the Lord himself does not satisfy?'

60. Ps 16:5
62. Gal 6:14
64. Cf. Jerome, Ep 125.20
67. Cf. Mk 10:29-30

Question of the disciples:

XCII. Prohibition of honor and rank below the abbot.

The Lord has replied through the master:

[1]The abbot must take care never to appoint anyone second to himself, nor to assign anyone to third place. [2]Why? So that by not causing anyone to become proud of the honor and by promising the honor of being his successor to someone who lives a holy life, he may make all eager to rival one another in doing what is good and in humility, [3]just as the Lord judged the apostles quarreling over first place when 'he brought a child into their midst and said: [4]"Let anyone who wants to be great among you be like this, [5]and let anyone who wants to be first among you be your servant"'. [6]And the Lord likewise said to his disciples: 'Whoever first keeps my commandments and then teaches them, he it is who will be called greatest in the kingdom of heaven'.

[7]Therefore, following this prescription for becoming humble, the abbot ought constantly to tell this to all the brothers: [8]'My brothers and sons, whoever among you exerts himself to be discerned as one who is obedient to the divine precepts in every regard and submissive to all that is contained in the Rule and conformable to what I do; [9]whoever strives to put my teaching into practice; [10]whoever does not subject his conduct to his own will and choosing but to obedience to God for correction through me, [11]that is to say, not to pride but to humility, [12]not to talkativeness but to silence, [13]not to hatred but to kindness, [14]not to deceit but to charity, [15]not to anger but to peace, [16]not to drunkenness but to sobriety, [17]not to satiety but to temperance, [18]not to discord but to patience, [19]not to murmuring but to obedience, [20]not to tardiness but to promptness, [21]not to contention but to agreement, [22]not to levity but to gravity, [23]not to idle talk but to words that are few and wise, [24]not to excessive and guffawing laughter but to tears of patience, [25]not to lust but to chastity—[26]whoever among you, then, practises all this to perfection will be designated, at the time of my death, not only by my judgment but

3–5. Mt 20:26, 18:2–4
6. Mt 5:19

also by that of God, [27]a master in God's school who shall expound to the disciples of Christ the divine art which he himself is already practising perfectly. [28]For how could anyone honestly strive for the honor of being a superior if he could not do what the divine precepts require for deserving that honor, [29]and how could he preside over the divine school if he could not translate into deeds what he learned by the instructions of the superior? [30]How could anyone who did not know how to amend his own behavior correct the vices of others? [31]And how could anyone who was unable to correct his own faults against discipline keep others under discipline? [32]Therefore unless one is first a perfect discile in every regard he cannot be a worthy master.'

[33]Having often said this openly to the community and not having assured anyone of the honor, let the abbot constantly change the order of precedence. [34]Let him have them sit beside him at table in turn, [35]let him bid all in turn to stand beside him in the oratory, [36]all in turn after him to intone the psalms, [37]so that no one may then be made proud of the honor of ranking second, and no one give way to despair because of ranking last. [38]Thus, if no one is raised above the rest to second place [39]and each one may look forward, in the suspense of expectation, to being considered for receiving the honor if he lives a holy life, and may be confident that [40]he can some day be chosen for the abbatial dignity because of his good deeds, it will come about that while all desire to attain this place of honor they will be eager to put the aforesaid precepts of God into practice, [41]since no one is designated for sure but the honor is promised to those whose conduct is above reproach and holy, [42]and all can make progress by competing with one another, [43]if not out of fear of the judgment to come, then at least for the sake of honor in the present life. [44]So if the community is large and none are ranked in descending degrees of dignity, with none having precedence, [45]the last one cannot despair about himself, [46]and likewise it will be impossible for anyone in second place, with everyone else ranked after him, to rejoice in his elevation and thereafter, assured of exclusive honor, neglect to bring God's

34. Cf. 84:2, 90:82

interests to fruition in himself because he is occupied with hoping for present rather than future gain; [47]for in general mankind is so constituted that it loves what it sees more than what it hopes for without seeing it.

[48]If then, as we said above, the abbot leaves everyone's rank undetermined and he sees all exerting themselves in their desire to attain this honor some day, [49]they will eagerly compete with one another to implement what is of God so that their good deeds may make them acceptable for appointment. [50]Consequently, with each and every one manifesting his works of holiness to the abbot and to God, they may look forward to the possibility that God and the abbot will be at one in passing favorable judgment on them in regard to this honor, [51]for they are all outstanding in their eager rivalry out of zeal for good and desire for the honor. [52]So they are compelled to manifest in themselves to God and to the abbot all that is holy and good when they start to hope for the reputation reserved for the perfect [53]and thereafter by their deeds give evidence in themselves of what they would like to teach the others by their words later on.

[54]Now, another reason why we have prescribed that all are to be of equal rank and that no one is to be assigned the honor of second place, is that it may happen—[55]as Scripture says: 'The last shall be first, and the first last'—[56]that before the death of the abbot some brother who has already met the test of some Rule may merit admission to the monastery, [57]or who indeed, as in the case of many we read about in the Lives of the Fathers, will be one of those who, secretly deserting their monasteries and communities because of a desire for humility, prefer to submit themselves to the command of another. [58]And because God 'does not withhold what is good from those who go their way in innocence' and humility, [59]and 'a city built on a hilltop cannot be hidden, [60]a lit lamp gives light when placed not under a tub but on a lamp-stand', [61]what if the abbot had already assigned one of his more lax brothers to second place [62]when a man of the aforesaid caliber

47. Cf. Rm 8:25
56. Mt 20:16
58. Ps 84:11
60. Mt 5:14

entered the school of this new monastery, his great worth hidden by humility, and his works of perfection then came to light day after day, [63]and while the new disciple of the monastery went about in contempt he were recognized from what he did as an old soldier of Christ? [64]When the abbot suddenly became aware of this man's being such, would he not regret having already appointed a lax monk as second to himself and, blaming his own judgment, think of undoing what he did, [65]since it is not right that the better should be subordinate to the worse and that the latter should give orders though he himself is incapable of putting the orders into practice?

[66]Therefore the place of honor is to be kept in abeyance for all, held in promise some day for those who show themselves well-pleasing. [67]The abbot should frequently give verbal assurance of this to his brothers, saying: [68]'The Lord will give the honor to someone who sways him by his holy deeds, and [69]"he will not frustrate the desire of him" who has not defrauded God himself of his due, [70]and through him God will provide the other disciples with what is needed, once he himself finds that he is lacking nothing in this master'.

[71]So while the abbot sees all the brothers panting with thirst for this honor and each one competing to evince in himself works of holiness in what is good according to the precepts of God, [72]he will continually be pondering in his mind and scrutinizing with his eyes which of them all stands out in the rivalry of observance as the most excellent and perfect. [73]And then at the time of his death, having called all the brothers into his presence, let him say to them: [74]'You have all done well indeed in holy observance. [75]You have always shown good behavior in the sight of God.' [76]And suddenly calling out the name and taking the hand of the one whom he has secretly always considered better than the rest in every perfection, let him say to the whole community: [77]'Hear me, sons: the Holy Trinity, by whose judgment this choice is being made, knows [78]that in the full observance of God's commandments, [79]that is, in silence, in obedience, [80]in

68. Ps 84:11
69. Ps 78:30

faith, in peace, in kindness, in patience, in goodness, in sin-
cerity, [81]in vigilance, in sobriety, in continence, in chastity,
[82]this man has always stood out as the best among you.'

Question of the disciples:

XCIII. THE INSTALLATION OF A NEW ABBOT CHOSEN BY HIS PREDECESSOR FROM AMONG ALL.*

The Lord has replied through the master:

[1]'Therefore by the judgment of God and my attestation he
is chosen as your shepherd, [2]appointed your abbot by the
Lord, whom he has always pleased by his good deeds. [3]He
will take charge of the Lord's flock and will give it back at the
judgment to come. [4]See to it, brothers, that no one take this
appointment with ill-will [5]and despise Christ, whose representative in the monastery this man will be for you.'

[6]As soon as this has been done, all say a prayer, and the
head of the Church in that area is immediately sent for. Then
with the clergy of his official household as witness, [7]the
bishop with his own hand transfers on the diptych the name
of the one chosen for the abbatial dignity, after the name of
his predecessor, [8]and then during Mass at the altar in the
oratory it is read out by the cleric, but the brother himself
presents the offerings. [9]But this [is done] only if the abbot is
not yet deceased and has not yet been removed from the list
of the living, otherwise after the name of the superior. [10]Then
after his death, when his name has passed to the list of the
departed, the name of the new abbot is written at the top.

[11]Then as soon as the celebration of Mass in the oratory is
finished, in the presence of the bishop and the whole body of
the clergy of his official household, as we have said, [12]his
predecessor gives the sign of peace to him, then to the com-

Ordinatio and *ordinare* have been translated 'installation' and 'install' in this
description of the ceremony. 'Ordination' and 'ordain' may be preferable,
especially as the terms are now used more widely in new liturgical texts. In
the minds of most moderns, however, they still mean primarily elevation to
sacred orders, and the abbot in RM is unquestionably a layman and remains
one.

munity, then he places into his hands this Rule [13]as well as the keys of the monastery's larder after asking the cellarer for them, and the inventory of all the goods and iron tools and books and all the furniture and everything anyone has donated by testament, in the presence of the bishop and under his seal. [14]In the presence of the bishop and all his officials and his own community, he shall say to him to whom he is giving this Rule:

[15]'Receive this Rule, brother, as the law of God, whereby you are to procure eternal life for the observant, threaten everlasting condemnation for the lax. [16]Here it is that the soul conquers or perishes, [17]here that life is either lost or saved. [18]Upon this depends God's demanding of you these souls under your watchful eye. [19]According to this inventory you, after me, will have to give an account of this flock at the Lord's judgment. [20]Remember, remember, brother, remember that "from him to whom more is entrusted, more will be required", [21]and henceforth be on your guard and do not feel safe from the voracious jaws of the wolf, [22]and [know] that there will be diabolical traps for your flocks but also remedies and exhortations whereby you will have it in your power to heal the wounds of souls and the ruination caused by faults. [23]Henceforth be as vigilant and cautious as you can, although until today you have been without anxiety.'

[24]This done, the abbot again addresses him as he is holding this Rule in his hands: [25]'Go into the oratory of the Lord and stand in my place with the community which is now yours. [26]By his prayers let the high priest make binding in the records of heaven what you have undertaken on earth.'

[27]And having said this, he hands him his own cloak. [28]After taking it, the recipient kisses the hand of the giver, [29]and as soon as he has done so the new abbot enters the oratory with the bishop accompanied by the community now his, and

13. This ceremony took place in the dormitory, where the abbot was bedridden. The sign of peace was given to the new abbot by the community in token of their acceptance of him. Later on he gave it to the community to signify his gratitude.

19. Cf. Chh. 3–6

20. Lk 12:48

27. Cf. 2 K 2:8–14

stands in the place of his predecessor. After the bishop has pronounced a prayer for him, [30]the new abbot immediately goes to the altar and places on it the Rule he has received. [31]And while he is doing so, the whole community in back of him says this verse along with him: 'Confirm, O God, what you have wrought in our midst' with the *Glory be* and the familiar chant. [32]Prostrating himself in prayer on the floor as soon as he has finished saying this, he asks the bishop to pray for him again. [33]In back of him the community likewise lies prone on the floor. [34]Then, the prayer finished, they rise and he kisses the knees of the bishop and stands up to be given the sign of peace by him. [35]Then he in turn gives the sign of peace to the latter's officials, then to the deans and all the community, [36]and afterwards makes his exit from the ceremony.

[37]Next he hands over the keys to the cellarer, goes immediately and prays with all, this time he himself and not the bishop says the conclusion and, having asked the blessing, he seats himself on the chair of his predecessor. [38]Thereupon the deans first and then all come and kiss his knees.

[39]Immediately afterwards he rises and goes to his predecessor lying there and bends over him for the sign of peace. [40]Having received the sign of peace from him, the former superior says to all: [41]'Brothers, pray also for me that on the day of judgment before the Lord my interrogator I may be able to present and faithfully report the entire final account of your souls as well as mine. [42]And as the Lord has made you steadfast on earth, so may he deign in heaven to look with favor upon my death.'

[43]Should it be that subsequently this abbot does not die but recovers, he resumes all authority and power of administration and his former magisterial dignity—[44]and rightly so, since God has restored life to him just for this—[45]and thereafter until the day of his actual death the one recently installed may lay no claim whatever to the dignity conferred on him.

31. Ps 68:28
36. *exeat disciplinae* (cf. 89:28)
37. The chair of his predecessor on which the new abbot seated himself may have been in the refectory (23:1, 27:12), but the abbot surely also had a chair in the dormitory where he read if he so wished (44:12).

⁴⁶Then when the actual day of his death comes, let there be no question about the one already installed in the bishop's presence some time ago succeeding him. ⁴⁷This, however, only if his worthiness has not fallen victim to pride and haughtiness, ⁴⁸if he has not therefore arrogated to himself any prerogative during the other's lifetime. ⁴⁹Rather let him with full determination of mind take it upon himself and with alert vigilance be on guard ⁵⁰not to let the appointed dignity meanwhile make him proud, ⁵¹but instead to give, before God and the brothers and all men, daily evidence of growing perfection in what he does in accordance with the precepts of God contained in the Rule. ⁵²And in this state let him from then on humble himself in word and deed more than the grace of this same humility bowed him previously, ⁵³so that everyone may consider him made more humble and of less account than all after his appointment to the dignity than before, ⁵⁴that he, as one who is perfect, may deservedly be seen to exemplify the maxim declared by the Lord: 'Let anyone who wants to be greatest among you be last as far as you are concerned,' ⁵⁵that he who humbles himself may deserve to be exalted.

⁵⁸Nevertheless let the previous and real abbot accord him special honor ⁵⁶because of his dignity which the bishop bestowed by prayers and because he with his own hand wrote his name on the diptych of the monastery after that of the previous abbot when he was ill, ⁵⁷and because the abbot by his own decision had chosen him. ⁵⁹And, what the Rule did not allow before, let him now be regarded as second in virtue of his installation by the bishop and the choice of the abbot himself, and especially because of his increased and more fully developed humility. ⁶⁰He has not arrogated this title to himself arbitrarily, but the merits of perfect observance have won it for him. ⁶¹Because of haughtiness and pride the Rule does indeed forbid the appointment of seconds. ⁶²But God has chosen, with the concurrence of the abbot, and the bishop has installed this man because of his practice of good observance and his very great humility, although the restora-

54. Mt 20:27
55. Lk 14:11

tion of life to his predecessor has as yet not allowed him to take charge. [63]Therefore from that day on let him, now a spiritual Caesar-elect as it were, sit next to the abbot, [64]preside over the other choir opposite the abbot at the psalmody in the oratory, [65]receive the cup after him at table, be regarded as second to him in everything and, [66]whenever the abbot goes anywhere, let his authority to substitute for him and to correct the vices of the brothers and to excommunicate be acknowledged. [67]Should an excommunicated brother refuse to make satisfaction to him in the usual way, let his transgression be reserved to the abbot, but he himself is to remain in the state of excommunication until his return. [68]By delegation of the abbot when he is on a journey he is to exercise all these functions and act in his stead in everything during his absence.

[69]He may not, however, of his own accord claim even this for himself, [70]but when it is officially granted him by order of the previous and real abbot, then he may feel free to make any disposition or to believe himself empowered to occupy this position of honor. [71]Indeed let him at all times consider himself to be on a par with everyone else and, if he wishes to be perfect and wants to deserve to attain that to which he is destined, humbling himself all the more [72]let him rather regard himself as inferior to everyone among his brothers, and in the depth of his heart believe himself of less account than all, [73]for the Lord understands how to exalt those who are like this. As Scripture says: 'He who humbles himself will be exalted'. [74]Moreover, this brother must always take care never to admit conceit of heart because of the dignity in store for him nor, [75]bursting with pride of some sort, to be in any way worse, in comparison with his previous observance, in practising any detail either of humility or of the divine mandate set down in the rule, feeling already assured of the designated dignity. [76]And if the abbot sees the one he has chosen frequently transgressing in any way, not making progress toward perfection but instead getting worse through negli-

64. 'Sit next to the abbot'= at table. 'Preside over the other choir' perhaps meant that he designated those who were to intone (22:13-14, 46:1-2).
73. Lk 14:11

gence, [77]and he does not amend when admonished by the abbot, [78]let him be quickly given to understand for sure both that any priest at all may delete his name from the diptych at the request of the abbot, [79]and that he upon his return to his group will be classed with the lax and subjected to excommunication in the customary manner because he does not shun faults. [80]He who through carelessness has squandered what he had gained should also get what he had left behind. [81]And as soon as he has been reduced to lower status let him be removed from the abbot's side, [82]and from that day on let the abbot with eye and mind seek among all the brothers another who is better than the delinquent. [83]In the case of this one too, after he has been secretly chosen day by day, let the abbot at the time of his death unmistakably point to him with his hand as the one who is to be rightfully and deservedly set over all by installation in the first place. [84]And as to those rejected because through negligence they fall from the topmost pinnacle of honor, let them listen to the apostle saying to them: 'You were running well; who stopped you? Satan,' who trips up the proud. [85]And before anyone changes over from diligence to negligence and becomes reprobate, let him listen to the warning Scripture addresses to him daily: 'Hold fast to what you have, lest another receive your crown'. [86]And let anyone who has heard and not heeded blame himself when he falls, [87]for the Lord puts down the proud, the negligent and the unworthy in order to exalt the worthy, the observant and the humble, [88]because with the Lord, the just judge, there is no respect of persons. [89]Nor does he want to give anything to the wicked, for he understands how to love only the just, the good and the holy, [90]and it is to them that he owes honor in the present life and the reward of an eternal crown.

---

78. A priest deleted the name from the diptych because the abbot, a layman, might not touch this cult object.
84. Gal 5:7, 1 Th 2:18
85. Rev 3:11
86. Lk 6:49, Deut 6:3
87. Lk 1:52
88. Rm 2:11, 2 Tim 4:8

Question of the disciples:

XCIV. How, IF THE ABBOT DIES SUDDENLY, A NEW ABBOT IS
APPOINTED FROM AMONG THE BROTHERS, OF WHOM NO ONE HAS
BEEN DESIGNATED AS BEST QUALIFIED DURING THE ABBOT'S
LIFETIME, BECAUSE OF HIS SUDDEN DEATH.

The Lord has replied through the master:

[1]Considering the unexpected misfortunes of human nature
and the onslaught of sudden death, as is so often the case, we
have deemed the following as the proper procedure for finding among the undesignated the one to be installed, so that
among the possibilities a definite method may be determined.
[2]Accordingly, since we have said above that each and every
person's rank in the monastery must remain unspecified and
that no one must be assured the dignity of second place,
[3]since then the abbot during his lifetime has not decided who,
having been found by experience better than the rest, is to be
installed as his successor, [4]what if the aforesaid suddenly
passes to the Lord; our response is: What then? [5]Lest a grim
and scandalous fight between factions turn the house of
peace into a battleground when, by his own judgment pre-
suming upon the succession for himself, everyone stirs up all
to dissension, [6]we give this decision: that the local bishop and
clergy settle on a very holy abbot, who shall live above the
community in the place of the former deceased abbot, [7]and
he, having received this Rule, [8]shall give thought, according
to the ordinances of this Rule, to whom he discerns as better
than all the others in all observances. [9]So on the thirtieth day
this abbot, having taken an oath on the most holy gospels in
the presence of the same bishop and clergy, is to declare that
he has been bribed by no one with promises and compliments
but that he is in all honesty revealing what he has found in
God's cause. [10]As soon, then, as the entire community is
standing before him, let him at once take the hand of the one
he has discerned as better than all others in full observance of
the commandments of God and the precepts of the rule,
[11]and now finally the installation of this man in first place by
the same local bishop and clergy is celebrated according to
what is set down in this Rule, as we have said above.

5. A grim and scandalous fight would hardly have been surprising in view of
the spirit of competition which the Master himself had unleashed!

Question of the disciples:

XCV. THE PORTERS OF THE MONASTERY.

The Lord has replied through the master:

[1]Inside near the gates of the monastery a cell is to be built for two brothers advanced in age. [2]Posted there, let them at all times close up the monastery behind those who leave and open it for those who are coming in, [3]and also announce arrivals to the abbot.

[4]Every day during the periods devoted to reading in the monastery, however, these two old men must see to it that they lock the gates and join the community to listen to the readers. [5]In like manner, when the signal for the Divine Office has sounded in the oratory they are to lock the gates and be present at the Work of God in the oratory.

[6]As to manual labor, let them be asked to do what they can according to what is possible at their age, [7]that is, either the arts and crafts if they are skilled in them or, [8]if they are not, at least they may assist the weekly servers every day as far as they are able to do so. [9]However, as long as opening and closing keeps them busy, no other work is to be asked of them. [10]They receive the food for the dogs from the cellarer and give it to them along with water and broth left over from the kitchen. [11]They take care of the animals within the confines of the monastery, assisted by the weekly servers during their respective week. [12]They clean the gate [13]and every day light the night lamp suspended and prepared inside it for the purpose of recognizing at the entry anyone who may chance to arrive during the night.

[14]These elders, as we have said above, are to eat with the abbot as a mark of respect for their age, [15]in accordance with the example of perfect humility given by St Eugenia when she said that she did not want to show herself superior even to these. [16]For to such perfect ones Scripture says: 'The greater you are, the more you should humble yourself, and you will find favor with God and man'.

---

10. Dogs were kept to chase away wild animals and to protect crops. Animals meant pack horses (58:7) and draft horses (87:48,72).
15. *Passio Eugeniae*, p. 394, ll. 2–4
16. Sir 3:20

¹⁷Everything necessary should be within, inside the gates, which means, oven, machines, lavatory, garden and all that is required, ¹⁸so there may not be frequent occasion for the brothers to go outside repeatedly and mingle with people of the world. ¹⁹Were we to appear before the eyes of the devout and be venerated as angels by them, it would more be to our damnation, ²⁰and it would be improper to say *Benedicite* to us unworthy of it, since we might be considered saints which we are not. ²¹Or, on the other hand, the holy habit would be cheapened by the ridicule of some unbelievers as it went about in public and on the streets.

²²Therefore, since all these things are located inside, let the gate of the monastery be always shut ²³so that the brothers, enclosed within with the Lord, may so to say be already in heaven, separated from the world for the sake of God.

²⁴This gate of the monastery is to have on the outside an iron ring in a bracket, which when struck by a visitor will indicate on the inside the arrival of anyone who comes unexpectedly.

END OF THE RULE OF THE HOLY FATHERS

ABBREVIATIONS

ACW	Ancient Christian Writers series. Westminster, Md. and London.
ALW	*Archiv für Liturgiewissenschaft.* Maria Laach.
AA SS	*Acta Sanctorum* (Bollandists). Antwerp, 1643–.
AS OSB	*Acta Sanctorum Ordinis S. Benedicti,* edd. L. d'Achery & J. Mabillon, 9 vols. Paris, 1668–1701.
CCh	*Corpus Christianorum, Series Latina.* Turnhout, 1953–.
Conf.	*The Conferences of John Cassian.*
CSEL	*Corpus Scriptorum Ecclesiasticorum Latinorum.* Vienna, 1866–.
DACL	*Dictionnaire d'Archéologie chrétienne et de Liturgie.* Paris, 1924–53.
DBS	*Dictionnaire de la Bible, Supplement.* Paris.
Dict. Spir.	*Dictionnaire de la Spiritualité.* Paris, 1932–.
Inst.	*The Institutes of John Cassian.*
LXX	Septuagint
NPNF	A Select Library of Nicene and Post-Nicene Fathers of the Christian Church. New York & Oxford, 1887. Reprinted Grand Rapids, 1952.
Passio S. Anastasiae	*Etude sur le Légendier roman,* ed. H. Delahaye (Subsidia Hagiographica 23:221–49). Brussels, 1936.
Passio S. Eugeniae	*Passio SS. Prothi et Hiacynthi martyrum,* ed. B. Mombritius, *Sanctuarium* 2:391–7. Paris, 1910.
Passio Sebastiani	PL 17
PG	J. P. Migne, *Patrologia cursus completus, series graeca.* Paris, 1857–66.

285

PL	J. P. Migne, *Patrologia cursus completus, series Latina*. Paris, 1844–64.
PO	*Patrologia Orientalis*. Paris.
RAM	*Revue d'Ascétique et de Mystique.* Toulouse, 1920–.
RB	*The Rule of St Benedict.*
Rev. Bénéd.	*Revue Bénédictine.* Maredsous, 1884–.
RHE	*Revue d'Histoire écclesiastique.* Louvain, 1900–.
RTAM	*Recherches de Théologie ancienne et médiévale.* Louvain, 1929–.
Sextus, *Enchiridion*	*The Sentences of Sextus,* ed. Henry Chadwick (Cambridge Texts and Studies, New Series, Nbr. 5). Cambridge, 1959.
SPCK	The Society for Promoting Christian Knowledge, London.
Visio Pauli	*Visio Pauli,* ed. M. R. James, *Apocrytha Anecdota* (Cambridge Texts and Studies, Second Series, Nbr. 3:11–42). Cambridge, 1893.

Scriptural citations have been made according to the enumeration and nomenclature of the Jerusalem Bible.

SELECTED BIBLIOGRAPHY

(We list here only works which have been cited in the abridged Introduction)

1. EDITIONS OF THE MASTER

S. Benedicti abbatis Anianensis, *Concordia Regularum*, ed. by H. Ménard. Paris, 1638 (PL 103:713–1380).

S. Benedicti abbatis Anianensis, *Codex Regularum*, ed. by L. Holstenius, Rome 1661; second edition, Paris 1663; third edition, with critico-historical observations by M. Brockie, Augsburg, 1759 (PL 103:423–664; the *Regula Magistri*, only mentioned in passing in PL 103:573–574, figures *in extenso* in PL 88:943–1052).

La Règle du Maître, Édition diplomatique des manuscrits latins 12205 and 12634 de Paris, by H. Vanderhoven and F. Masai, with the collaboration of P. B. Corbett. Brussels-Paris, 1953 (*Les Publications de Scriptorium*, 3).

La Règle du Maître, Introduction, Text, French Translation, and Notes by Adalbert de Vogüé, Concordance by Jean-Marie Clément, Jean Neufville, and Daniel Demeslay. (*Sources Chrétiennes*, no. 105–107). Paris: Cerf, 1964–1965.

2. ANCIENT AUTHORS

Ambrose, *De officiis Ministrorum libri tres* (PL 16:25–193).

Arnobius Junior, *Commentarii in psalmos* (PL 53:327–570).

Augustine, *The Works of St Augustine*, 8 vol., trans. by Marcus Dods and P. Schaff. (*NPNF*). Buffalo and New York, 1887–1892.

Aurelian of Arles, *Regula ad monachos* (PL 68:387–394); *Regula ad virgines* (PL 68:399–404).

Avitus Viennensis, *Poem.* 6 (PL 59:369–382).

Basil, *The Ascetic Works of St Basil*, trans. by W. K. L. Clarke. London: SPCK, 1925. Also trans. by M. M. Wagner, *The Fathers of the Church*, ed. by R. J. Deferrari. New York, 1947ff.

———, *Saint Basil, The Letters*, trans. by R. J. Deferrari. London and Cambridge, Mass: Loeb Classical Library, 1926–1939; reprinted 1950.

Caesarius of Arles, *Sancti Caesarii Episcopi Arelatensis Opera Omnia*, 3 vol., ed. by G. Morin. Maretioli, 1937.

Capitulare Euangeliorum, ed. by Th. Klauser, *Das Römische Capitulare Euangeliorum*. (*Liturgiegeschichtliche Quellen und Forschungen* 28) Münster, 1935.

Cassian, *The Works of John Cassian*, trans. by E. C. S. Gibson. (*NPNF*, vol. 11) Oxford, 1894; reprinted Grand Rapids, 1955.

Chrysostom, *Letters to Pope Innocent*, trans. by W. R. W. Stephens. (*NPNF*, vol. 9) Buffalo and New York, 1889; reprinted Grand Rapids, 1952.

Decree, Gelasian, ed. by E. von Dobschütz, *Das Decretum Gelasianum de libris recipiendis et non recipiendis* (*Texte und Untersuchungen* 38) Leipzig, 1912. Reproduced by H. Leclercq, 'Gélasien (Décret)' in *DACL*, 6:740–745. Also in PL 59:105–180.

Faustus of Riez, *Hom. ad monachos* (Pseudo-Eusebius 38; PL 50:841–843); *Ep 7 ad Ruricium* (PL 58:857–858).

Gregory the Great, *Dialogues*, ed. by U. Moricca, *Gregorii Magni Dialogi*. Rome, 1924. Trans. from a different Latin edition by H. J. Coleridge. London, 1874.

Gregory of Nyssa, *Gregorii Nysseni Opera Ascetica*, vol. 8, ed. by W. Jaeger. Leiden, 1952.

Hippolytus, *Apostolic Tradition*, trans. by G. Dix. London: SPCK, 1937.

Jerome, *Letters*, trans. by W. H. Fremantle and others. (*NPNF*, vol. 6) Oxford, 1893.

John the Deacon, *Ep. ad Senarium* (PL 59:399–408).

Liber diurnus romanorum pontificum (PL 105:11–182).

Liber pontificalis, ed. by L. Duchesne. Paris, ²1955.

Maximus of Riez, *Hom. x* in *Bibliotheca Veterum Patrum*, 6:665–666. Lyons, 1677.

Ordines Romani, ed. by M. Andrieu in *Spicilegium Sacrum Lovaniense* 11, 23, 24, 28 (*Études et documents*). Louvain, 1931–1956. Trans. from a different Latin edition by F. Atchley (*Library of Liturgiology and Ecclesiology for English Readers*, vol. 6) 1905.

Palladius, *The Lausiac History*, trans. by R. T. Meyer, (*ACW*, no 34). Westminster, Md. and London, 1965. Also trans. by W. L. K. Clarke, London: SPCK, and New York, 1918.

Passio S. Anastasiae, ed. by H. Delehaye, *Études sur le légendier romain* (*Subsidia hagiographica* 23:221–249). Brussels, 1936.

Passio S. Eugeniae, ed. by B. Mombritius, *Sanctuarium*, 2:391–7, under the title *Passio SS. Prothi et Hiacynthi martyrum*. Paris, 1910.

Passio SS. Iuliani et Basilissae, ed. by P. Salmon, *Le Lectionnaire de Luxeuil*, p. 27–56. Rome, 1944. See also AA SS, Januarii, 1:575–587.

Paulinus of Nola, *Letters of Paulinus of Nola*, vol. 1, trans. by P. G. Walsh. (*ACW*, no 35). Westminster, MD. and London, 1966.

Pelagius I, *Pelagii I Papae Epistolae*, ed. by P. Gassó and C. Batlle (*Scripta et Documenta* 8). Montserrat, 1956.

Pomerius, Julianus, *The Contemplative Life*, trans. by Sr Josephine Suelzer (*ACW*, no 4). Westminster, MD., 1947.

Regula Cuiusdam (PL 66:987–993).

Regula Ferioli (PL 66:959–977).

Regula Pauli et Stephani, ed. by J. Vilanova (*Scripta et Documenta* 11). Montserrat, 1959. Also in PL 66:949–959.

Rufinus, *Historia monachorum* (PL 21:387–462).

Sacramentary, Gelasian, ed. by L. C. Mohlberg, *Liber Sacramentorum romanae æcclesiae ordinis anni circuli* (*Rerum ecclesiasticorum Documenta, Fontes*, 6). Rome, 1960.

Sacramentary, Gregorian, ed. by H. Lietzmann, *Das Sacramentarium gregorianum* (*Liturgiewissenschaftliche Quellen und Forschungen* 3). Münster, 1958.

Sextus, *The Sentences of Sextus*, trans. by H. Chadwick (*Texts and Studies*, New Series, 5). Cambridge, 1959.

Vies Coptes de S. Pachôme et de ses Premiers successeurs, trans. into French by L. Th. Lefort. Louvain 1943.

Vie de Schenoudi, Une Version syriaque inédite, trans. into French by F. Nau. Paris 1900.

Visio Pauli, ed. by M. R. James, *Apocrypha Anecdota* (*Texts and Studies*, 2, 3). Cambridge, 1893. Trans. from a different Latin edition under the title *Revelation of Paul* by Alexander Walker, *Apocryphal Gospels, Acts, and Revelations* (*Ante-Nicene Christian Library*, vol. 16:477–92). Edinburgh, 1870.

3. MODERN AUTHORS

The complete list of studies on the problem of the relationship between the RM and RB up to 1958 is given by G. Penco, *S. Benedicti Regula* (Florence, 1958) pp. xi–xviii.

Alamo, M., 'La règle de S. Benoît éclairée par sa source, la Règle du Maître', *RHE* 34 (1938) 739–755.

Albers, B., *Consuetudines monasticae*, t. 1. Monte Cassino, 1907.

Altaner, B., *Patrologie*. Freiburg, ³1951.

Andrieu, M., *Immixtio et Consecratio*. Paris, 1924.

———, *Ordines Romani* (see ANCIENT AUTHORS).

Bardy, G., 'Gélase (Décret de)', *DBS*, 3:579–590.

Cappuyns, M., 'L'auteur de la Regula Magistri: Cassiodorus', *RTAM* 15 (1948) 209–268.

Corbett, P. B., 'The *RM* and Some of its Problems', *Studia Patristica*, 1. Berlin, 1957.

Delehaye, H., *Études sur le légendier romain*. Brussels, 1936.

Deseille, P., 'A Propos de l'epilogue de Ch. vii de la Règle', *Collectanea OCR* 21 (1959) 289–301.

Egli, B., *Der vierzehnte Psalm im Prolog der Regel des Hl. Benedikt*. Sarnen, 1962.

Froger, J., 'Les anticipations du jeûne quadragesimal', *Mélanges de science religieuse* 3 (1946) 207–234.

———, *Les origenes de prime* (*Bibliotheca 'Ephemerides Liturgicae'* 19). Rome, 1946.

Gindele, C., 'Die römische und monastische Ueberlieferung im Ordo Officii der *RB*', *Studia Anselmiana* 42 (1957) 171–222.

———, 'Die Strukter der Nokturnen in der lateinischen Mönchsregeln vor und um St Benedikt', *Rev. Bénéd.* 64 (1954) 9–27.

Hallinger, K., 'Papst Gregor der Grosse und der Hl. Benedikt' in *Studia Anselmiana* 42 (1957) 73–104.

Hanslik, R., *Benedicti Regula*, (*CSEL* 75). Vienna, 1960.

Hegglin, B., *Der benediktinische Abt.* St Ottilian, 1961.

Heiming, O., 'Zum monastischen Offizium von Kassianus bis Kolumbanus' in *ALW* 7 (1961–1962) 89–156.

Holzherr, G., 'Die Regula Ferioli', *Studia Anselmiana* 42 (1957) 223–229.

———, *Regula Ferioli*. Einsiedeln, 1961.

Janeras, V., 'Notulae liturgicae in *RM*', *Studia Monastica* 2 (1960) 359–364.

Jong (de), J. P., 'Le rite de la commixtion dans la messe romaine', *ALW* IV/2 (1956) 245–278, and V/1 (1957) 33–79.

———, 'La commixtion des espèces', *Questions liturgiques et paroissialles* 45 (1964) 316–319.

Leclercq, H., 'Gélasien', *DACL* 6:735–740; 'Gélasien (Décret)', *DACL* 6:740–745; 'Lectionnaires', *DACL* 8:2270–2306; 'Naples', *DACL* 12:691–776.

Masai, F., 'La *RM* à Moutiers-Saint-Jean', *A Cluny*. Dijon, 1950.

Mohrmann, C., *Études sur le latin des chrétiennes*, tt. 1 and 3. Rome, 1961 and 1965.

Morin, G., *Études, textes, decourvertes*, t. 1. Paris, 1913.

Payr, Th., 'Der Magistertext', *Studia Anselmiana* 44. Rome, 1959.

Penco, G., 'Origine e sviluppi della questione della *RM*', *Studia Anselmiana* 38 (1956) 283–306.

———, *S. Benedicti Regula*. Florence, 1958.

Riché, P., *Éducation et culture dans l'Occident barbare*. Paris, 1962. [ET *Education and Culture in the Barbarian West: Sixth through Eighth Centuries*. Columbia, S.C., Univ. of South Carolina Press, 1976.]

Schmitz, Ph., *Histoire de l'Ordre de Saint Benoît*, t. 1, Maredsous 1942.

———, 'Règle Bénédictine', *Dictionnaire de droit canonique*, 2:297–349.

Schuster, I., *Regula Monasteriorum*. Turin, 1945.

Steidle, B., 'Das Inselkloster Lerin und die *RB*', *Benediktinische Monatschrift* 27 (1951) 376–387.

———, 'Domini schola seruitii', *Benediktinische Monatschrift* 28 (1952) 397–406.

Vagaggini, C., 'La posizione di San Benedetto nella questione semipelagiana', *Studia Bendictina* (*Studia Anselmiana* 18–19 [1947]), 17–86.

Vogüé (de), A., *La Communauté et l'Abbé dans la Règle de Saint Benoît*. Paris, 1961. (English translation in preparation)

———, 'Le sens d'antifana et la longeur de l'office dans la *RM*', *Rev. Bénéd.* 71 (1961) 119–124.

———, 'La Règle du Maître et les Dialogues de S. Grégoire', *RHE* 61 (1966) 44–76.

———, 'Scholies sur la Règle du Maître' in *RAM* 44 (1968) 121–160, 262–292.

———, 'Problems of the Monastic Conventual Mass', *Downside Review* 87 (1969) 327–338.

The editors of Cistercian Publications thank the following monastic communities for their encouragement and support in the publication of The Rule of the Master.

Assumption Abbey, Richardson, North Dakota
The Benedictine Sisters, Boerne, Texas
The Benedictine Sisters of Perpetual Adoration, St Louis, Missouri
The Benedictine Sisters, St Mary's, Pennsylvania
Corpus Christi Abbey, Sandia, Texas
Marmion Abbey, Aurora, Illinois
Mount Angel Abbey, St Benedict, Oregon
Mount Saviour Monastery, Pine City, New York
Mount Saint Scholastica, Atchison, Kansas
New Camaldoli, Big Sur, California
Saint Andrew Abbey, Cleveland, Ohio
Saint Andrew Priory, Valyermo, California
Saint Anselm Abbey, Manchester, New Hampshire
Saint Bede Abbey, Peru, Indiana
Saint Benedict Convent, Bristow, Virginia
Saint Charles Priory, Benet Hill, Oceanside, California
Saint John's Abbey, Collegeville, Minnesota
Saint Joseph Abbey, St Benedict, Louisiana
Saint Mary's Abbey, Morristown, New Jersey
Saint Meinrad Archabbey, St Meinrad, Indiana
Saint Peter's Abbey, Muenster, Saskatchewan
Saint Procopius' Abbey, Lisle, Illinois
Saint Scholastica Convent, Fort Smith, Arkansas
Sacred Heart Priory, Richardson, North Dakota
The Sisters of St Benedict, Crookston, Minnesota
Westminster Abbey, Mission, British Columbia
Weston Priory, Weston, Vermont